ZEN IN THE VERNACULAR

"*Zen in the Vernacular* wonderfully points out and elucidates how Buddhism is always awakening in new language, language which can speak directly to us and from our own lips, as we discover how our narrative weaves its way through the countless narratives of our world: intimately connected, yet often at odds. How will we navigate our way? How can 'things as it is' inform and clarify our narrative along with the world's? Let's listen to what Coyote has to say."

EDWARD ESPE BROWN, AUTHOR OF *THE COMPLETE TASSAJARA COOKBOOK*, *THE TASSAJARA BREAD BOOK*, AND *NO RECIPE: COOKING AS SPIRITUAL PRACTICE*

"In *Zen in the Vernacular*, Peter Coyote brings us along on his Zen path and with concise language shares his unique understanding of Buddhism, birth and death, mind and body, and daily life. In engaging with things as it is, he delves into the social and political issues that he's passionately concerned with. In these chapters, based on a series of talks he gave during the pandemic, Coyote speaks with remarkable intelligence and compassion about how to awaken to truth far greater than our small mind while not turning away from the suffering and turmoil that surrounds us. All the while his fire is fueled and peace of mind maintained through Zen practice and meditation and an unwavering commitment to all beings."

DAVID CHADWICK, AUTHOR OF *CROOKED CUCUMBER* AND EARLY STUDENT OF SHUNRYU SUZUKI ROSHI

"This large book full of wisdom provides an updated and nuanced presentation of basic Buddhist teaching. Peter shares personal stories from the depths of Zen communities and from a range of friends: Governor Jerry Brown to American Zen pioneer Gary Snyder to a Mohawk poet and artist working as a logger in the Northwest. Peter employs his wide experience to envision Zen practice and life anew for modern contexts, something American Zen folks now work to express this worthy ancient tradition for contemporary application. Peter's vernacular Zen, stripped of exotic trappings, is an important contribution to this project. Peter gets down into the weeds. He faces loss and grief with open dignity amid our present afflictions of the pandemic and climate fires as well as in poignant situations of personal loss. But perhaps his greatest gift to an American vernacular Zen is his affirmation that Buddhism is not about 'spiritual bypass' or mere self-help programs, turning away from the challenges of societal oppression. Rather, Zen is a practice of universal awakening. Returning to his early inspirations from Gary Snyder, Peter Coyote expresses how a modern Zen can offer support and some settledness to engage with systemic suffering."

TAIGEN DAN LEIGHTON, AUTHOR OF
CULTIVATING THE EMPTY FIELD: THE SILENT ILLUMINATION OF BUDDHIST ZEN MASTER HONGZHI

"This is a wondrous and generous book. Peter Coyote honorably follows D. T. Suzuki and Paul Reps, who both sought two generations ago to introduce Zen Buddhism to a curious United States. Coyote goes a step further, contextualizing the practice from within American life and culture, deftly reconciling contradictions, challenging the solipsistic to look inward. A thunderous ovation from my one hand!"

KEN BURNS, FILMMAKER

"This book is written by someone who has had a deeply rich life. It is full of anecdotes from that life, told with humor and clarity, that serve as metaphors for teaching Buddha's dharma. It acknowledges and confirms a path for non-monastics—lay people immersed in daily life. It shows us how we can organize everyday life as the practice of liberation. This is a deeply compassionate book, joyously written by an accomplished storyteller. This book will help the West envision what Buddhism could look like 300+ years from now. Enjoy."

SOSHIN TEAH STROZER, FOUNDING TEACHER
AT THE BROOKLYN ZEN CENTER

ZEN IN THE VERNACULAR

THINGS
AS IT
IS

PETER COYOTE

Inner Traditions
Rochester, Vermont

Inner Traditions
One Park Street
Rochester, Vermont 05767
www.InnerTraditions.com

Cataloging-in-Publication Data for this title is available from the Library of Congress

ISBN 978-1-64411-975-4 (print)
ISBN 978-1-64411-976-1 (ebook)

Printed and bound in the United States by Lake Book Manufacturing, LLC

10   9   8   7   6   5   4   3   2   1

Text design and layout by Virginia Scott Bowman
This book was typeset in Garamond Premier Pro and Gill Sans with Zeitung
Micro Pro, Gala, and Myriad Pro used as display typefaces

To send correspondence to the author of this book, mail a first-class letter to the
author c/o Inner Traditions • Bear & Company, One Park Street, Rochester, VT
05767, and we will forward the communication, or contact the author directly at
sfzencoyote@gmail.com.

Scan the QR code and save 25% at InnerTraditions.com.
Browse over 2,000 titles on spirituality, the occult, ancient
mysteries, new science, holistic health, and natural medicine.

◉ ◉ ◉

*For Marilyn Jean McCann, who
introduced me to Zen practice.*

*For Gary Snyder, who modeled what
a Zen life might be like.*

*For Lew Richmond, my teacher, who allowed
me just enough helium to float between
earth and sky.*

*For Shunryu Suzuki-roshi—the inspiration
crossing Space and Time.*

*For David Harris,
who left us in 2023:
Honor, facing the fangs of the world,
Courage facing Death—
the conscience of our country.*

We are not made of different stuff from the people we might choose to scorn.

DAVID BRAZIER, *THE FEELING BUDDHA*

Contents

Foreword by Lewis Richmond   ix

PART I

What the Buddha Taught

Introduction: Orientation   2

1   The Four Noble Truths: *Dukkha*   6

2   The Four Noble Truths: *Samudaya*   17

3   The Four Noble Truths: *Nirodha*   22

4   The Four Noble Truths: *Marga,*
the Eightfold Path   26

5   Marga Part II   41

6   An Introduction to the Precepts   51

7   The Precepts Part II   60

PART II

Things as It Is

Introduction: Infusing the Ordinary   78

8   What Is This Thing We Call the Self?   88

9   Form and Ceremony   102

10 Emptiness and the Heart Sutra   115

11 Enlightenment: Seeing the Unseen   130

12 Believing in Nothing   141

13 The Three Treasures:
    Buddha, Dharma, and Sangha   146

14 The Role of Faith in Buddhist Practice   161

15 On Time: Host and Guest   171

16 Fuketsu's Speck of Dust   180

PART III

Engaged with Vernacular Zen

    Introduction: Flashing in the Dark   192

17 On Anxiety   204

18 On Busyness   222

19 Wild Body, Wild Mind   236

20 Misunderstanding Emptiness   253

21 Values Not Embodied in Behavior
    Do Not Exist   268

22 Karma   277

23 On Loss: Issa's "And Yet . . ."   294

24 Contradictions   307

25 Buddhist Anarchism   318

    Acknowledgments   327

    Annotated Bibliography of Further Reading   329

    Index   332

Foreword

Lewis Richmond

I HAVE KNOWN PETER COYOTE for more than forty years, as a friend and fellow devotee of the Buddhist path, and I believe that the one word that describes him best is *integrity.* Peter has integrity, in both senses of the word—someone who is both moral and honest as well as whole and undivided. He's always been that way, I think. Throughout his life in various guises and careers, Peter has always stuck up for the underdog, whether it be Native Americans, union workers, poor people, or struggling minorities. Part of Peter's Buddhist name, Jishi, means "compassion warrior"—in Buddhist terms a *bodhisattva,* a being who consistently puts others' material and spiritual needs above his own. That's Peter.

Over the course of a long and varied life, Peter has been a master of many crafts: actor, improv teacher, award-winning poet, musician and songwriter, political activist, administrator and advocate for the arts, longtime Buddhist meditator, and now Buddhist priest—the list goes on. Although he has acted in more than 160 films and many TV shows, these days he is best known as the narrative voice of Ken Burns's many documentaries on aspects of American society and history. Some have called Peter's voice the "voice of America." It is a voice of integrity and care. People trust that voice.

Now he has written this book, combining the best of his activism

with the best of his Buddhist teaching, which he calls "vernacular Zen."
Zen has been an element of American culture and artistic life since the
1950s, and Peter is right to reference Gary Snyder in this connection.
Gary was Peter's first Zen mentor, and Gary and his generation of beat
poets and truth seekers were the first progenitors of vernacular Zen;
Peter is their rightful successor. In the sense of the fusing of two precious metals—such as silver and gold—this book is an amalgam of all
that Peter is and has been. The "silver" of his passion for social justice is
fused and blended with the "gold" of his dedication to the deep wisdom
that Buddhist practice teaches.

These essays—originally lectures given on Facebook during the
Covid years—are filled with right-to-the-point Buddhist teaching inter-
leaved with Peter's reflections on those teachings' applications to the
wider American society and the causes of social justice dear to his heart.
In his mind, they are connected and continuous, and he is gifted in the
way he persuades the reader of this connection. I think he succeeds, not
only because he is articulate and compelling, but because his whole life
has been a testament to that connection. Indeed, the Buddha himself
was a social revolutionary. Casting aside the rigid caste rules of the society of his time, dispensing with all the rites and rituals of worship that
were so prevalent then, the Buddha created a community of honesty
and simplicity, a congregation with no rank or caste; all were equal in
the eyes of awakened mind.

Peter teaches in that spirit.

LEWIS RICHMOND,
AUTHOR OF *AGING AS A SPIRITUAL PRACTICE*

PART I

⊙ ⊙ ⊙

WHAT THE BUDDHA TAUGHT

Introduction to Part I

. . . . .

Orientation

IN RESPONSE TO NUMEROUS REQUESTS from people suffering from anxiety and seclusion related to the Covid-19 pandemic, I began offering a series of weekly and then biweekly dharma talks on Facebook between March of 2020 and March of 2021. Reviewing the talks, I felt that the translation of Zen Buddhism into an American vernacular required the physicality of a book, with its portability, permanence and ease of bookmarking. There is something user-friendly about a book that does not require whizzing back and forth through the videotapes of lectures stored on an online channel. Furthermore, crafting and shaping a book allowed me to refine my thoughts and clarify my sometimes loopy expression during improvised dharma talks.

Although I am ordained as a priest in the lineage of Shunryu Suzuki-roshi, founder of San Francisco Zen Center, and first trained there in a monastic setting and am currently a transmitted teacher in that lineage (granted independence by my teacher), my life and practice are primarily secular. Consequently, I thought that secular spiritual life might be the appropriate vantage point from which to investigate my lineage of contemporary Zen thought and practice and examine its utility in the daily reality of the United States, particularly during the Covid pandemic of 2020 and 2021.

Part 1 of this book will discuss the Four Noble Truths, the Eightfold Path, and dependent origination—Buddha's foundational teachings. However, rather than explicate each in depth, I'll establish some general principles and examples and refer those who are interested to excellent explanations already committed to print by teachers I respect and from whom I learned.

Part 2 of this book, "Things as It Is," is concerned with secular Buddhist practice, the dominant practice of most American Buddhists. The expression "things as it is" was a favorite of Suzuki-roshi, and when I first encountered it, I considered it a charming grammatical error on the part of someone still struggling with English. Some years later, more deeply immersed in practice, I realized that the torqued syntax perfectly expressed the fusion of what the ancient Chinese referred to as "the 10,000 things," with the truth of a single, unbroken, interdependent Universe in which nothing exists solely alone. There is only one reality. From the vantage point of our personality, it appears to be multiple things, but when our limited personality expands to include deep wisdom, there is only one pulsing something, some energy, common to every expression of its multiplicity.

Part 3 of this book, "Engaged with Vernacular Zen," examines political and social issues ranging from the murder of George Floyd to the impossibility of avoiding negative consequences in our struggles to create positive change. Because politics is, at root, concerned with relationships between human beings and all beings and their environment, it seems neither a stretch nor a misapplication to consider political and social issues through a Buddhist lens.* The passions, fears, and fixed political ideas that led to that conflagration are still exacerbated and vivid, and so it is precisely the milieu in which calm and reflection might do the most good.

This book concentrates on the way Zen practice and perspective can be helpful to contemporary, secular life, making Zen more accessible and interesting to Americans. I would like to clarify that many of the

---

*Particularly in the aftermath of a violent attempt to block a legitimate election, overthrow an elected president, and place democracy's head on the chopping block.

mental/physical states achieved by Buddhist practice—including kensho and enlightenment—are human experiences that transcend cultural differences. They are a human legacy available to all who commit to the rigors of self-examination and practice. Many Americans may already be familiar with them but perhaps never considered their experiences as spiritual. It is my hope that reviewing their experiences through a Zen lens might offer the consolation of familiarity to experiences they might have felt were at odds with our cultural norms.

O

During the nearly three thousand years since the Buddha lived, his teachings spread around the globe, and in each culture they have been pruned and modified to ensure harmony with local customs, laws, values, and cultural structures. I refer to such modifications (or adjustments) as "gift wrapping," translating the gifts of Buddha's teaching in manners and means sensible to particular cultures in particular times. This gift wrapping is what allowed Buddhism to enter foreign lands, cross political and cultural borders, and establish reestablish and reinvent itself in new cultures. Despite common core principles and practices, these culturally appropriate gift-wraps are why Indian, Tibetan, Vietnamese, Japanese, Chinese, and Indonesian Buddhism have significant differences.

When Suzuki-roshi first began teaching eager young Americans, he included only minimal ceremonies—bowing to one's seat and bowing to the room, along with a few short chants. I was not a Zen student at that time but have been told by his disciples that this ceremonial simplicity was purposeful, to allow space for his American students to internalize his teachings and adapt them to their own culture. He taught what he knew, which was formal Zen, a Japanese expression of Buddhist thought and practice, but he also clearly understood that the transplantation of Japanese Zen roots into American soil would eventually produce its own native varietals.

Like Nature, Buddhism expresses itself according to principles of diversity. Most Buddhists do not meditate. Not all Buddhists are celibate, monastic, or married householders. Not all wear robes or shave their heads. Not all Buddhists believe in reincarnation. Some sects of Buddhism stress the existence of prior Buddhas in ancient times, also turning the wheel of dharma. The Buddha did not invent meditation, but his awakening is the first recorded instance of a person achieving enlightenment solely by their own efforts. You will also come to understand in these pages why Zen people are not overly concerned with reincarnation.

Because Buddhist practice around the world mirrors the diversity of humankind, rather than claiming one iteration as superior to all others, I think that Zoketsu Norman Fischer, a well-known and respected senior teacher from San Francisco Zen Center, had it exactly right in this quotation from a dharma talk he gave entitled "On Being A Priest."

> Some priests may follow a traditional path, complete dharma transmission, and become Zen teachers in a traditional way. Other priests may make service or craft their practice. Some priests may remain for many years, or a lifetime, in large Buddhist institutions. Others may practice residentially only for a short time. Some may start large or small centers of their own. Others may fold into the world at large without beginning a group, practicing with others in a less visible way. Some may become monastics or hermits, practicing quietly and without taking much direct responsibility for the practice of others. The choice of a path within being a priest will depend on circumstances, temperament, and dialogue with friends and teachers. Paths may change within the course of a lifetime of practice. The role of the teacher within this relationship can be that of mentor, spiritual friend, or traditional hierarchical teacher.

To me, this statement epitomizes a method of checking in with the Buddha's precepts (guides to behavior), in an authentic but not rule-bound way, recognizing that nearly everything boils down to kindness and service. I would be content if, by its end, readers felt similarly about this book.

1

The Four Noble Truths: *Dukkha*

BUDDHA'S FIRST TEACHING AFTER his enlightenment is referred to as the Four Noble Truths. According to legend, this occurred forty-nine days after his enlightenment, while the Buddha wrestled with his fears that what he had just learned might be too subtle or difficult for most people to understand.

While I was constructing this section, an old friend and Zen teacher, Paul Shippee, an early disciple of Suzuki and then Chogyam Trungpa, sent me a copy of *The Feeling Buddha,* a book by David Brazier, a British psychotherapist and Buddhist teacher.

The book was an engrossing revelation because the author identified, analyzed, and clarified what I have long suspected to be a misunderstanding of Buddha's first teaching. Brazier's knowledge of Sanskrit and Pali (the languages in which Buddha's earliest talks were recorded) has aided his offering of clear and succinct guidance concerning the Buddha's meaning.

As they are conventionally translated, the Four Noble Truths are arranged as a metaphor of a doctor diagnosing an illness, as follows:

The First Noble Truth: *Dukkha*—Suffering exists.
(The illness is suffering.)

The Second Noble Truth: *Samudaya*—There is a cause of suffering.
   (The diagnosis is that *desire* is the germ causing the illness.)
The Third Noble Truth: *Nirodha*—There is an end of suffering.
   (The illness can be cured by extinguishing desire.)
The Fourth Noble Truth: *Marga*—Following the Eightfold Path ends
   suffering.
   (The curative prescription is to live an enlightened life, free from
   desire.)

I struggled with this analysis and presentation for years. It appears
to be internally logical, but what does one *do* with it? Buddha himself
once said, "I teach only dukkha and the elimination of dukkha," and
I could never fully grasp how the Four Noble Truths expressed that
teaching. To state the obvious, Buddha did not speak in English, and
one of David Brazier's contributions was to parse the Buddha's original utterances as if he were panning for gold, and he turned over some
extremely valuable nuggets.

Dukkha is an ancient Pali word—the literary language in which the
first and earliest expressions of Buddhism were recorded. These expressions were advanced as the actual words of the Buddha. *Dukkha* was
initially translated by early Western scholars as "suffering," a word with
profound resonance for Christians (the faith of the early translators into
English), but many scholars resisted this translation on the grounds that
it did not accurately reflect the Buddha's meaning. Dukkha accompa-
nies everything that lives, certainly everything with a nervous system.
I imagine it sometimes as a global wind filled with pepper. Brazier
chooses the word *affliction* as a more accurate definition of dukkha.
Some people prefer the word *unease,* others *dis-ease;* I am partial to
affliction because it stresses something that happens to us for which we
are not responsible.

An orthodoxy about this teaching evolved, which often made me
uncomfortable. The first implication chafing me was the common

assumption that the Buddha was primarily discussing mental suffering and not physical events, as if he were saying, "Being sick is not the
problem. Fretting about being sick is the suffering." It's obvious to anyone who's ever been ill that both are a problem.

More problematic for me was the implication that suffering is caused by
craving (to my ear, a moralistic and Christian-tinged word). Consequently,
if we end the craving, we end the suffering and live from that point on
pain-free. That has always flown in the face of my own experience.

The suffering of the Buddha *after* enlightenment is a public part
of the historical record—his painfully infected foot, his grief when
his friend King Bimbisara was executed by his son, and his subsequent
death from eating poisoned mushrooms. When I began my study of
Buddhism, I was often propelled by the hope that if I could just achieve
enlightenment, my life would be clear sailing from there on. Suffering
would cease. I would float around in some blissful Buddhist Disneyland
in nirvana. I know better today.

Buddha left a precise record of what he meant. In the text of his
first recorded speech, the Dhammacakkappavattana Sutra (the First
Turning of the Wheel), Buddha defined *dukkha* as follows:

> This is the Noble Truth about dukkha: Birth, old age, sickness,
> death, grief, lamentation, pain, depression, and agitation are dukkha.
> Dukkha is being associated with what you do not like, being sepa-
> rated from what you do like, and not being able to get what you
> want. In short, the five aggregates* of grasping are dukkha.

---

*The five aggregates (*skandhas*) sum up the totality of a mental and physical existence
without positing an ego. Traditionally they are Form, Feeling, Impulse, Sensation, and
Consciousness. The idea of a self or soul can't be identified with any one of these parts,
nor can we describe a self as their sum. They are the subject of our mindful observation,
and yet grasping them, trying to fix or hold on to them, is one aspect of suffering. We
learn to live with the body, allowing it to be the body, allowing feelings to be feelings,
understanding that all the wisdom of evolution is within us and learning how it
communicates with us.

If Buddha's teaching was calibrated to destroy desire, what is the relationship between desire and dukkha? If the supposition is that suffering is caused by desire, then birth (included as dukkha by Buddha) had to have been previously desired. This appears to be an after-the-fact justification for a prior existence, supporting the contemporaneous Hindu belief in reincarnation, but I could never understand what it had to do with suffering.

When you read the Buddha's actual words, it's a relief to learn that he never said that. Enlightenment was certainly never going to end birth and death, and the belief that a soul (*atman*) body-hops from lifetime to lifetime is fraught with assumptions and difficulties. It is also at odds with the Buddha's original teachings. Yet that has not slowed the rush of millions to achieve enlightenment because it is widely believed to be a panacea.

If enlightenment is supposed to end dukkha, it didn't do so in Buddha's case. He suffered and died after his enlightenment, so I must either believe that Buddha was wrong in his definition of dukkha or that his interpreters were. For my part, I cannot believe that previous translations of the Four Noble Truths reflect what Buddha intended to transmit to us.

Buddha's teaching of "dependent origination" implies that nothing has a solitary, independent existence. Literally it means, "No this, no that." No tree, no apple. No leaf, no tree. No sunlight, no leaf, no apple. No water, no tree, no leaf, no apple. It's easy to understand that what we refer to as an "apple," and consider to be a singular physical object, is composed of numerous non-apple parts. Furthermore, no matter how gingerly I might dissect an apple, I will never find any physical entity that represents its supposedly unique, singular, quality—the core of its "appleness." This syllogism is equally true for our own existence. The self that we sense and feel is similarly supported, interdependent with and composed of nothing less than the world itself. (We will return to this in more depth later in the book.)

From this, it would appear that the assumption of a self (by any name—soul, spirit, or atman), or any supposedly independent identity traveling into the future without losing its unique identifying signs, is at odds with the Buddha's teachings. I might be comforted by believing in reincarnation more than I do, but I don't have to assert that it is any more true than Santa Claus. The truth is that we don't need any theories of reincarnation to understand Buddha's teachings. He did not speak much about reincarnation and, in fact, was very clear in expressing that there was no soul or self (*annatā*) tying us to rebirth.

I won't dispute the subject of reincarnation and will leave that to others, but it is fair to say that Zen people don't overthink the subject, preferring to concentrate on what's occurring right here in this present moment where we are all on the greener side of the grass in this very moment. Everything else is a belief, guess, hunch, or hope.

Nothing Buddha taught will save us from the consequences engendered by an earthquake, feeling physical pain if we are wounded, or grief if we lose a child or pet. If Buddha was speaking only of mental formations, why did he include birth, death, and illness in his definition of dukkha? Those are *physical* events. If dukkha can be *eliminated*, what do we make of death and birth? If we can't escape dukkha, what does this mean for our lives and practice and our quest for enlightenment? Why study Buddhism?

As a preamble to this discussion let me offer that when we save someone from drowning, we do not eliminate water but instead save the victim from the *effects* of it. Similarly, the phrase "saved from all suffering" does not indicate that all suffering was destroyed. It can be logically restated as "saved from the effects of suffering."

If we believe that enlightenment will catapult us across an imaginary fence into a Buddhist Disneyland synonymous with the Christian heaven or Islam's paradise and float worry-free on clouds of bliss, it means that we have misinterpreted what the Buddha taught and could profit from investigating our own wishful thinking. The Buddha's father, according to legend, tried to design a life for his son, giving him every advantage behind the palace walls and going to great lengths to see that he was protected from the pain of authentic unmoderated existence. The Buddha's curiosity led him out into the world and revealed to him the truth that his privileged, sheltered life was not authentic. It was in the quest for his authenticity that Gautama (Buddha's pre-awakened name) left his wife, child, and palace grounds to study.

Living in the jungle with fellow religious ascetics, he pushed himself to great extremes to deny the primacy of his body, hoping that might liberate his spirit. For six years he pushed himself so hard that one day he passed out in a ditch and lay dying of malnutrition. He was spotted by a young servant girl carrying an offering of rice and milk to her local temple. She spontaneously offered him the food she carried, which was intended as an offering for her temple.

The food and her spontaneous generosity revived the Buddha and revealed to him that his extremism and denial of his body was folly. Moved by her gesture, Buddha realized that his six years struggling with desire, attempting to create a life without dukkha, had failed. That path had led him to the doorway of death. Reenergized by the girl's food and selfless act, he sat beneath the shelter of a Bodhi tree, vowing not to arise until he had achieved enlightenment.

Some time later, as the morning star was rising, the perceived distance between it and himself disappeared. He had pierced the fiction of a separate, permanent self, and he reached out and touched the Earth, asking it to be the witness to his enlightenment.

After his enlightenment, when Buddha returned to his five ascetic friends, he was not famous. He was not the Dalai Lama or Deepak Chopra; he was an ordinary man who had broken agreed upon rules, so his companions were cool toward him for indulging himself with the creamy rice the milkmaid offered. But as he approached them, they observed him and perceived immediately that he was a changed man, and they begged him to teach them. His very first teaching was the Four Noble Truths.

Buddha cautioned all who would listen against seeking childish, romanticized relief from our actual lives. The idea that a spiritual quest should be a search for some state or condition *other* than our lives is still often accepted by spiritual seekers as the legitimate goal of study and may have much to do with why, at the end of the day, so few people seem to find lasting relief from their varied spiritual pursuits.

David Brazier is shrewd in pointing out to us that Buddha described dukkha as a Noble Truth. He reminds us that the word *noble* means "dignified" and "worthy of respect." *True* obviously means "real." There is no need to escape or be ashamed of what is noble. Our infirmities and imperfections, our pains and discomforts *are* our real life. They do not indicate a lack of spiritual development. In fact, they are the building blocks of our development. The implications of the Four Noble Truths suggest that the first and second (samudaya) are the energetic fuel for keeping life active and in motion, and in spiritual terms, for driving that life toward the noble vision of saving all beings.

◯

In the thirteenth century, the great Buddhist master Dogen, who brought Zen from China to Japan, clarified the Buddha's words this way:

> The most important issue for Buddhists is how to get a completely clear appreciation of birth and death. Buddha (Enlightenment) exists within birth and death. So, birth and death (as a problem) vanish. Birth and Death (as reality) are Nirvana. If you see this you will not seek nirvana by trying to avoid birth and death. This is the way to be free from birth and death.*

In my immature understanding, I often considered my suffering to be my internal junkyard dog, vicious, unruly, and threatening my destruction if he wasn't placated. Efforts to pacify that bullying dog led

---

*From Shusogi ("Meaning of Enlightened Practice"), a document compiled after Dogen's death by students hoping to offer a concise example of his teachings.

me into numerous distractions and bad outcomes: hard drugs, perpetual unease, illicit or careless sexual relationships, and disregard for the needs and suffering of others. The bars are full of such people, and impulsive searches for relief may manifest as addiction to gambling, incessant feuds, self-aggrandizement, obsessions with the smartphone, TikTok videos, tweeting all day, or compulsive shopping. All such flights inevitably debase our dignity and distract us from self-examination. They are the antithesis of being noble and dignified.

In our culture—particularly as it has overfed on superstition and the substitution of belief for fact—it is often subtly expressed that if we are having problems, somehow, it's our fault. If we hadn't eaten gluten, had only eaten more garlic and less dairy, been less stressed, slept more, had only practiced yoga, or imbibed ayahuasca and psilocybin we wouldn't be in this fix. There's often an implied judgment that when we suffer we are neurotic or spiritually undeveloped. John Wellwood refers to such nonsense as "spiritual bypassing" and reminds me of a time during the sixties when I barely restrained myself from strangling a young *spiritualista* blithely asserting that a Vietnamese peasant napalmed by our government while feeding her children was "only working off past karma."

The truth is that affliction is part of reality. I struggled with hepatitis C for forty-odd years as the result of sharing syringes during a decade of heroin and cocaine use. I can't catalogue the number of insistent suggestions about cures for this virus I received over the years—each expressed with unshakeable certainty—if I just tied red thread around my wrists or took coffee enemas or bought Dr. Nosebleed's 7 Critical Supplements, dosed myself with the correct electronic frequencies, ate walnuts, or did liver purges, my affliction would disappear. Needless to say, it did not, and it was not until I was past seventy that modern science produced Gilead's Harvoni, which cured me in twelve weeks, with no side-effects or recurrence. While I still favor herbs and supplements for daily health, I must observe that every friend I ever had who insisted on alternative-only treatments for grave diseases is dead.

Certainly judgment, anxiety, anger, jealousy, arrogance, and the like are dukkha. Buddhist philosophy labels them poisons (*kleshas*) because they not only poison our thoughts and our relationships with other people, but they also cloud our minds to the degree that we can no longer sense our original clarity and enlightenment. They are hypnotically absorbing, and the distinction that my personal experience has confirmed from Buddha's first teaching is that we never totally rid ourselves of affliction, even after enlightenment. That is not bad news, however, because the other Noble Truths and zazen meditation teach us how to contain it and save ourselves from their consequences. Once we have the knack, by following the Eightfold Path (more on this later) we can model the life of a Buddha with our own—a life of dignity, calm, and helpfulness to others.

If enlightenment ended dukkha, the Buddha would not have died of food poisoning or Suzuki-roshi of gallbladder cancer. After fifty years of Zen practice and several "waking" experiences, I still struggle with restraining my family legacy of choleric temper, impulses that tend toward violence, and condemning others as stupid or venal when I disagree with them. I am replaying the behaviors I learned in my childhood home, where it was better to be a thief than to be stupid. It is clear to me today that the Buddha's teaching of saving all beings described something other than *eliminating* suffering.

The idea that enlightenment will save us from all suffering raises false expectations because we cannot live permanently in an enlightened state. It *will* save us from the unnecessary suffering caused by fear, greed, and delusion. In the world of form and contradiction, enlightenment is a kingdom we can visit and remember that alters our worldview profoundly, alerting us to connections and relationships with everything from a different perspective. However, it's important in this world of ceaseless change to understand that we're not *supposed* to live there. Our spiritual practice should not be dedicated to substituting our *idea* of enlightenment for our everyday reality. *Satori,* or *kensho* or enlightenment, is a temporary stop. But it changes everything. We don't have to travel far. Several inches of movement, if it takes us around a corner, affords us a radical change of perspective.

An important takeaway from the First Noble Truth is that we are not neurotic when we suffer affliction. This is a phenomenon that happens to everything with form—earth is eroded by water; mountains are shaped by windblown sand, raised by magma flow and eruption; the Universe, despite its patterns, is always involved with ceaseless change.

When our lives don't correspond to how we imagine we are supposed to feel, we may feel ashamed and embarrassed by that and practice appearing unruffled and above the fray. Understanding dukkha as Noble Truth should put that self-criticism to rest. How can one remain ashamed of what is real? How can we feel ashamed of what is noble? Buddha chose his words carefully and explained quite clearly what *dukkha* meant.

It's true that Buddhist practice leads to happiness, but that destination is not a happiness free of disturbances. We don't achieve happiness by destroying dukkha but by finding our happiness *within* it. If I were dead, I wouldn't feel anything. So even if I'm sick, I understand I'm alive, and, though suffering, still in contact with the mystery and beauty of the Universe.

For many years I suffered from wanting to be happy. I spent most of my time bemoaning the fact that I was not happy and cataloguing the symptoms of my sorrows. One day, I gave up caring whether I was happy. I began to relate to my emotional states as if they were internal weather—sometimes sunny, sometimes frigid or cloudy, and bingo, I realized I was happy most of the time.

Korean Zen master Kyong Ho lived in the latter part of the nineteenth and early part of the twentieth centuries. He alluded to a revelation something like this when he said:

Don't ask for perfect health. That's just greedy. Make medicine from the suffering and illness. Don't hope to be without problems, that's just laziness. Accept life's difficulties, it's your path to be free of obstacles. Without them, the fire of your enlightenment will go out. Find liberation within the disturbances themselves.

O

Where is this leading? Consider dukkha as energy. It could be likened to the gasoline required by an engine. If we ignite gasoline on the ground, it burns off or starts a conflagration. If we contain it within the limitations and structural rigidity of a gasoline engine, the energy is transformed into useful work. This is where Buddha is directing our attention.

But first we need to understand what the energy does.

The Four Noble Truths: *Samudaya*

THE SECOND NOBLE TRUTH, usually translated as "There is a cause of suffering" was expressed by Buddha as *samudaya,* which means "arising." When we are in the world and are afflicted by desire, loss, or the like, feelings and impulses arise. We can't help it. We can't help dukkha, and we can't help its initial consequence—samudaya. Both are spontaneous events. Someone cuts us off while driving, and anger or fear arise; we may flip them off before we even know what we're doing. We see a sexually attractive person, a dangerous dog, a cute puppy and our responses arise automatically.

The conventional explanation of the Four Noble Truths says that desire is the cause of our suffering. When we fall ill, sickness is very clear. Our sinuses are stuffed, we have a fever, we have a headache. We think, "Oh god, I'm sick. I have so much to do today. I'm going to be unable to work for a week. How'll I pick up the kids? My boss will be angry. This is going to be terrible." Those mental processes are afflictions, but Buddha was very clear that he was including the physical symptoms as dukkha as well. He included birth, old age, sickness, death, and pain. He was not suggesting that all phenomena could be transformed by a change of mind.

When strong emotions arise in response to events, the fact that Buddha defined them as Noble Truths also informs us that they are natural and real. They are true (real), and they are noble, worthy of being respected. What arises are responses from the human spectrum. They are not "yours" or necessarily indicative of character and development. It's not shameful or crazy to feel anger, shame, or lust. No feeling is crazy. What's crazy is feeling something and not wanting to feel or admit it. All such feelings arise in response to dukkha, and being mindful and acknowledging them keeps us grounded in the raw ground of our humanity.

If we abandon shame, we can deal with our *reality* in a straightforward manner without obscuration or avoidance.

When we are angry, we have to acknowledge that anger is present, but we needn't own it to the degree that we feel responsible for it. We don't need to lash out or speak cruelly, or pretend that we're not angry when we are, because we are just experiencing human nature. Similarly, when we see someone or something we're attracted to, we don't simply seize them or begin a pursuit. But neither do we pretend that we are not attracted to them. We don't pretend that strong feelings are not working within us. We don't deny or repress what we feel, but neither do we give free rein to self-indulgent behavior.

In the early sixties, running with an anarchist group called the Diggers, I used to wear a pin that read, "Do Your Thing." Remembering that today, it's a little horrifying to consider how wide a range of indulgent behavior that afforded me. Though I intended it as a reminder to stay authentic to my true feelings and intentions, because I had already defined myself as a "good guy," I remained oblivious to the shadows I and every human being carry and unwittingly create. Our actual nature is not other than the full breadth, width, and depth of the energy of the Universe. From that perspective, it's clear (or should be) how dangerous human beings can be when they do not monitor their inner lives.

When we lose something, we experience loss. When death snatches someone we love, it is not shameful to grieve. It is not evidence of being unenlightened or spiritually undeveloped. Such losses remind us of the insubstantiality and impermanence that make *everything* precious.

This is why Buddhists often wear little skulls on their beaded malas, to remember impermanence. Everything is changing, everything is impermanent. The person we were yesterday is changed today. It's a fundamental truth of reality. When we can come to terms with that, when we can come to terms with insubstantiality, with the impermanence of everything, we can experience grief and loss without being undone by it, because it too is impermanent.

Impermanence does not mean insignificant. Quite the opposite. Almost no one has particularly strong feelings about artificial flowers, because the flowers are not dying. It is their transcience that confers value to them, and every single thing on Earth, within its own time frame, is passing away just like flowers.

Clear-eyed recognition and appreciation of how natural this is, is what spurs us to empathize with and help others, or request help ourselves. If I feel helpless, why should it be a source of shame to request help? It's samudaya. Something has arisen in response to dukkha. Why can't I ask for help? Or why can't I give it? I can't speak for everyone and all instances, but in my own case, I was usually embarrassed at being (or perceived as being) unable to "handle things" or weak. David Brazier addresses that subject directly when he says, "The idea that an enlightened person is one without needs and feelings is one of the most dangerous of all the pitfalls that lie scattered along the spiritual path."

I've spoken before, in other dharma talks, about John Wellwood and his term *spiritual bypassing,* which is a sort of camouflage behavior that some people assume when they are troubled. Their behavior is calibrated to signal that they have risen above such undeveloped feelings, are too spiritually evolved to wallow in the petty muck where you and I dwell. They would have us believe that they are too evolved to express grief, anxiety, or envy. Such behavior is a high-status behavior cloaked in spiritual drag. It is dishonest and harmful to the degree that it induces others to feel ashamed of their own feelings.

It is our personality orchestrating our normal responses to feelings, denying or revising them to present the best version of our idealized self to others. When we operate through that personality, instead of just being open and transparent to the world, expressing how we actually feel (which does not have to be expressed intemperately), we are actually being dishonest and refusing to share who we actually are with others because our behavior might threaten our carefully constructed and idealized image. I like to remind my students not to assume any "Buddhist persona"—any special personality different from their own, which they employ only when they are behaving as Buddhists.

At the point we discover that the self is not an organ or gland with any specific form, color, and location but is an *awareness,* we are balancing on the edge of absolute freedom. A self without fixed qualities and limits allows us to understand not only the insubstantiality of the self but that nothing in the realm of language can harm us. We have been defending a fiction. Furthermore, without any sort of internal armature other than the spine, qualities about ourselves we dislike or disapprove of can be remedied by practice.

We live in a very emotional country. Americans give free rein to their passions as opposed to, say, a culture like Japan. When we say, "I'm angry," that is like saying the totality of myself is angry. Tibetans say, "Anger exists" or "There is anger," because they do not extend the quality to their entire self-consciousness. Such an expression is less conclusive and absolute, less connected to an identity, so there is more room to negotiate.

When Tibetans say, "Anger is present," there's no "I" included. Anger is there but not dominating the sense of self. When we consider a fixed self and are troubled, rising emotions are bound to the self that has arisen within us to experience it. We lose sight of its impermanence and surrender to the fiction of a continuous narrative describing "The Adventures of Me." Even aversion (pushing away) is merely another way of maintaining attachment as in the old Buddhist adage "The ground we fall down on is the ground we push against to rise."

Common to all similar statements is a temporary blindness to our myriad connections to the Universe, which we habitually consider "outside" of us. Because both affliction and arising happen to everyone, since they are both Noble Truths (i.e., real and worthy of respect), perhaps the most interesting questions are *Why* are they worthy of respect? Whose respect?

If we are cold, we move closer to the fire or raise the thermostat. If we are too hot, we move farther away or take off a sweater. This is the manner in which arising serves us as a motive energy, keeping us and the Universe in motion and changing. Because arising is fundamental to the Universe, *is the Universe itself,* it is of course worthy of respect. It is no different from respecting a mountain or a wolf as emblematic of life itself. Once we have fully understood that nothing is permanent and that everything changes, it's only a short step to understanding that every emanation of the Universe is a *nonrepetitive* occasion and that what has been generated is an inexplicable miracle.

If there were no affliction and arising there would be no spice or heat for the cook-pot, nothing to knock us off our game and afford us the opportunity to review and revise that game. It is why "navel gazing" is such an inappropriate misunderstanding of Buddhist practice, which always remains wide open to the energies of the Universe.

This arising extends and focuses the energy of dukkha behind curiosity, behind learning, and (pending our response) behind suffering. It is indivisible from the fabric of life, and recognizing that is recognizing their importance to us. That is a good temporary basis on which to build respect. So, too, is the understanding that everything has the same common denominator in the formless energy of the Universe—Buddha-nature.

In the early Brahmajala Sutta, reviewing sixty-two beliefs held by ascetics, including the belief that form and perception transcend death, Buddha marked them as "wrong views." It's an orthodoxy that enlightenment is going to free us from that cycle of rebirths, but what kind of religion states as its highest goal the eradication of life? It's an orthodoxy, but is not really Buddha's teachings. Buddha wants us to live well in *this* life. Who knows about other lives? Past lives? It's all say-so.

3

The Four Noble Truths: *Nirodha*

AFFLICTION (DUKKHA) AND ARISING (SAMUDAYA) lead directly to the Third Noble Truth, which is conventionally translated as "truth of the end of suffering" (which inflects to my ear like an advertising pitch). Often presented as "the destruction of desire," that is not the manner in which the Buddha described it. For the Third Noble Truth, Buddha used the word *nirodha*. It does not mean "destruction" but is often translated as "cessation," but not necessarily of desire. In modern Hindu, a language descended from Sanskrit plus local vernaculars, *nirodha* is a word for "condom." The Buddha's idea of containment was of a very specific order, and it would have been apprehensible to any village peasant where the custom was to contain fire by building a protective clay wall around the fire pit to prevent the flames from leaping out and incinerating the village. Buddha traditionally referred to the three poisons—greed, hatred, and delusion—in terms of fire. The fire contained by nirhoda is the energy generated by affliction (dukkha) and what arises (samudaya). I stress my gratitude again to Rev. David Brazier for supplying the image nirodha represents. Such a barrier would have been well known to people in the Buddha's time, and, understanding its purpose, they would also have understood the fires of unruly emotions Buddha wanted us to contain. The method of containment is meditation, which is continued until a high confidence develops that whatever arises in the mind can be contained by the practitioner, and it is at that point that one can walk the Eightfold Path with confidence that one is modeling the Buddha's life in our own.

Without discipline and restraint, affliction and arising can and often does send humans fleeing into self-destructive (and certainly undignified) escapes. Among the things we learn from the study and practice of Buddhism is that the "I" who wants to control everything, who wants to be always comfortable and happy and considers itself the most important thing on earth, is something we have assiduously empowered and transformed into an identity that we believe to be a separate existence, an isolated integer in the vast Universe—the most common delusion of humans.

If we wonder exactly what it is that we are containing, Buddha describes it as a *thirst* for either an object or a state relative to that object; either a thirst to possess or escape, to cleave to something pleasant, or to flee the unpleasant. It is the thirst to change our state, our life, to end illness or some condition we don't like.

The prescription for containment is *to immediately sever the feeling from the object that generated the emotion.* If someone makes us angry, for instance, we are urged to sever that person from our thoughts as a cause and own the anger our mind generated. That allows us to investigate our response itself without either the distraction or confusion of continually referring outside ourselves, confusing the source that triggered that feeling as the cause of our own personal emotional response.

Practicing nirodha develops the confidence that we can contain our feelings and that they cannot harm us. Meditation demonstrates to us that our feelings are ephemeral and transitory, and, like them or not, they will arise and disappear from our mind screen to be replaced by something else. They do not exist as separate powers and forces outside of ourselves. Buttressed by our zazen posture and mindful attention to our awareness and breath, we learn to contain the energies of our inner life and prevent the destructive nature of negative thoughts and feelings and past traumas from compelling us into behavior we may regret.

The Buddha says that we don't have to repudiate any feeling. We can take it as the subject of examination and not confuse the emotion with the person or events that caused it. There is a magnificent compassion released when we stop judging and begin considering our emotions as phenomena worthy of critical examination. So, the next question should be: Once we have accomplished this, what is the Buddha's work?

Buddhist practice concentrates on using energy—transforming the chaos of dukkha and samudaya into constructive purposes—to help others and to model a noble and dignified life. Our passions resemble tidal engines, harnessing the restless oceanic energies of the Universe to generate positive actions. As we oscillate back and forth between pleasure and pain and states between, on some level, it's all just energy, all oscillation and change. Those changing states are the raw fuel powering our engines to express the life and the large story of the Buddha in our own lives.

David Brazier, in his *Feeling Buddha,* puts it this way:

> We capture our own inner fire to change the world. When we notice greed arising, we notice what it is directed toward. And we unhook it. Unhook the feeling from the object, and we work on the feeling. We conserve the energy for a higher purpose.

That's what Buddhists vow to accomplish. We are not trying to make ourselves less than human, flesh vessels shorn of emotions and feelings we may not understand. We are not being urged to live lives of diminished feelings and emotions. We might think of it like burning garbage to generate electricity. If we are concentrating on feeling good all the time, we are self-centered and self-referential, not performing a spiritual practice at all. We are expressing greed in another manner. Because that's at odds with the "things as it is"—the innate generosity of the Universe—it's never successful in the long term.

It's not necessary to remember any past life to practice Buddhism in this life. Rebirth is not a necessary prerequisite to understand the

Four Noble Truths. Nirvana is not a metaphor for the peace of death or escaping this mortal coil. It is a practical term for a life in which the fire inside us is contained and an understanding of our innate freedom, which allows us, in the next moment, to drop our personal history and narratives, becomes something completely new and different. *That* is radical freedom. We don't get frightened when the furnace goes on in our house or our car engine runs, because we know its power is contained. Our task is to commit the requisite discipline of nirodha to the force of habit.

Anger may rage in us, and we need to know it. But we don't shoot somebody to express it. We can admit that "I'm experiencing anger" but don't have to surrender to its demands or allow ourselves to be thrown off course. Examine it while we are in it. It won't last forever. This is what banking the fire means—separating the emotion from the trigger, understanding the experience in ourselves and expanding our vocabulary—emotionally and physically—to become more skillful at understanding others as well. The only control of events available to us is our own intention. I can't control your ignorance, virulence, or delusions. I can control it in myself. I can ensure that it does not pass my teeth or animate my body. I refuse to allow them to mobilize me physically to do harm to others.

The process of transforming what has afflicted and consequently arisen within us into an ethical, dignified life that is helpful to others—the life Buddha modeled for us—which is a grander, larger story than our own moment-to-moment pastiche, is the practice of harmonizing our personal life with the Universe itself, of which it is indissoluably composed, and this is the concern of the last of the Four Noble Truths.

4

The Four Noble Truths: *Marga*, the Eightfold Path

THE FOURTH NOBLE TRUTH, *marga*, means "path" or "track." It is the practice of living as a Buddha and expressing our lives as Buddha. It is the practice of living a life that others can observe and model if they choose, thereby transmitting the model from generation to generation until all beings have been saved from ignorance. The prescription for the "illness" is a path and set of practices that sustain an enlightened life.

The Eightfold Path is expressed as a list but describes a circle. Each of the steps are interdependent. This simultaneously expresses the *description* of an enlightened life designed from Buddha's own enlightenment and in subtle ways expresses enlightenment itself.

Buddha modifies his description of each step on the Eightfold Path with the word *Right*. Right Understanding, Right Speech, Right Effort, and so on. The Buddha intended "right" to mean corresponding to the absolute truth of the Universe, but in English the word connotes the opposite of wrong and so might appear judgmental of other spiritual paths. For this reason my teacher substitutes the word *Buddhist* for "right," to indicate that this is *our* way, not the only way. So, I follow Chikudo Lew Richmond's practice of designating the actions in terms of *Buddhist* Understanding, *Buddhist* View, and so on—to mean that this is the way Buddhists understand things.

While studying this, I learned that some scholars trace the derivation of the Pali or Sanskrit word translated as "right" to a current flowing in the middle of a river, which I like. Along the shoreline of a river, back eddies can create interruptions to the river's flow, which could be likened to self-defeating behavior in which internal conflicts create tension and disharmony. In the center of the stream, the water is lined up and moving without impediment. This notion of being harmoniously in union, and not being divided against oneself, is what we are seeking to emulate.

Most people, whether or not they're aware of it, have a *fundamental intention,* a long-term, abiding intention operating in the background of their consciousness. It is often something they do with each breath— perhaps a competitive worldview, or an intention to stay out of trouble, or an impulse to be of use. In the case of dedicated Buddhist practitioners it often becomes a desire to mimic the Buddha's intention to save all beings.

Buddha's original disciples were very varied, what they possessed in common was this intention and their authentic response to its demands. They stepped aside from their personal preferences (ego) to let the power of the Universe (usually transmitted through intuitions) support and guide them. They learned to meditate. They learned not to fear powerful emotions but instead to harness them and use their energy to liberate others.

That's what the final Noble Truth (marga)—the Eightfold Path—is about: a series of reminders and consultations with our our inner wisdom before speaking, acting, or working, checking in to ensure that the choice under consideration is in accord with the Buddha's precepts. There are no Buddhist police or irrefutable authorities hiding in the bushes, tracking us to insist on any orthodoxy. Many who've gone before us have written insightfully about the Eightfold Path, and their writings will deepen your understanding (which is why I've provided the bibliography at the end of this book). Ultimately, however, it is we Buddhists who police ourselves.

Our first training is to identify our suffering, anxiety, and dissatisfactions; to identify our greediness, prejudices, and anger;* and to recognize that we are fully inhabited by the *total* human spectrum of emotional possibilities, not just the ones we approve of or consider worthy. Let me state one thing clearly here—Buddhist history is filled with vivid, colorful, outrageous, fully alive people. Courageous people. Some were murderers. Some were thieves, but inspired by the Buddha they transformed themselves into enlightened men and women, morphing their negative energies into powerful tools dedicated to serve the dharma. Any idea that such men and women employed enlightenment to transform others into repressed expressions of spiritual vanilla is foolish.

One of the towering figures in the story of Zen is an eighteenth-century master named Hakuin, of the Rinzai school. Hakuin was a cartoonist, author, and songwriter and applied every capacity he possessed to elucidate Zen teachings and make them accessible to everyday folk by expressing them in vernacular language. He had many kensho (enlightenment experiences) during his life, but what he referred to as his final enlightenment was understanding the critical importance of the Buddha's Eightfold Path. He came to believe that following the Buddha's precepts and forms of practice *was* enlightenment itself, not just a path to lead people there.

The Middle Path (between mortification of the flesh and indulgence) that Buddha discovered after his rescue by the servant girl who found him unconscious harnesses the energy of dukkha and samudaya (affliction and arising). Once contained, they can be transformed into noble and worthwhile human lives, transforming our brief residency in physical form on Earth into a vehicle that besides being helpful to

---

*A discussion of how to do this and deal with these emotions can be found in chapters 6 and 7.

others actually plants the seed for a more compassionate future. The Eightfold Path is the template for that achievement.

Based on the Buddha's enlightenment, he explained the path as:

Buddhist View
Buddhist Thought
Buddhist Speech
Buddhist Action
Buddhist Livelihood
Buddhist Effort
Buddhist Mindfulness
Buddhist Samadhi

Each practice aids us in hewing to the measure of Buddha's original model, chipping away and smoothing our own rough edges. Each title of the Eightfold path is also a mnemonic device to aid us in decision making and focusing our intention on the universal love and care of all beings. Though it's described as a path, it is more literally a circle where each station connects to all the others. There is much discussion of the Eightfold Path available in Buddhist literature, and I've included some titles at the back of this book for those who may be interested in a deeper dive into marga, making it easy for us to check our understanding against the great minds that have preceded us.

Even if we begin with baby steps, we can practice tolerating and understanding ourselves, being kind to interior states without flinching or shame. This process may generate powerful emotions that require courage to face directly, but you will also come to understand that there's no *there* there, no fixed interior self to be redefined, no physical expression of a fixed self to be permanently marred, harmed, or damaged. We needn't do more at first than recognize, accept, and investigate what arises within us, which also means resisting the fight-or-flight impulses that arise when we are tweaked by discomfort or anxiety. By studying ourselves closely when anger or sadness arises in us, we can learn to understand the physical sensation defining those states. When we can relax with them, they relax and pass on like cloud formations. They are our interior weather.

We can't grasp either our suffering or our liberation, because our thoughts and emotions, like everything else, are subject to ceaseless change. We can't hold on to a good mood and consequently needn't fear bad moods taking up permanent residence in our psyches. Understanding and compassion for ourselves will help us bear what arises. Meditation helps us to develop the requisite strength and stability to become aware of these mental events and realize their ultimate insubstantiality. You can't harm an empty bamboo tube.

Meditation itself is a form of enlightenment. The Eightfold Path itself is enlightenment. Observing the Four Noble Truths is enlightenment. They all model the Buddha mind, which is not different from your own mind and the mind of Nature. By detaching from our small personality, we can become intimate with our original nature, which is beyond our control. A kayaker does not need to control the river but instead plays on its energy. We can go with it. We have some choices about speech and behavior, but not so much about what does and does not arise within us.

The meditation we practice is called *shamata,* which means "stopping." You don't have to count your breath (though it's very helpful, particularly for beginners). By sitting still, we are depriving the mind of stimulation and not generating karma (more accurately, allowing our karma to work on emptiness). At Thich Nhat Hanh's Plum Village in France, they have bells that sound every fifteen minutes. When they chime, everyone stops and conducts a small self-query: "How am I feeling? How am I doing?"

Discover your own times and places to stop during the day. The fire of our passions and feelings won't become destructive behavior if we catch them before they have grown too powerful.

This is a good place for me to urge you to look into the Eightfold Path on your own. Take one of the books I've suggested in the further reading list at the end of this one and get a sense of how different people have deepened and expanded these guide rails of behavior over the centuries. There is no need, nor would it be possible, for me to recapitulate here the breadth of wisdom you'll encounter by further reading, but perhaps a few examples about how subtly a precept can be observed might be illuminating.

I was once having a tea and chat with a longtime dharma friend Fu Schroeder at Green Gulch, the farm and monastic center in Marin County, California. Fu and I had come to Zen Center at around the same time, and she continued her strict monastic practice after I left to earn a living as an actor. She remained at Zen Center, evolving and growing until her practice was well recognized by her peers and she became the abbot of Green Gulch Farm Zen Center. She's an extremely amusing woman, and we were catching up as old friends. Happy to be in her company, I was storytelling and describing someone to her sarcastically and carelessly, being amusing. Looking back, I can see I was trying to entertain her at the expense of a person we might both consider a fool. She listened politely, but when I was finished she said softly and without judgment, "Wow, that certainly doesn't make me want to meet them."

Her gentle pause switched on a light, revealing to me that I had been paying more attention to entertaining her rather than being concerned with how I was using the power of speech or how I might have told the story in a manner that was more charitable toward the subject. I was privileging my own experience of that person as reliable, not offering an objective review. I was sarcastic and withholding from him the benefit of the doubt. Fu made no judgment of me, but her succinct and accurate representation of my story in the light of Buddhist Speech generated what we in Zen practice call "a turning word"—a moment that makes you see things differently. It's easy to gloss over such moments on your own, but friends who are also practicing (such groups are known as *sanghas*) can help keep us straight.

Habits such as these are deeply buried and often subtly disguised in us.* Staying alert for them is a prerequisite for any kind of spiritual

---

*It helps me to remember this when I sometimes say, "The problem with Buddhism is . . . there are people in it."

growth. It was certainly not an example of good practice on my part, and, uncomfortable as it was to have revealed my carelessness so nakedly, I was grateful for the correction. Purifying a lifetime of bad habits is endless work.

Whenever I get too fascinated with my own point of view, I'm helped by remembering the Dalai Lama's response to a question about whether he harbored bitter feelings toward the Chinese.

He answered, "The Chinese have taken everything from me. I am not going to allow them to steal my state of mind." This remark was made by a man who was forced to flee his country; who saw his temples burned, his monks tortured and killed, his people reduced to a minority in their own land; and who spends most of his waking hours comforting people, many of whom have arrived in India after performing thousands of full prostrations—bowing, extending the body, standing, and bowing again—inch-worming in this way across Tibet, to Dharmsala India, where His Holiness lives. Recalling his remark is always enough to right my listing ship.

It's a fundament of Buddhist belief that *everyone, without exception,* is inherently a Buddha. Our Buddha-nature (and certainly I include myself here) is blocked from time to time by unresolved greed, anger, or delusion—negative energies known as kleshas. Disturbing as it might be to admit, I am not so unlike our former president or political figures for whom I have difficulty feeling compassion. I am a product of the same Universe, breathed by it, my heart beats according to its laws and principles. I also have the same brain, nervous system, and sense organs as those I ridicule.

It requires effort for me to perceive the Buddha in Donald Trump, but here's a test: Can you name a president in your memory who made it more graphically clear to millions of citizens the overriding importance of honesty, character, transparency, law, and social norms than Donald Trump? He taught by negative example, but the lessons were clear and irrefutable. His occupancy of the White House was instructive, and if elections are to be believed, more people agreed with me than didn't, because the predicted "red wave" of Republican victories did not occur.

When I am harshly critical or judgmental of others, I forget that I'm reinforcing the fiction that *I* don't also possess in my nature the qualities that I'm skewering. To do this, I have to pretend that I possess only the positive aspects of the human spectrum. This is why I've come to believe that *we are always the problem we are trying to solve in the world.*

The offloading of our own negative characteristics onto others is called projection. This is how wars, divorces, and feuds are nurtured. This is the way I can make myself feel virtuous and powerful and disguise my anxieties and difficult moral conundrums, such as "What is the difference between terrorists bombing an urban hotel filled with women and children and my country's warriors committing the same act?"

It is healthy to consider ourselves worthy of respect and love, but that is not identical with a blanket statement such as "We're the good guys." We are human beings, and as such we each possess the total spectrum of human thoughts and emotions. We may all have Jesus and Buddha within us, but we also have Hitler and Vladimir Putin. When we forget that, we abandon the necessary monitoring of ourselves to keep those negative parts of our humanity appropriately restrained.

In Buddhist Speech, we try not to aggrandize ourselves, try not to make ourselves better than others. We understand that in some way, everybody is trying hard, struggling with things like mortality, change, illness, loss, and stress, and, like us, waiting to one day board a train that never returns. A friend of mine reminds me that "we're all bozos on the bus," and this is why Fu called my attention to my carelessness.

The first three steps on the Eightfold Path—View, Thought, and Speech—identify Buddhist Conduct. The next three steps—Action, Livelihood, and Effort—relate to Buddhist Action: *what* we do and how we behave in the world.

Our behavior, our physical and mental acts, express our understanding of Buddhism more accurately and succinctly than our speech. When we pay less attention to our personal concerns, we liberate bandwidth to become more aware of and care for others, and the planet itself, of which we are an obviously inseparable part. People try to hold on to what they cherish (including the idea of their "own" life) and flee or evade what they don't. Everybody is in some sort of trouble. Everyone is in the cage of their own body, struggling against the implacable limits of time and health. When we divert our attention from our own problems, we can begin to observe this clearly, begin to see others as luminescent and beautiful as flowers, illuminated in the process of passing away.

Anyone having a faith, a practice, or a discipline also has something like a sailboat's keel, assisting them in returning to upright after (not if) they list off-center. The surest way to alleviate our own suffering is to help someone else, and it works with a near-magical efficiency. The moment we shift our attention from ourselves to others and begin actively strategizing how to help them, our own problems recede and diminish in importance.

I once narrated the voice-over for a video called "Never Alone," to be played at a media event in Paris. It was conceived and run by two women, one of whom is a close friend, an actress named Gabriella Wright. Gabriella possesses such luminous beauty and personal grace, you might think she had been born into a blessed spiritual dimension, unscathed by struggle or suffering.

Her sister committed suicide, and the act shattered Gabriella's life. Deep contact with her own relentless grief led her to transform it into an organization and a public event titled Never Alone: Worldwide Suicide Prevention Movement, designed to teach young people how and where to reach out for help when they are struggling. By shifting her focus from the personal to the universal, Gabriella effectively transformed her personal suffering into an instrument to relieve the suffering of others.

The facts are staggering. The Chicago Tribune reported that in the United States between January 2020 and Oct. 13, 2023, between 1.1 and 1.2 million people have died from the Covid pandemic. Half of

American adults are obese and obesity is described as the "epidemic crises of our time."* Overdose accounted for the deaths of 96,700 people in 2023,† and alcoholism accounted for 261 deaths every day, taking 40 percent of all hospital beds in the United States and killing 95,000 people annually from all causes—health, drunk driving, and so on—in 2023.‡ Worldwide, 4 million people a year die of it. Another 50,000 people die from gunshot wounds. Crystal meth is currently used by approximately 897,000 teenagers and adults in America, and approximately 5 million Americans regularly use cocaine. Since 1999 more than 932,000 people have died of drug overdoses.§

Each of these deaths was someone's son or daughter, aunt, uncle, mother, father, nephew, or niece enmeshed in a network who knew and loved them. Each of them was suffering in visible or invisible ways, and trying vainly to disguise it. Ripping a life from its network causes catastrophic ruptures in the social fabric. Gabriella dedicated her personal suffering to others, to concern for people who were alone and depressed during the pandemic. Living alone, without comfort and support, many became dangerously receptive to suicide. Gabriella's efforts are a clear example of Buddhist Action.

I would rather make a sandwich for a hungry person than give a speech about hunger to an audience of ten thousand, because making a sandwich is replicable behavior. Many people are too shy to speak before crowds, but anyone can make and distribute sandwiches, and anyone can model that behavior, multiplying its effect and extending its repercussions through time.

Buddhist Livelihood is trickier to discuss.

It might appear obvious that not many Buddhists are drug dealers (though I've met several Buddhist ex-drug dealers) or weapons

---

*Dr. Christos Mantozoros in the article "Over 4 Million Deaths per Year Caused by Obesity: Safe, Non-Invasive Treatments Could Help End Epidemic."
†Statistic from the website of the National Institute on Drug Abuse.
‡Statistic from the Centers for Disease Control.
§Statistic from the website of the Center for Disease Control and Prevention (current to 2020).

manufacturers. However, I have known Buddhist soldiers, Buddhist convicts, and others practicing in situations that would normally make practice extremely difficult.

Livelihood needs to be understood as more than one's occupation. If we take Buddhist vows seriously, we are attempting to harmonize our awareness and intention with the Buddha's own. This is the deep meaning of the very first of the Three Refuges Buddhists vow to follow— *I take refuge in the Buddha.* It expresses the understanding that these teachings are more reliable shelters (refuges) and protection against the vagaries of existence, changing our minds, or being victimized by our own greed, anger, and delusions, as opposed to wealth, power, status, political ideas, or transient emotions.

Difficulties arise because we live in and support (whether or not we want to) a culture whose depredations of the Earth are magnified by wealth, power, and indulgence. No matter our ideas about it, our lives benefit from and support an extractive economy that regards most of creation as *resources* to be exploited by humans for human purposes. This cultural common denominator makes it difficult to carefully assess the effects on our world of all the products we buy and use.* Virtue signaling and half measures are obviously no longer going to save the planet from the climactic fires, droughts, and floods brought about by the overheating of the atmosphere. Our elevation of the economy to primary importance among competing concerns is a codependency running contrary to kindness and regard for other species, and contrary to the fact that we and the environment are not isolated entities. Like waves in the ocean, we may appear discrete and "other" than elephants, jaguars, and the rest of the natural world, but we are all a part of the same ocean. We have hoodwinked ourselves into believing that because

---

*I might have used *environment* instead of *world,* but I try not to overuse the word because of its implication that we and it are separate. Language allows us to discuss subjects like pollution as if the consequences affecting plants and animals are not also part of our own suffering. The term reduces our complex interdependence to a much simpler form of phoney objectivity that allows the extractive economy, and its source in human greed for wealth and comfort, to continue with impunity.

they are identified by different names they exist independently.

Like it or not, whether going along with it or resisting it, we are *all* a part of human culture's exploitative and extractive cost to the world. There are none of us that use no plastic, are not dependent on fossil fuel motors, and bear some responsibility for the wars over rare minerals that power our cell phones and computers. There is no place to stand outside of all-of-it. We are not saved by disagreeing with our cultural values or remaining critical or working to change them. They are the matrix in which we exist. Society, as it's currently constituted, does not offer us many alternatives.

I had a friend, now passed, named Peter Blue Cloud, a Mohawk ironworker, poet, and artist. When he relocated from his native New York State to the Pacific Northwest, he worked as a logger. Because he loved cowboy songs, we used to sing together sometimes, and one afternoon, after a number of beers and songs, because he knew I considered myself an environmentalist, he confronted me, asking, "Do you resent me for cutting down these huge old trees?"

Some part of me felt, "Sure, I resent anyone cutting these majestic trees," but I had to consider his question seriously. He was a spiritual man, a mentor to many in the resurgence of Native American political consciousness, a warrior, and important artist in his community. I knew intuitively that it must have pained him to cut down these grandfather trees.

Sensing my thoughts, he continued: "Look, I'm an artist. I have few material resources and even less money. I have a house I rent. I have a family to support. This [work] is what I have to do. It fits my skill sets, and my comfort in the woods. But, before I fell one of those great trees, I take the time to make a bed of branches, so that they don't explode when they hit the ground. I say a prayer. That takes time, and the mill owners don't appreciate that. They want us to drop these old grandfather trees as fast as we can, but building those cushions is what I can do and how I demonstrate my respect."

When we are responsible for others, we may not always have the clear and simple choices many moral arguments demand. When I knew Peter, I had very little money and was living on about $2,500 dollars a year. My needs were minimal, and voluntary poverty seemed like a gift I could pay forward for the planet and model for others. It required lots of collective, communal effort to keep myself, companions, and the children fed, sheltered, and safe.

Years later, during the pandemic, I would read similar arguments from blue-collar employees on the slaughterhouse lines in Iowa and Nebraska. The governor of one of those states informed workers complaining of unsafe working conditions and their fears of infection that if they refused to come to work, they would be fired and she would personally cut their unemployment money. These men and women spend their days hacking up cattle, chickens, and pigs on assembly lines moving so rapidly that they sometimes were forced to wear diapers because they were not allowed bathroom breaks at work. (Consider that for a moment.) Obviously the governor's priorities were the health of the corporations, not the citizens of her state.

Such workers suffer low wages* and brutal schedules because we, as a nation, are addicted to cheap meat and goods and privilege our personal economy's over the well-being of our community. The primary concern of the corporate masters is offering good returns on the investments of their shareholders. The primary way we keep meat cheap is by exploiting the labor and farmers who are the base level of the pyramid of production. Are we to assume that such concerns are not the province of Buddhist practice, which declares its intention to save *all* beings?

While upper-middle-class people, including myself, are safely sanctuaried at home, doing dharma talks on Zoom and writing this from my little farm in rural Sonoma County, millions of workers on these factory lines and in shops and stores have been arbitrarily designated as *essential workers* and forced to report to work, pandemic or no pandemic. They are literally risking (and losing) their lives to keep the ready flow of cheap meat and products available to consumers—just as friends of Peter Blue

---

*A $7.00-an-hour legal wage affords an individual $14,560 if they work 52 weeks a year. That's nearly the exact figure of $14,580 the government calculates as poverty for an individual. At $15.00 an hour, the same 40-hour work week affords $28,000 a year, which is less than the governments' poverty income of $30,000 for a family of 4.

Cloud died in logging accidents while stripping the hills of living trees (and flooding the creeks with topsoil that washed down after the protection of the trees was removed). We are all in this together, and yet because the consequences fall disproportionately on the poor and undereducated, concern for a living wage has not reached the level of a national consensus.

Where the rubber meets the road in life, things are rarely clear or pure, and facile judgments backed by ideology solve very little and help very few. It is a mental pet to assume that just because we oppose and critique practices or processes as exploitative or destructive, somehow our resistance immunizes us from responsibility for their consequences. We're all a part of an immense, inconceivable organism, and every option, every choice, every moment is an inextricable admixture of positive and negative valences. Pretending that we are not responsible for the practices of the corporations we buy from is a self-induced blindness. The best we can do is to reach for the most enlightened possibilities *available* to us, without closing our eyes to the inevitable negative consequences hitchhiking along on the backs of those choices like remora riding sharks.

It would be comforting to believe that because I have LED lights in my house, and solar panels and battery backup, and because I drive an electric car I am somehow "better" than a log-truck driver or mill hand doing whatever they have to to survive. My efforts are incalculably small, and I can't offset the larger cultural indulgences I participate in by pretending that I have balanced the scale. I live in a 1,700-square-foot house on an acre and a half of land, by myself. In Guatemala this space might support ten people.

Simply by being an American—even a poor American—we consume an inordinate share of the Earth's resources. There is no way to avoid complicity with the destructive effects of our extractive economy offering us the endless bounty of cars, smart phones, snowmobiles, and yachts. That is our culture. The least we can do is stay conscious of the real issues and press for change by keeping them in the forefront of awareness. To do more than the least, we need to be actively urging discussions and plannings to reduce our net use of energy, per person, in a way that does not produce squalor.

I have to take responsibility for my garbage. I have to take responsibility for what the industries I buy from do to their workers and their waste. When my old computer or TV is sent to China to be pillaged for parts by the poor and their children, am I not related to the fact that those performing those tasks are sickening and dying from the poisons inherent in their disposal? I can pretend to be exempt from those consequences, but I am just comforting myself and allowing myself to avoid looking closely at my own life. (Part 3 of this book, "Engaged with Vernacular Zen," addresses such questions in greater depth.)

Mutuality and interdependence with the rest of creation means that we will always be required to expand our awareness even while we constantly fail in our efforts to minimize harm. If we are trying to fix our intention in a changing Universe, we have to reinstate it hundreds of times a day. This is what Buddhists refer to as "living by Vow." We'll never be perfect, but having admitted that, we can still press our political system to make the manufacturers of televisions and computers and cell phones reclaim them when discarded and force them to recycle the parts. Yes, this will shave points off stock shares, but those pennies on the dollar will also accumulate in effect, so that the poisonous byproducts of industry don't leak into our common environment.

We can press the system to amplify our recycling, push the limits of what we currently consider possible—minimizing our cultural use of plastic, for instance. None of us living in the higher levels of the privilege pyramid can afford to be proud and self-congratulatory of our own achievements, as if we were disconnected from the industrial and mental processes that generated our wealth.

What should also be implicit in this struggle is enough humor and compassion for ourselves that we can still enjoy the miracle of our lives and not torture ourselves for our failures. If we hope to model the pleasure the Buddha also taught, we have to remember that nowhere in Buddhist literature that I have read does it say that bodhisattvas were intemperate, judgmental, and guilt-ridden while trying to save all beings.

5

Marga Part II

THE EIGHTFOLD PATH IS A CIRCLE in which the eight points all revolve around an inner center of Buddha-nature. Any single designated practice interconnects with the rest. We all have to win our livelihood, no matter what culture, economic system, or geography we live in. When wealth was once measured by strings of wampum, people collected shells, ground and polished them, and their *labors* actually generated their wealth. When the means of creating wealth was freely acquired one could possibly assert that the poor were lazy (or untalented, or handicapped, or widows). Today, when the manufacture of money is controlled by the government and the government and our political system are organized around money, the situation is entirely different. Poverty is generated and controlled by ideologies often designed to protect great wealth and political power. The government forbids copying the money and maintains strict control over its creation and distribution. In a nation where most people do not own property, patents, or processes to generate capital, describing ourselves as a capitalistic culture is more of a misnomer than an accurate description.

We can no longer *make* our money today but instead must trade *something*—labor, service, acquired wealth, or products—with those who have amassed it. Despite its utility as a medium of exchange, for all its convenience and fungibility, more and more people on Earth find themselves denied access to the means to produce wealth, and life for the majority has become increasingly fraught.

I've never understood the supposed dignity in having to beg for a job. In my experience, humans love to work and will work without compensation when left to their own devices. People remodel their homes; create enormous gardens; build machines, guitars, furniture, cabinets, boats, and more; and generally thrum like members of a bee colony. A *job,* on the other hand, appears to be labor so odious one must be *paid* to do it. It is often neither ennobling, encouraging, interesting, meaningful, or personally fruitful. We have to do it, and occasionally the arguments of my old Socialist relatives come to mind, reminding me that conditions we consider unalterable today were made by people and can be remade or undone by them.

Employment by others is a relatively new condition in this country. As recently as immediately after the Civil War, most Americans made or grew what they required or traded for their needs without the intercession of money. Most of the early settlers were indentured for five to seven years to pay off the cost of their passage here from Europe. They cleared the forests, built the mills and granaries, grew the crops for their wealthy benefactors. When the time came to vote for representatives, it would seem only natural to vote for people with the wealth to effect change.*

People with spiritual intentions must further refine the question of livelihood by demanding of themselves that their sustenance be won in a way consistent with their values. It's never so easy that we can afford to consider ourselves ethically superior to people who may not make the same demands of themselves. The first thing to admit is that any idea of a "pure" place to stand outside of the culture is imaginary.

I flick the same light switch as Donald Trump. My Tesla required the mining of steel, copper, and rare minerals just like any other vehicle. My refrigerator runs on electricity that, despite my paying a premium for green power, may well be damaging watersheds or polluting the air.

---

*Douglas Fitzgerald Dowd, *The Twisted Dream: Capitalist Development in the United States since 1776* (Cambridge, Massachusetts: Winthrop Publishers, 1977).

When I visit one of those internet sites that calculates energy use and informs you how many planet Earths would be required for everyone to live as I do—despite my solar panels, LED lights, battery-powered car, and no-meat diet—the number I received was that it would require five planet Earths for everyone to live as I do. That realization pummels self-righteousness! It leaves me only three choices—ignore the subject, think and work more diligently about lowering my footprint, or join the destructive culture in "being all that I can be" at the expense of the Earth and its creatures and my fellow humans. In other words, everything works out well if I stop thinking.

Understanding that we have no separate place to stand means that our ideas of personal purity are inevitably inaccurate. Purity is an idea—a nice idea, but there's nothing save emptiness uncontaminated by the presence of other elements. Remember *dependent origination*? If this exists, that exists? My computer exists because the army exists, because the Pentagon exists, because the highways exist, because the trucks exist, because mining exists, because business exists, and on and on. That's reality. That is the world in which we live and strive. Enlightenment is *included* in that reality. But none of that implies that we are helpless and can simply be resigned to the world being reduced to garbage and ash by our use of it. By being bound to the culture we have some leverage on it. As in martial arts, the "fall" does not go to the biggest, but to the most aware.

So what can we do? Nearly fifty years ago, while considering the possibilities of earning my living as an actor, I realized that in leaving the counterculture where I'd just spent a decade, I was going to be getting my hands dirty in the "straight" world of money and ego. (That I never considered my counterculture use of heroin, consorting with the Hell's Angels, indiscriminate sex, drug and alcohol use, or getting my hands dirty should be a testament to my youthful myopia.) I was troubled by questions like: "What could I do to mitigate harm or damage of films with which I disagreed? How could I protect myself from falling prey to value systems I considered unhealthy?"

With five or six years of meditation under my belt by then, I had begun to understand that each moment we live is always an admixture of positive and negative valences, like the Universe itself. Without a "pure" place to separate myself from everything, I reasoned I could at least search for the most enlightened option available *in each instant*. That implied that I could not control, for instance, the *content* of the movie I was making or alter its political perspective. If I found its argument to be odious, I could always refuse to do it, but, like Peter Blue Cloud and most of my fellow Americans, I had mortgage(s) to meet; children to educate, clothe, and feed; and bills to pay. Like anyone else without property or inheritance, I was scrambling for a livelihood.

After much wrestling with the subject, I came to understand that I *could* control *how* I made the movie. I could, for instance, treat each and every person I met with respect and dignity. I could treat the lowliest assistant in the same manner I greeted the director or star. I could be the first actor ready on the set each day. I could be thoroughly prepared with the day's work. I could resist expressing impatience or competition with my peers and coworkers and try to ensure that, to the best of my ability, the working environment remained cooperative, light, fun, and safe. Those things were in my control, and therefore I could assume responsibility for them—regulating world capitalism and neoliberalism were not.

I followed those decisions rigorously, and as a consequence of those decisions, on virtually every film I made (160 by retirement) a coworker or colleague would ask me: "Hey, do you have some kind of religion or something?" When I inquired why they asked, it always turned out that they had observed the consistency of my behavior and found it compelling. Their observation and questions afforded me the opportunity to discuss my practice and beliefs with them, and remind them that they could imitate my behavior if they chose without changing their religion or becoming Buddhists.

That's how the Buddhist precepts operate, as moment-to-moment self-queries about what Buddha might do in similar circumstances. In its deepest implications, the word *nirvana* (the imagined perpetual bliss that attracts so many to Buddhism) means that we are actually untethered and physically free to be radically different in the next instant. If we practice that (which is another way of saying renewing ourselves in each moment) consistently, and we consistently choose the most enlightened options available, we are doing Buddha's work.

Every moment presents a wealth of choices for us. If we want to minimize the damage our existence causes to self, other, and the planet, if we want to be kind and not use the world harshly, if we would like to model peace and equanimity between people, we can constantly review the Eightfold Path as we act—at least until the time our good intentions are fixed as habits. But even then, knowing that we're fallible, why not check? Sometimes there may not appear to be any ideal option, but we still have to act. Even doing nothing is a choice.

You can go to a monastery, and, in my experience, monasteries are extraordinary examples of people living with a minimal impact, but they are still populated with humans—which is to say, with all the errors to which humans remain prone. Monastic institutions are not free of status competitions, jealousies, and struggles for power, but usually they know it, and such subjects are relegated for discussion and work. The monks and nuns, laypeople and priests consume food and books, many have families and relationships, and all participate in the larger economy. They're doing their best.

The story that follows is an example of Buddhist Effort, which I learned years ago.

There was a fellow (and friend) named Harry Roberts at Green Gulch Farm Zen Center while I was living nearby. He was an agronomist and a biologist, but he'd had a storied and complicated life. At some point he'd even been Ginger Rogers's dancing partner.

We became friends while I was there because he'd been raised by a Yurok Indian* shaman from childhood and formally trained as a

---

*The Yurok people live along a 44-mile corridor surrounding the Klamath River in Del Norte and Humboldt Counties. They're one of the few tribes in North America that have never been removed from their native homeland.

shaman's apprentice. I knew the country where he grew up intimately, since I was part owner of a commune called Black Bear on the edge of the Trinity Wilderness Area near the confluence of the Klamath and Salmon Rivers. I had close friends in the Karuk tribe who were immediate neighbors to the Yuroks and had hunted, gambled, and reveled with them, in the process of studying the bounty of the Klamath and Salmon River watersheds. (*Yurok* in the Karuk language indicates "downstream people," while *Karuk* itself means "upstream.") One of our Black Bear sons married a Karuk girl, and Harry and I had native and Zen friends in common; I think he was relieved to be able to speak to someone for whom his background was not an oddity.

Both Karuk and Yurok people have a healing ceremony called the Brush Dance, performed for tribal members who are ill. A sick person would be set in the center of the dancing area and surrounded by the entire tribe. Beforehand every participant would spend days cleaning and ensuring that their ritual regalia was impeccably perfect—each feather rendered perfect or replaced. Soiled buckskin and bindings meticulously cleaned, beads in perfect order, and so on.

Once, Harry told me, when he was a boy, he was fretting at the diligence required for such repairs. He was working alongside his stepfather, the shaman, and became restless, whining to his stepdad: "Why do we have to be so perfect, this way? Nobody's going to know."

His stepfather did not respond, nor did he utter a word to him for three days, letting Harry stew with the problem without guidance. (This is pretty much the Native American way I gathered, without overmuch worry about precious little psyches being damaged.) Harry would have referred to the silent treatment as "building character."

After several days of silence, Harry's stepfather sat him down and addressed him: "D'jou think on why I haven't spoken to you?"

Harry nodded that he had.

"So you know why I was cross with you then?"

Harry shook his head, indicating, "No, I don't."

His stepdad explained, "This ceremony only works because the sick person is convinced that *every* member of the tribe, those he likes and those he doesn't, all put out their very best effort to indicate how important to them the health of that sick person was. If you cheat, or take the easy way out, you'll imagine that others might cheat, too. So, if you get sick and need help, you'll be out there and filled with doubt. You won't trust the good feeling and support you're being given. You won't have that support as healing energy to help you. You won't believe that everyone in the tribe did their absolute best to help *you*."

One of the ways we express our affection and respect for and to the world is by offering our best. Taking the time to be impeccable. This is not to say that we will always operate at the same peak level. On some days we're not up to snuff, but we can still do the best that we are able to on that day. Because Buddhism does not posit a god separate from her creations, there is no superior power to judge us, nor any hells but those on earth and of our own minds to which we can be condemned. So, to remain free of external edicts and commandments from others, we must consult our own innate wisdom and strive to do our best, moment by moment and day by day.

There was a time around my sixty-fifth birthday that I surrendered to a spasm of greed—I wanted an old 12-cylinder Ferrari before I died. It's laughable today, but I thought about it, researched, and prepared to buy one, readying my garage and so forth. In the end I couldn't do it. I could have plundered my savings for the money, but in the end I denied it to myself, because I didn't want to promote such an affluent symbol as a worthy goal that might stoke the envy of others. I considered the health of my children and granddaughter, the foxes, red-shouldered hawks, and great horned owls where I live. I let it go for everything that breathes oxygen, for all the non-human beings who need clean water, and forests, and habitat. It's laughable as a personal sacrifice, but it was something I had envied since my teens. However, if I make less than my best efforts, I'm failing to "clean my regalia," wishing the world would be different while taking advantage of its current form.

The penultimate station on the path is Buddhist Effort. In terms of spiritual practice, the effort to be *mindful,* to pay attention, has a specific meaning. We monitor our internal states because we know that we can express any impulse on the human spectrum—positive and negative. If we're not paying attention, we can easily follow an aberrant impulse and cause harm, no matter how spiritual we believe we may be. Envy floats through our human DNA. Rage as well. Disgust. Judgment. Passions that can destabilize us or our community are an instant below our serene and affable social surface.

It's our responsibility to keep our internal house in order; to do the housecleaning; to dust and clean and sweep out all the corners; to prevent harsh words from leaking past our lips or harmful impulses from animating our muscles. That's what we can control. In fact, it's the *only* thing in this Universe we can control. The governor of that control is our *intention:* our intention to be kind, our intention to be responsible, our intention to be developed, dignified, useful people. Given the quixotic nature of the human mind and the internal lawlessness of our psyches, training that intention and focusing it until it becomes a habit is no small task.

If you've ever meditated, you've observed how difficult it is to do something as simple as sit still and pay attention to your own posture, breath, and hand position. Some beginners cannot count their breaths past three before becoming distracted. Some may be congratulating themselves on getting to ten and, in the next round, will be lost in fantasy. It's okay. We're training our intention and housebreaking our personalities as if they were puppies. These are the only things we can control but to do that we must counteract a lifetime of indulgent habits and believing everything we think.

In the same way that our culture often extracts the active ingredient from a wild herb, synthesizes and merchandises it, there is current movement seeking to extract mindfulness from its spiritual context and utilize it as a device to help corporate employees work more efficiently. That's an efficiency technique disguised as a spiritual practice, designed to produce more widgets, sales, contacts, or services with less counter-productive employee interactions. It is basically an extension of greed, sidestepping any considerations of the moral or ethical nature of the work that's being done, or the side effects it might be producing in the culture. It's like cutting the heart out of a dove to study its nature.

Mindfulness cannot be severed from its most important task of monitoring our awareness and behavior to consistently express compassion and care. Making employees "mindful" to be better at their jobs (whatever that job may be) is like being attracted to someone because of their talent or charisma and disregarding their character. The bureaucratic model may employ concentration to make work more effective, aiding the bottom line, but it has no inherent moral valence, and, like intelligence, can be applied to immoral or amoral practices with equal facility. Naming such practices "mindfulness" is an expropriation of a spiritual word to camouflage an extractive intention.

Buddhist mindfulness reminds us of two things. While we may not be responsible for what happens to us in the world (dukkha) and what arises in us as a consequence of that affliction (samudaya), we *are* responsible for containing the effects of both and ensuring that negative energy does not spill out over our barricades and cause conflagrations in the world (nirodha). We are also responsible for transforming our negative states into wholesome and positive ones. All this is in the service of a Grand Story of which we should not lose sight—the Buddha's intention to save all beings from suffering.

The final step, closing the circle of the Eightfold Path, is Buddhist *Samadhi,* which literally means "concentration," "absorption," or "meditation." The texts refer to this as a one-pointed state of mind, when it is concentrated and focused enough so that mental chatter slows and one might say that mind merges with the object of attention. At that point there may well be a moment where the self temporarily disappears, and the world stands revealed as impeccable and perfect without it. That is a description of a temporary visionary state, however. We can't live there permanently. On a more permanent level, we might say that it radically alters one's perception of being central to the Universe, of being first among equals. Freed of that responsibility of maintaining self-importance, we are liberated to find our authentic purpose in life and responsive to following the directives of our Buddha-nature.

Each of us is a nonreplicable event. Buddha was not trying to make everyone like himself but instead urged them to see clearly who they were and how they could use that identity and awareness to be of help to a troubled world. His teaching was not a question of amassing knowledge at all. Particularly Zen (and I write this fully aware of the irony of it), which despite the thousands of books published about it, does not require a great deal of intellectual learning to practice.

Buddha's cousin Ananda, who memorized every word the Buddha uttered and was his closest companion, was reputedly never enlightened until many years after the Buddha's death. No one could possibly have had greater access to the Buddha's teachings, and if enlightenment was simply a problem to be solved by knowledge, Ananda was perhaps the person in the best position to do that.

It's also worth mentioning that just as the Buddha stresses Right Samadhi, there can be wrong samadhi. People like Stalin and Hitler, who have had visions of grandiosity and self-importance and organized their lives as a quest to fulfill those visions, were fueled by a kind of samadhi-like power. Right Samadhi always includes the well-being of all creation—all people, all species. Once you experience such a vision you will forever see, feel, and assess events differently. Your choices will be regulated by fidelity to Buddha-nature as it is expressed in your life.

6

An Introduction to the Precepts

THE BUDDHA WAS SUCH A CHARISMATIC FIGURE that the record reveals that just one conversation with him was enough to change people dramatically. His original spiritual companions, who had accompanied his six years of study in the jungle, had been cross with him for accepting the bowl of rice and milk from the servant girl who'd saved his life. Yet legend informs us that as he approached them on the road after his enlightenment, they perceived that he was a radically changed person, even before he spoke.

When he spoke, he articulated the Four Noble Truths, the Eightfold Path, and Sixteen Precepts in easily remembered forms, offering instructions as to how these might express enlightenment in their own lives. I want to thank my friend and dharma brother Gary Gach, a Buddhist writer whose works you should read if you haven't, for urging me to include discussion of the precepts here, and particularly my old friend and transmitted teacher Teah Strozer, founder of the Brooklyn Zen Center, for a particularly lucid translation of the precepts.

Buddhism is a vast shelter, and it's worthwhile remembering that among the extraordinary diversity of Buddhists around the world, secular or monastic, married or single, all Buddhists follow the Three Refuges and the precepts. A precept is a guide for moderating behavior. It's not a commandment like the Ten Commandments and they do not share their very authoritarian tone—"Thou shalt have no God before me." This statement describes a reality that includes other gods and creates a heirarchy among them. The god giving the commandment commends himself to us as the most important one (in much the same manner our ego convinces us that we are the first among equals). His commands and authority derive from being the Creator of the Universe, and he accepts no deviation from that loyalty.

There is an arbitrary nature to all such creation myths: Genesis, the Kalevala, Old Man Coyote—each culture has its own narrative about how the world and its varied life-forms arrived into being. The Abrahamic religions (Judaism, Christianity, and Islam—all descendants or "children" of Abraham) are built around dualities of Good and Evil, Light and Dark. Christianity has the God of Good, and Satan—the God of Evil. Satan, with his goatlike legs, horns, tail, and cloven hooves, is a judgment on nature itself. The God of Good lives somewhere in the formless reaches of the heavens, apparently either unbound from earthly concerns, which may cause the demise of millions, or otherwise deep in the weeds with us, theoretically looking over each of us personally.

Buddhism does not have such contradiction at its core. Its belief in Emptiness, the formless, pregnant energy underlying and simultaneously creating the entire Universe, addresses the largest, most absolute underlying Unity. Perhaps this focus on the pre-formed common denominator to everything has saved Buddhism from some of the underlying conflicts that afflict other religions. In Christianity, for instance, the story concerning Jesus's virgin birth and many doctrinal disagreements of Christian faith were not clarified until three centuries after Christ's death. The website GotQuestions.org describes what occurred at the Council of Nicea as follows:

[Emperor] Constantine . . . called for a meeting of bishops to be held in Nicea to resolve some escalating controversies among the church leadership. The issues being debated included the nature of Jesus Christ, the proper date to celebrate Easter, and other matters. The failing Roman Empire, now under Constantine's rule, could not withstand the division caused by years of hard-fought, "out of hand" arguing over doctrinal differences. The emperor saw the quarrels within the church not only as a threat to Christianity but as a threat to society as well.

One of the issues resolved at the coucil was the issue of Mary's virgin birth, with the banishment of a priest named Arius, who asserted a normal birth for Jesus.

None of this is a judgment of Christianity. Buddhism is as chockfull of mystical narratives as every other faith and underwent its own major revision about five hundred years after Buddha's death. At that time, Buddhism was concentrated on personal enlightenment (referred to today as the Hinayana school, the Small Vehicle) and the upwelling of interest from artists, craftspeople, and laymen expanded the philosophy to include all beings (the Mahayana school, the Great Vehicle). It also has its share of mythical events—asserting that immediately after Gautama's birth, he stood up, took seven steps north, and uttered:

> *I am chief of the world,*
> *Eldest in the world.*
> *This is the last birth.*
> *There will be henceforth for me*
> *no more re-becoming.*

Furthermore, according to myth, every place the baby Gautama set his foot, a lotus flower supposedly bloomed, and the shadow of the trees sheltering him followed his ambulations. Tales such as this reveal the embroidery of the human mind itself, digging ever more deeply into a subject.

Many people worship the Buddha in the same manner Christians and Jews worship God and Yahweh as holy beings. But such faith-based legends are not fundamental or required for Buddha's teaching, and he certainly ascribed no such magical qualities to himself. There is nothing in the Buddha's teachings that requires us to believe in anything that we cannot ascertain for ourselves, except the fact that once upon a time in ancient Nepal a young man named Gautama lived and attained enlightenment. All such tales are arbitrary, wonderful, fanciful, uplifting, and inspiring—but fashioned, repeated, and transmitted by humans in different circumstances at different times and places. The Buddha addressed himself to operations of the universe that anyone could observe if they took the time.

Buddhist precepts are quite different from the Ten Commandments in another way as well. Most Buddhists don't conceive of a creator as separate from creation itself or, in other words, any distinction between a god and his/her works. Perhaps what most closely corresponds to the sacred in Buddhism is what Buddha described as Emptiness and his adherents have named Buddha-nature—the primordial energetic formlessness, beginningless, and endless, underlying (and composing) all phenomena, eternally gestating itself into infinite forms in astronomical cosmic play.

For Buddhists, the Universe is a singular, seamless interactive event. And despite the apparent singularity of what the Chinese refer to as "the 10,000 things"—the *apparently* separate trees, birds, jellyfish, dolphins, hummingbirds, insects, thoughts, mountain ranges, and leopards—none can exist independently of all of it. None possess a germ of identity discoverable as the "self" of that object or named occurrence. Consequently, Buddhists describe them as *empty* (of self).

It would be equally true to say that nothing exists *only* singularly. Every apparent singularity, including myself, is a composite of elements, some of which are apparently personal—body, personality, the content of some thoughts and feelings. But "mine" is an assertion that cannot be definitively proved, because the "I" we refer to so habitually is also composed of numerous "non-I" elements such as sunshine and oxygen, water, microbes in the soil, pollinating insects, and the like, which are distinctly impersonal and yet indivisible from our personal life. There is no existence separate from them. When "I" die, these elements do not, so it is as logical to assert that "I" am as eternal as I am time limited.

Buddhist literature often refers to our singular existence as an illusion because it accounts for only the self-centered perspective we perceive through our own personality and not the vastness supporting and nourishing it and of which it is equally composed.

The precepts relate to the relationship between the two, between our conduct and the larger reality. In the same way that a small pebble dropped in a still pond can extend ripples of influence, the "I" we seem so certain about, if we look, is limited to three possibilities about any event, object, or circumstance we relate to. Our "self" can either like, dislike, or be neutral about circumstances and objects. This is a very tiny room in which to be constrained in the vastness of the Universe.

A free person understands that they have access to the entire spectrum of humanity within them. Those who understand this and realize that aberrant (or antisocial) thoughts and impulses can strike any of us are usually among the first to seek some form of guidance. For Christians it is the Ten Commandments, for Muslims the Koran, and for Jews the Torah, which the ancient Rabbi Hillel whittled down to "What is hateful to yourself do not do to your fellow-man" (Babylonian Talmud, Shabat 31a). For him, this is the entire Torah, the rest is commentary.

For Buddhists, the precepts are the commentary on what could be considered variants of the fundamental instruction of compassion. They all also address the gap (when it exists) between what we believe and what we do.

The first precepts are called the Three Refuges because a person vows to take refuge in the Buddha, the dharma (his teachings, and truth), and sangha (his community of followers). We normally think of refuge as a shelter from some affliction or danger, and the Buddhist sense of the word does not stray far from that understanding. To seek shelter within the Buddha is to remind ourselves of our deepest wisdom—what the Brooklyn Zen Center translates as "the vast stillness, clarity, and kindness that is the true nature of all life." It is the largest possible unifying common denominator, generating everything we can name in the Universe, including time.

When we remember these precepts, the Buddha himself and all the wise and honored bodhisattvas, male and female, are transformed from long-dead icons into living presences, a vast congress of clouds, waves, mountain ranges, and hiccups, exerting influence through the flesh-and-blood medium of human forms practicing their dedication to the Buddha's way. We are Buddhas when we perceive as Buddhas, when we think as Buddhas do, and when we behave like Buddhas. The precepts and the Eightfold Path are our maps. They are not commands from an all-potent authority.

Understanding and countermanding the delusions of an isolated fixed self and understanding dependent origination, are the basis of Buddha's assertion of "no fixed self." This is often overlooked by those who concentrate perhaps overmuch on reincarnation. The notion of an independent, fixed identity, body hopping through time, is something more than an error, because it actually cleaves the Universe into opposite parts, sundering its original wholeness. I would never challenge teachers as eminent as His Holiness the Dalai Lama and the Tibetan tradition Masters. I am speaking of the Zen sects who do not emphasize reincarnation. It could be true, or not, but it is always "received" wisdom, something we are told; not something we experience in this life. Most spiritual traditions have similar distinctions over various points of orthodoxy. I have had this conversation in Lhasa, Tibet, with several Rimpoches, people reputed to be reincarnated Lamas. When I asked them about it, they giggled and responded, "I don't know. This is what I was told."

Origination and the concept of Emptiness are the masculine, intellectual side of Buddha's teachings. They are useful and beguiling, but until they are fused with their feminine counterparts of kindness and compassion (where the rubber meets the road of the world of ordinary life), they remain intellectual conceits. The precepts are the Buddha's warm and compassionate heart expressed as action. We are reminded of this in figures like Avalokitesvara (Kwan Yin), the Buddha in compassionate form who is often represented as either male or female, open to and responding to the suffering of the world.

To "take refuge in the Buddha" means to seek shelter from the world's afflictions in the wisdom of Buddha's worldview and teachings, which are factual, dependable, and easily observable. They do not require belief in miracles and leaps of faith or the supposition that people long ago were markedly different from those today.

Some sects of Buddhism follow faith practices similar to the Abrahamic religions—for instance, repetitive chanting of Buddha's name—but the results of Buddha's practices can be personally affirmed by the devotee practicing them and do not necessarily require the intercession of priests and elders. For this reason, and the fact that the Buddha was pointedly human and not divine, many people do not consider Buddhism a religion but instead a practice for living a tranquil, dignified life of service to others.

The second of the Three Refuges, "refuge in the dharma," can be stated as "the teaching of the way of life, day by day, that accords with Buddha." Dharma can mean either the nature of reality or the truth of things, and adherents of the Buddha have confirmed for themselves that this description of reality and how things work accords with their own perceptions.

Practicing zazen meditation is the practice of constructing a personal doorway into Buddha's mind, which is your own mind, your own clear knowing. It is a personal undertaking to explore your inner geography, the vagaries of your thoughts and feelings with rigor and precision. What might that mean? As an example, consider that when someone angers us by word or deed, that person may trigger our emotions. The trigger did not cause us to feel as we do in that moment, which means the emotions themselves are ours. Normally we blame the trigger as the cause for the emotion vexing us, and we shift our attention from our own experience to other's behavior. In fact, the emotions are our own, and only we can study, understand, and moderate them. Concentrating on the trigger, while a common human practice, is a convenient distraction for those afraid to face the truth of their inner lives.

In Buddhist practice, we don't separate primary truth from ethical behavior. The means *are* the end—meaning, the manner in which we pursue our goals *is* the goal we are actualizing, no matter what we think we're "saying." People who may have debased themselves pursuing a compelling goal, amassing great wealth, position, or power, remain debased after they have achieved those goals, and may still be searching in vain for the anticipated rewards they expected.

The precepts are guides through mazes like this. Like posture in zazen, they offer us standards against which to check ourselves and our intentions. Our Buddha mind (usually expressed as intuition or feeling) is where we seek refuge and consultation to see whether what we are about to do accords with the Buddha's way.

The questions we pose to ourselves as we "take refuge in the sangha"—the community of beings that is our refuge and support—will emanate from our Buddha mind, not the limited understanding of self, our normal personality. It does no good ultimately to look outside ourselves, though consulting with therapists, senior practitioners, and teachers and studying what other teachers have concluded may well reveal subtleties and patterns of behavior we might not recognize immediately. I'll discuss this in greater depth in the next chapter.

The Buddha to whom practitioners refer, bow to in gratitude, and honor with beautiful statues, altars, and flowers is not the physical Buddha regarded as a supernatural, holy being. The gestures of respect practitioners make are to Buddha-nature, our own innate wisdom and the inherent wisdom of the Universe. Looking deeply enough, our own wisdom and the wisdom of the Universe *are not different from Buddha's.* Refuge in the Buddha is refuge from the delusion of selfishness and self-concern. A refuge is a shelter from the buffeting of daily life, from confusions of the mind, from the consequences of past behavior. The precepts are more like boundaries of the territory we hope to inhabit to ensure that we are following the Buddha's path and stepping in his footprints.

Dharma refers not only to the Buddha's teachings but also to "the truth" as it manifests itself in all times and places. To take refuge in dharma means to concentrate on what may be learned from Buddha's teachings (study) as well as from our internal resident Buddha, communicating to us through our hunches and feelings. It is the truth of the world itself, as it is, which is why poet Gary Snyder sometimes evokes *wilderness* as the model of dharma—Nature expressing itself for its own ends and purposes, outside of human will and intention; dharma clarified from a regard beyond the restrictive perimeters of our ego.

A word about ego. Our ego is not our enemy. If that were the case, it would never have survived the crucible of evolution. However, its work on our behalf remains so focused on self-preservation, self-interest, self-promotion, and prioritizing the Universe into what it likes and what it dislikes that it cannot be relied upon as an objective translator of "things as it is." Similarly, because it considers itself first among equals it is not always a reliable instructor on how to behave with others.

Meditation is the mind-body practice that allows us to occasionally slip the ego's boundaries and achieve intimate contact with things as it is. It is a prerequisite of wisdom, and if there is any cultural or spiritual practice that does not in some manner employ meditation, I can't identify it.

To take refuge in the sangha means to prioritize the advice and friendship of those who follow the Buddha's teachings. The sangha also includes the community of great wisdom seekers from the past and our comrades in this day and age with whom we study and grow. It is not essentially different from Christian, Jewish, or Islamic communities of the faithful and observant, except that a Buddhist sangha does not require fealty to a particular mythology, costume, or much adherence to dogma. It is a wisdom tradition more than a religious tradition.

Buddhist Action organizes our lives to follow these vows, which are never separate from our moral commitments. The Buddha was very clear about this. Rather than being a church one visits once a week to reaffirm our spirituality, Buddhism is more like a church one inhabits moment by moment.

7

The Precepts
Part II

THE SECOND SET OF PRECEPTS is called the Three Pure Precepts. They are often expressed as:

> *Avoid all evil.*
> *Cultivate all good.*
> *Actualize all good for others.*

The First Pure Precept forces us to depend on a relative expression—the Second Pure Precept of "I vow to do good"—because without referencing its opposite, good can be rendered meaningless: kindness is good, charity is good, chocolate is good, music is good. Adding its opposite clarifies the field of play but creates a semantic confusion. The terms *good* and *evil* suggest fixed, easily identifiable states that theoretically mean the same thing to all people. Everyone who has reached adulthood has experienced topics that some define as good and others deplore: abortion, the death penalty, sexual preference, gender, liberals, conservatives, to name a few. When we can replace *good* and *evil* with less general, more specific words, we should do so, concentrating on *behavior* as opposed to suggesting that the *essence* of someone has the fixed quality of good or evil. Of course it is good to feed the hungry, but do we still feel that after we have declared those people enemies?

It is good to care for abandoned animals, but do we support feral cats until they eat all the songbirds, or puppy mills generating thousands of puppies that may or may not be sold and will then be put to death?

The word *evil*, besides being an English word, does not translate what the Buddha really said. The word he used was Akusala, which means unskillful. It is a word that concentrates on behavior and not one's essence.

Most people agree that torture and deliberate cruelty are evil. However, their definitions always rely on context. However, their definitions are never precise nor universal. When our nation recently euphemized torture (the Dark Side) and told citizens it was a "necessity" during the Iraq war, the nation never considered it evil because we don't consider our side capable of evil. The euphemism helps us disguise the fact that every human possesses the capacity to express everything—including rage, hatred, and desire for revenge—that any other human can express. It is less confusing to be more specific and use precise language like *deliberate cruelty* and *revenge* when that is what we intend. Describing such actions (in others) as evil lulls us into believing that, even when we are behaving identically, we are somehow exempt from the consequences. *We* could never behave that way, and it gives us the latitude to disguise our actions with euphemisms. Words like *cruelty* and *vengeance* are sharper, more specific and pungent than *enhanced interrogation*. They allow us less room to delude ourselves. *Deliberate cruelty* allows us no inoffensive disguise for what is being proposed and perpetuated.

Humans *exactly* like us have participated in massacres and genocides, carpet bombed civilian cities, placed bombs in baby carriages, always believing that their god had given them dispensation to destroy the children of other gods. People exactly like us are the only state actor on Earth who dropped two nuclear bombs on heavily populated cities in Japan.

I vow to do good may mean any and all of the following: I vow to be continuous at this effort. I vow to foster actions that engender insight, happiness, and clarity. I vow not to lie. I will try to discover loving kindness within myself. Each and all these meanings devolve from being in contact with one's *innate* nature. We're not going to read it on a cellphone app. It's not going to come from reading an article. It's not going to come from my teaching or a Ted talk. Ultimately, it's going to be perceived, accepted (or not), and adjudicated by your own awareness and your own measure of dedication to service and helpfulness. The time-tested method for enhancing such perception is to regularly sit in meditation.

The Third Pure Precept is "I vow to save all beings"; in other words, I vow to live for the benefit of all beings. It's not that Buddhists will bring you "the good news" as a liberating bulletin from God. We hope you'll discover that your own nature is an authentic expression of the Universe, and we vow to help you achieve that in whatever way we can.

One of the great philosophical contributions of Buddhism to human thought and culture is the concept of the bodhisattva—beings so dedicated to the welfare of others that they vow to postpone their own enlightenment until all other beings have been saved. To save all beings ultimately means to aid them in discovering and expressing their own nature. It's not an edict to be imposed on them. It's not "a right way." Our practice has forms that I'll discuss at length later, particularly the forms of sitting zazen. But the old Zen adage expresses the goal most concisely—"Formal practice/Informal mind." We govern and restrain the body so the mind can be soft and free. And freedom from habits, dark thoughts and impulses, attachments to a fixed identity, self-ishness, and prejudice is what the Buddha's life exemplified.

Disciplining the body is a direct way to discipline extraneous mental impulses. One way to calm overexcitement in the mind, allowing it to slow down and observe fogs of dialog, grudges, envies, resentments, and passions without being hooked by them, is meditating—sequestering enough awareness by paying attention to your posture and breath in an uninterrupted communion with body and mind. This reservation of awareness gives us a safe perch from which to watch the flow of our thoughts and feelings without being snagged.

Originally derived from monastic rules governing behavior at the

earliest Buddhist temples, there used to be more than two hundred precepts (depending on the school) for monks and about three hundred
precepts for nuns, which a number of scholars suspect were political
accommodations to a male-dominated culture to win permission for
women to practice at all. In the tradition that took hold after Dogen,
that number was reduced to sixteen, with the first six being the refuges
and Three Pure Precepts.

The third set of precepts in my lineage is known as the Ten Clear
Mind Precepts, sometimes referred to as the Ten Grave Precepts. They
exist to refine our understanding and offer us ethical guidelines for
our lives.

THE TEN CLEAR MIND PRECEPTS

A First Look

I vow not to kill, which includes not creating the cause for others to
kill. For strict practitioners this would include not colluding against
any other sentient beings, doing everything possible to avert war as
well as not supporting the meat trade.

I vow not to take what is not given. In the realm of perfected dharma
practice this precept of not stealing would include holding no
thought of gain.

I vow not to misuse sexuality. This would include not coveting and certainly not creating a veneer of attachment. A corollary to this might
include accepting responsibility for bringing new life into the world.

I vow not to lie means to communicate truthfully. In the realm of the
inexplicable dharma, the precept of not speaking dishonestly might
include putting forth not one word. It calls to mind the student in
ancient times, challenged by his teacher to demonstrate his knowledge, who replied, "If I speak, I lie. If I don't speak, I'm a coward."
We have to speak, but we have to speak with the understanding
that anything we say about Buddha-nature is at best a partial explanation and therefore never completely truthful.

I vow not to intoxicate mind or body of self or others. This does not mean enjoying wine or alcohol but instead refers to anything that might alter or obscure our original pure nature and inherent clarity. It can also refer to harboring delusions and ideas to the point of intoxication, even proselytizing Buddhism in an uncritical or overly emotional manner.

I vow not to slander, which means either lying about or speaking ill of others. Slander is something more than simple falsehood, because it also includes the intention to harm others in some manner. The positive corollary would be to encourage one another to behave helpfully, charitably, and kindly.

I vow not to praise self at the expense of others. This is also a caution against comparative thinking. Each of us is a perfect expression of ourselves, which is why Suzuki-roshi once observed, "You're perfect just the way you are . . . *and* you could use a little work." We say perfect because each of us represents a long chain of karma and influences, which, like evolution itself, has worked on us until we have become a perfect expression of that karma. However, because we can consciously vow to change our behavior, we are never locked forever in the consequences of what we have done or thought and can change those consequences by changing our thoughts and behavior.

I vow not to be possessive of anything. This operates on a number of levels. Primarily it urges us not to be stingy with wisdom, generosity, or helpfulness, particularly concerning dharma. We are urged not to hoard for our own benefit that which might help others. On a deeper level it is an inquiry into our ideas of who we consider ourselves to be and what we believe we might lack. Who is it that owns? I don't believe it is an admonition to give your shoes away to a barefoot person, but in some circumstances it might be. It is certainly an admonition to be generous with our wealth and our understanding, but on a deeper level it reminds us that the Universe has given us everything we need, and therefore we might consider what it is we believe we lack.

I vow not to harbor ill will. On the simplest level this is a violation of the vow *to save all beings.* To harbor ill will is to be stuck in a narrative usually related to a moment in time that has passed. Someone did something to us that we took personally and we can't release our resentment or anger. The person or event was a *trigger* for our negative reaction, but the emotion is actually *ours.* As Buddhists, we are urged to change our focus from the person who triggered us to understanding and liberating ourselves from our negative feelings. Keeping the experience locked onto the trigger prevents us from seeing things clearly and impersonally, obscuring events in a narrative that locks us perpetually in the past.

I vow not to disparage the Three Treasures. Since the Three Treasures, Buddha, dharma, and sangha cover everything from wisdom to interactions with others, this might appear to be a no-brainer. What is to be gained by trash-talking wisdom, teachers, and the teachings? It's also a caution to not privilege your teacher or beliefs over all others, not to engage in needless disputes about dharma or other sangha members, distracting yourself from your own practice. They are called treasures for a reason.

If we fight with or disparage others, with whom will we live? If we cloud wisdom with ignorance we are actively disrupting the harmonious flow of the Universe and breaking our vows. Perhaps you had a bad experience with a teacher or sangha. There may be a temptation to blame them for your difficulties, but when we point our finger at others, we often forget there are three fingers pointing back at ourselves. The path of wisdom dictates studying our own faults more diligently than those of others.

Each of these precepts has three levels. Let's discuss the refuges first, then the precepts, though please remember, the refuges, the pure precepts, and the Clear Mind Precepts are all simply precepts.

The Three Poisons

Buddhists refer to energies and impulses preventing us from expressing our natural enlightenment as kleshas, or the Three Poisons, dark thoughts and impulses. In ancient cartoons for nonliterate people, the Three Poisons were depicted as a rooster, signifying greed; a snake, signifying ill will; and a pig, signifying ignorance. One of the reasons that we meditate is to become intimate with those impulses so we can recognize them and prevent them from escaping our control.

The most useful description of how to do this was sent to me by Teah Strozer, a transmitted Zen teacher and one of the founders of the Brooklyn Zen Center. It is so lucid and practically helpful, that I'm presenting it here as I received it (with tiny edits). Its title is an acronym spelling RAIN:

R stands for Recognizing what is happening in this moment. Someone just walked too close to you on the sidewalk or didn't give you what you feel is your "right of way" and boom, you're angry. The R is simply to notice what is happening, to be present enough to know that something is happening. This is not a small thing. Many people are immediately reactive—and worse, they blame the other person for causing their reaction. The point is to be awake, to pay attention.

A stands for Accepting. This does not mean that you wanted what just happened to occur. It simply means that you acknowledge that it did. You name it—for example, "anger is here." The idea is that although you are not going to indulge the emotion or thought with further thinking, self-righteousness, or some other emotion, neither do you resist, avert, or distract yourself from the event. You simply acknowledge and name what is happening and remain willing and open to whatever it is.

I stands for Investigating the sensations in the body. This step is primarily a physical noticing. What does anger feel like? The heart beats faster; there can be a flush of energy and heat and a tightening of certain muscles. These physical events are what we label as "anger." This energetic-emotional component has to be willingly and thoroughly felt until the body returns to open relaxation. You breathe and wait, and breathe and feel the body, at first tight and then slowly change, relax, and open, letting go. If this is not thoroughly done, then we haven't fully experienced the emotions triggered by the initial thought. Then that energy gets stuck in the body and adds to the conditioned structure that was triggered in the first place. This openness to the physical event is what integrates the energy, dissipates it, and, if it is practiced over and over, eventually dissolves that particular egoic structure, which has no concrete core. The realization that the egoic system will eventually dissolve if we don't add more thought or energy to it is a wonderful one when first experienced, and a real taste of the potential freedom to come if we continue with practice.

· N stands for Not identifying. There's no need to identify a "me" in what just happened. It was a passing mental and emotional event, like watching a scene in a movie or the clouds as they move through the sky. It was not a permanent fixture of the psyche. We don't have to build and rebuild a "me" on the content of the mind-body that rises and falls ceaselessly. Instead we can stand as the observer of the event. This not-identifying can be tricky, but when the first change of identity shifts from the content of mind to the observer, we can see that the content is not who we are. This is the first real shift of freedom. Eventually, identification as the observer drops away as well, but to simply make the shift is a good place to start.

With RAIN we remember that waking up, reconnecting with life as a whole, is a possibility for each of us. It is our birthright.

Once recognized and owned, as described above, the kleshas become harmless and we can observe them as they rise and fall in the mind. We don't have to be afraid to receive them if we have learned to control them (nirodha). It should be an obvious corollary to understand that we can do nothing with kleshas if we define ourselves as good and purge them from our consciousness, identifying them only in others.

PRECEPTS

....

A Deeper Pass, Three Examples

Another way to express the First Clear Mind Precept—**"I vow to not kill"**—is "A disciple of the Buddha does not kill." The syntax of this is not a command, more like a reminder that if you want to be a Buddhist, this is how we behave. This is the *first* precept in Buddhism. It's the sixth commandment in Judeo-Christian tradition, following not coveting your neighbor's wife and holding no god before Yahweh or Jehovah, so we can understand by its placement that this is of the highest concern to Buddhists.

Harmlessness is the very first edict of Buddhism, and so not killing or taking life is the surface meaning. It's impossible to get through life without killing something, but still, that's our intention, and Buddhist vows always aim at the impossible for fear of falling short of the possible. Saving all beings, for instance, is the work of eons, but by actualizing that intention, others will see and model what we do, and pass it on through time.

You will have to negotiate for yourself whether you are going to have someone else kill the animals you eat. If you eat meat, it will be up to you and your diligence to determine whether the meat you eat has been humanely raised and slaughtered. You may decide to limit your protein to grains, legumes, and vegetables and not eat sentient beings. I try to avoid eating mammals, but occasionally the desire disguised as bacon will foil my best intentions. Cutting broccoli is taking a life, but because there is no option *but* to eat, we say grace and eat with gratitude and the full knowledge of the double-bind in which we exist—to sustain our own lives we must use others. A popular Buddhist grace states:

> *We venerate the Three Treasures.**
> *We're thankful for this food*
> *The work of many people*
> *and the suffering of other forms of life.*

---

*Buddha, dharma, and sangha.

Following this train of thought will eventually lead you to consider how much of the planet you feel you have a right to exploit for your own existence and indulgences. Each precept will have to be moderated by your understanding and conditions. In the world of form, where we live as individuated awareness, our conduct will express our understanding and our conditions may differ from others. Just as no two snowflakes are identical, neither are two human lives. The precepts are not one-size-fits-all rules to be followed in lock step but instead require mediation, nuance, and adjustment to be responsive to the particularities of your life.

Recently the Dalai Lama, a life-long vegetarian, was ordered by his doctors to eat some meat for his health. Life is fluid, and we must be, too. Conditions change, and we need to follow those changes, not the thoughts we may have about them. In our practice we often say, "Put no head above your own." That means when your head is clear and when it is calm, your feelings and intuitions will tell you everything you need to know. Be skeptical of everything, even your own teachers. All the questions and answers you need reside in Buddha-nature, into which your spinal telephone is plugged. Zazen is where we take the time to answer our calls.

In the realm of dharma, the deeper implication of this precept is that we don't give rise to the *idea* of killing. We cut off thoughts of anger and vengefulness, thoughts of envy. We cut them off by recognizing them, feeling them, and letting them go, by changing our mind, by pouring a cup of tea. When we meditate, we recognize what comes up, but we just observe what arises with it, and if we don't seize it, it will depart. Suzuki-roshi once said, "It's okay to let your thoughts in. You don't have to invite them to tea."

The idea of not killing is a seed that sprouts below thoughts. Physical violence and abusive behavior like threats and displays of anger are also a kind of killing. They kill peace. They murder the clarity and calm of others. They kill silence. They kill friendship. So, once again, we must decide for ourselves: How do I, as a Buddhist, negotiate disputes and differences?

The Second Clear Mind Precept states, **"A disciple of the Buddha does not steal,"** and its corollary is to practice the perfection of giving. The deeper, more internal aspect arises from thoughts of gaining and loss. We already have everything we need to live. We have sunlight, oxygen, water, flowering plants, the entire panoply of life revealed by sunrise every day. What are our actual thoughts about gain? What do we need to gain badly enough to take what is not given?

I can think of circumstances where desperate people steal to feed their children or because they're starving, or need medicines they can't afford. I would prefer to indict the culture and laws that deny people these basic human needs, because in such instances I'm not going to judge such thievery. Yes, they've broken a Buddhist precept; so would I if my children were hungry. Once again, you have to decide on your own authority and ethics how strictly you will observe Buddha's way. I once crossed the country without money, cleaning the bathrooms in gas stations for my gasoline; making and selling earrings I crafted from the pelt of a road-killed pheasant. My friend Pete Knell, president of the San Francisco Hell's Angels, crossed the country, earning what he needed by painting farmers' mailboxes and stenciling their names on the fresh paint, just to demonstrate that he was not a thief.

The Third Clear Mind Precept, **"A disciple of the Buddha does not misuse sexuality,"** is a statement concerning ethical relationships. It doesn't declare that sex is immoral (a tough case to make since the species' survival and much of its pleasure depends on it). It does declare that relationships can be abused. Sexual attraction can prompt dishonest statements of affection, break wedding vows, and engender jealousy and violence. It is not a trivial force to contend with. The precept's corollary is to honor the body—one's own body and the body of your lover, wife, or husband—and also to manifest good faith in relationships. No veneers of feigning more affection for someone than you actually possess. No false promises. We have to decide what our own limits will be.

As debate rages throughout the nation about abortion and who has the right to terminate a pregnancy and under what conditions, it might be instructive to explain how the thinking of an early Zen teacher of mine named Robert Aitken, an extremely upright man, evolved on this issue.

He began his teaching career firmly opposed to abortion as a violation of the first precept against killing. Over time however, he was so moved by the suffering of his female students that he left decisions about termination of pregnancy solely to the mothers. However, if one of his students elected to terminate her pregnancy, he requested two things of them. First, that they join him in performing a naming ceremony for the child, to clarify the issue irrefutably and honor the life that was to be terminated. Afterward, he would perform a funeral ceremony. I was impressed by his handling of this issue because, unlike a number of my liberal political friends, Aitken-roshi did not skirt the moral issue of taking a life (the First Clear Mind Precept). Unlike many in the "pro-life" movement, however, he was completely consistent in his beliefs, being opposed to war and the death penalty and certainly never considered violence levied against doctors or nurses who performed the abortions.

The funeral service honored the life that was being interrupted and offered closure to the mother, creating a frame so that the mother could formally accept the consequences of her decision, say good-bye, and adjust to the consequences of her decision. This is something that some in the pro-choice movement fail to fully acknowledge. Abortion *is* terminating a life, even a life that is unable to exist outside the mother's body. It is not regarded as a sin, a transgression against God. It accepts that there are times when such choices are unavoidable for the health or well-being of the mother, or because she is not prepared to be a mother at that time. It does not shame her for being sexually active or being careless. It seems to me that his compassion for the mother also included the moral suffering of pro-life people, who cannot accept the termination of the life of a fetus. It should not be easy, but he felt that such choices should be the mother's and not his. Rather than arguing that a fetus is merely a cluster of cells (I know no woman who ever had an abortion who ever made such a cavalier assessment of it) or dismissing the moral quadrant, it seems to me more honorable and consistent with Buddhist practice to face reality head on and deal with what suffering is within one's jurisdiction with appropriate ceremonies and leave the rest to the mother, without judgment or blame.

Continued expression of sexual interest after someone has expressed that they're not interested is a misuse of sex. Trying to overcome someone's resistance is not compassionate treatment. Extend such behavior far enough and it becomes rape. The male strategy of thinking, "If I keep trying, maybe they'll say yes," is not respectful. It's a misuse of someone else's space and privacy or may take advantage of their attraction to you, even though you have never touched them.

Using sexual relations to gain power or status or to manipulate one's partner is both a misuse of sexuality and a kind of theft of that person's sovereignty. To avoid unintentional harm, it's also necessary to consider: What is the effect of my sexuality on another person? If one is serious about modeling harmlessness and responsibility, the question is not simply getting what you want but checking in with yourself (the precepts) to determine if you are using your sexuality as a lever to pry open that person's will. Especially in a community, it's important to consider: What effect will my sexual behavior exert on the community?

I was a member of a Buddhist sangha that was riven and wracked with pain because of the inappropriate sexual behavior of the senior teacher. It sundered the community, threw a number of people off their practice, and caused lasting pain to others, affected families negatively, and made future governance of the institution difficult. It's no easy feat to stay on top of hormones. In my 20s, in the thrall of the counterculture and drugs, I was careless with a number of young women. That callowness returned to haunt me later in life and required painful amends to be made. As the man said, "There's no such thing as a free lunch."

The entirety of this book could have been dedicated to the precepts, so I'll stop this discussion here and urge you to review the bibliography at the book's end. There are many discussions of the precepts there. You've seen something of my mind and intuitions working to interpret them; now check out some other minds. The precepts are always useful to review.

O

Buddhism is a very intuitive, felt practice. The world is so complex, it's so interdependent that logic is not always a reliable instrument for negotiating it. Intuition is a far more ancient aspect of mind that includes emotion, memory, and intellect and ignites large areas of the brain. It's directly related to our success as a species and often will help us understand complex situations more readily than logic.

A bodhisattva makes a commitment to live from a generous heart. We already possess the entire Universe and more than we can use, so it should also be clear by now how misusing status and authority, when we have power over someone, is a form of stealing. Once again, we unpack such events, investigate them, apply the RAIN formula (see pp. 66–67). We keep our intentions on the back burner of the mind. We refer to them to judge our own conduct.

When we begin to practice a spiritual life, specifically as Buddhists, the precepts are the things we agree to do. It makes sense to trust the wisdom of elders and enlightenment as an ultimate teacher. For that reason, in Zen practice we do not treat our teachers like gurus to be worshipped but tend to treat them like wise aunts and uncles who've been scouting the trail ahead of us, perhaps made similar mistakes, and are offering us their condensed wisdom as guidance.

Teachers are not irrefutable sources. When we bow to a teacher or when we bow to a statue of the Buddha, it's sometimes misperceived by others as subordinating ourselves to someone of higher status with more sacred juju than ourselves. In fact, we are bowing to wisdom. When we bow, we are honoring our own inner wisdom, *and* the Buddha's, *and* the continuity of clarity, awareness, and wisdom on Earth. We don't have to change our previous religion to practice in this way, because there is nothing inherently antithetical to any religious beliefs (okay, perhaps nix human sacrifice or cannibalism) in Buddhism.

In discussing the precepts, Suzuki-roshi instructed us that "Zen and precepts are one." Non-Buddhists may think of precepts as externally imposed laws, commands, and judgments like the Ten Commandments, but they are not the utterances of a god. When we are living our daily life, we call the practice "precepts," but when we are sitting zazen they are "Zen."

I'm responsible for what I do. It's pretty simple. It means I have freedom to choose. When I make some decision, I will live out the consequences (and so, too, many others). So the precepts resemble safety rails on the highway, or a mountain climber's rope and carabiners, which, if used correctly, can save the climber from a fatal fall.

Some Native American tribes make it a practice to consider the consequences of their actions on seven generations. We can imagine how different our world would be today had our forefathers practiced the same discipline with the environment.

We consult the precepts again and again and again, as we live, moment by moment by moment, until they become fixed as habits. We have the absolute freedom to do that, and, in its deepest implications, that is what nirvana means—the absolute, unfettered freedom to, in the next second, make a choice to do something radically different from what we've ever done before. I don't *have* to choose to follow them, but the precepts are there to guide me if I want my life to approximate the Buddha's. If I remember that they are the products of an enlightened mind, just like the Eightfold Path, why wouldn't I choose them?

Having spent nearly the previous half of my life ignoring most directives and instead following my own whims and impulses and having suffered the consequences, and caused others to suffer the consequences of my poor choices, I find a deep utility and purpose in these precepts. The footprint of a single life is small on the sands of time, but if I consider myself a Buddhist, and act as consistently as the Buddha would, I am moving his great dream of universal enlightenment forward.

We consult the precepts because we have confidence based on the evidence of our teachers and other practitioners that they create a dignified, liberated, and helpful life. They minimize harm. They maximize kindness and compassion. They create a world that is deeper and more profound than only intelligence can offer against our innate greed, anger, and delusion.

When you sit zazen, you are violating no precept. When you follow the Eightfold Path, step by step, you are consulting the precepts, step by step, and will do minimal harm and generate minimal negative and unintended consequences. When we sit zazen, we let our karma work on emptiness, where it remains harmless.

You don't have to declare yourself a Buddhist to do these practices. His Holiness the Dalai Lama has said publicly that there's no necessity to change your religion. We are modeling behavior, not proselytizing. You can judge for yourself whether the practice serves you. Trust that the answer to every question resides in your Buddha-nature. It contains every possibility, so it's a more reliable place to search than the world of dialectics and contradictions. The length of this book demands that I limit the discussion of the remaining precepts. I have tried to give you an idea of how they operate and have included recommended reading in the bibliography. I'm content if your interest is piqued, and there's no need for me to recapitulate the brilliant work of teachers who have informed me. You should taste the flavor of their tea for yourself.

PART II

◦ ◦ ◦

THINGS AS IT IS

Introduction to Part II

. . . . .

Infusing the Ordinary

AT THE TIME OF MY ARRIVAL at San Francisco Zen Center in 1974, several years after Suzuki-roshi's death, the elaborate formal Zen aesthetics, brought to San Francisco by the Japanese teachers Suzuki-roshi had invited, were a welcome balm to my wounded body, barely clean of drugs. My spirit was also wounded by a decade in the disordered wilds of the counterculture and communal life, frequent use of heroin, and the helter-skelter turmoil of the streets' free-fall communes. The assassination of black leaders and multiplying burdens of unregulated capitalism were stressing the fabric of daily life. While a part of me still longed for the ecstasies of counterculture freedom, the discipline and order of Zen was indisputably calming my sense of despair, personally and politically, and restoring me to health.

Meditation in the cool, unhurried calm of Zen Center was a blessing. Fragrant yellow grass tatami mats covered the floor in orderly, black-rimmed rectangles. The air was lightly perfumed with subtle incense. Identical black mats and cushions rested side-by-side, minimally intrusive visual punctuation marks on the tatamis, perfect for seated meditation. On the altar a beautiful Buddha appeared to embody the benevolent benefactor I sought—a wise person unperturbed by the world outside our thick walls. Inside, silence was a physical balm, and in the safety of that environment, I felt as if I had returned to my true self . . . perhaps.

The Japanese aesthetic, including the robes and daily wear of most students, the near absence of expressed emotion, and nearly universal high seriousness—I assumed that *was* Zen. Wanting to fit in, I sublimated my cranky questions about why Americans were wearing Japanese robes and addressing one another with Japanese titles I could never keep straight: *Ino, Doan, Doshi*—terms that might as well have been *Beano, Donut,* and *Dosey-Do*.

I eventually settled down, both into the posture of zazen and acceptance of the monastic routines and discipline. After a number of months, I traded my crotch-constricting jeans for comfy black fat-pants and a soft, unstructured *hippari* jacket, which fastened with ties instead of buttons or zippers. After about a year, I bought a used set of black robes to wear in the zendo, and their comfort was a revelation. I was on my way to becoming a Zen student.

As I relaxed and accepted the practices of Zen Center, my understanding of how the prescribed forms of sitting, standing, walking, and bowing evolved and, as it did, my resistance diminished. Clearly, they were not punishments designed to force my freedom-loving American spirit into compliance. They proved useful in helping me express and self-critique the development of my practice and became a gateway into understanding the utility of discipline generally.

Zen Center's abbot, Richard Baker-roshi, ordained and transmitted* by the late founder, Suzuki-roshi, had a talent for translating Zen to Americans in a manner that made it current, stylish, and culturally important. He was particularly skilled at communicating with cultural and financial elites. As a form of outreach, he facilitated a monthly luncheon nicknamed the Invisible University, for which my wife was one of the primary *chefs du jour*. The guests were artists, poets, politicians, cultural thinkers, and intellectuals, and my invitation was more likely due

---

*Transmission refers not only to the deep intimacy of understanding between teacher and disciple but also to the transfer of the teacher's authority and confidence to the student, who is then empowered to teach independently and ordain their own lineage of priests.

to my wife's position and my friendships with well-known poets Gary Snyder, Michael McClure, and culture wizard Steward Brand than any cultural importance. It certainly did not hurt that at the time I worked for the current governor of California, Jerry Brown (a friend of Richard Baker), also interested in Zen.

That confluence of relationships afforded me a bifurcated view of SF Zen Center from a number of perspectives—as guest at this elite luncheon, as social peer of Roshi Baker (he was not my teacher), and my marriage to one of his students with an extensive social network among Zen community members. This multidimensional perspective made it inevitable that I would eventually become aware of some contradictions between San Francisco Zen Center's stated and applied values, problems that plague most institutions.

Some students rose at four in the morning to bake the acclaimed Tassajara bread sought by fine restaurants and sold to the public in Zen Center's Tassajara Bread bakery. These students had little time to meditate. Their work was arduous and demanding and their compensation very small. Others were building and operating Greens, an elegant vegetarian restaurant built in an abandoned building at Fort Mason, a former military installation recently repurposed for community activities. The difference between the students' earnings and the actual value of the work they performed (what Karl Marx referred to as "surplus value") was dedicated to supporting the institution.

This system of unequal compensation, status, and benefits became difficult for me to ignore or justify. While my wife and the other students dedicated long hours to the institution and their teacher, their ability to meditate and practice was curtailed. From within the abbot's circle, I observed his luxurious lifestyle supported by numerous student servants, the finest accoutrements, and a top-of-the-line BMW sedan to speed him to his many appointments.

Fairly or unfairly, I began to associate the elaborate Japanese ceremonies, the dazzling lacquer, tea implements, ornate brocades, and museum-quality Buddhas with these social imbalances. The overstory of the institution, including the abbot and his immediate family and entourage, had a decidedly aristocratic flavor, and, drinking tea in the abbot's well-appointed quarters, I often overheard condescending views of the students, one of whom was my wife.

I began thinking of these aspects of the practice as High Anglican Zen, and feared being flattered into complacency, or worse. I began to wonder if the exotic Japanese costumes, props, and practices might also replicate Japanese attitudes toward hierarchy and authority and did not know yet if they were fundamental to Zen practice, because Buddha was not Japanese, so neither were his original practices.

My observations were at odds with the progressive social values and liberation that had inspired my political work and my studies in Buddhism. Over time, I became less forgiving about the cool aloofness considered appropriate behavior in Zen Center's culture and frustrated by witnessing too many instances where formality and ritual appeared to have been privileged over kindness and empathy. It bothered me that I was being afforded privileges and respect I had not earned within the institution because of my relationship to the governor. I did not believe that enlightenment was antithetical to genuine human expression and wondered what had become of the vivid, eccentric, and authentic characters—Manjushri, the drinking and fornicating Ikkyu, cranky Dogen—I encountered in my Buddhist reading.

Eventually, I came to believe that the aspects bothering me about this generally admirable community of thoughtful, dedicated people might be due to a confusion, conflating the elaborate Japanese gift wrapping—Japanese aesthetics and formalism—with the Buddha's core teachings. Since the Buddha had been born into a Hindu culture in Nepal, I realized that this could not be the case, and this observation spurred me to begin investigating a more colloquial, American expression of Zen.

During my counterculture years, I had become quite close to Gary Snyder, the poet and Zen practitioner whose poetry and essays had inspired me as a teenager and, later, whose political broadsides and poems were passed from hand to hand during the burgeoning days of Haight Street.

I'd met Gary through mutual friends after coming to California. Their admiration for him was palpable and piqued my interest in the fellow who appeared to be a first among equals with the Beats. Jack Kerouac built an entire novel—*The Dharma Bums*—around his character Japhy Ryder, based on Gary. Gary had lived in a Japanese Zen temple for nine years, traveled widely in Japan, read and spoke Japanese, and had married a Japanese woman. I was attracted to the fact that Gary was a Wobbly,* a member of the International Workers of the World, where he had registered as a poet. He lived in the Sierra Mountain foothills in a humble farmhouse, far from the city's turmoil, and remained dedicated to the Wobbly ideas, the environment, and social justice. I was determined to learn whatever he would share with me on the subject of Zen.†

Despite having no formal arrangement with him, I still consider Gary my first teacher. For him, the title "teacher" bears specific connotations in his Rinzai practice, so he would not describe me as his student. Notwithstanding that, he was the person who introduced me to what a life grounded in Zen practice might look and feel like in an American idiom and what values it might be dedicated to. I did my best to understand and emulate his example on numerous levels and grew to appreciate his lay Buddhist practice, which was disciplined but also relaxed and fun.

---

*The IWW opened its membership to all workers, regardless of skills, race, or gender. Its goals were similar to the Knights of Labor, a socialistic union from the nineteenth century, and was the only union to represent unskilled labor. The Wobblies are well worth any time spent learning about them. A good start might be the documentary film *The Wobblies,* directed by Deborah Shaffer and Stewart Bird, renewed and recently released.

†The semi-comic details of our first meeting, hosted by fellow poet Lew Welch, are recounted in my first book, *The Rainman's Third Cure.*

At some point during our growing friendship, Gary returned to formal Buddhist practice to finish the koan studies he had been unable to complete in Japan. He chose to work with Robert Aitken-roshi, an American teacher from the Harada-Yasutani lineage—a meld of Soto and Rinzai Zen practices that strongly emphasized kensho (awakening). Because Gary, by then, was lighting the path toward what a lay Zen practice might be, I began to study with Aitken-roshi as well.*

Once, during a *sesshin* (a seven-day intensive meditation retreat) with Aitken-roshi at his Diamond Sangha temple in Hawaii, I encountered the following quotation by Yamada Mumon-roshi, a Zen master from his tradition, which affected me in a very definitive way. Without my understanding it at the time, it formed the germ of my incentive to write this book. It confirmed my intuitions concerning an American expression of Zen.

> I expect original words from you. But we have to be careful at this point. This word must be expressed by a person who comes to the same mind as Shakyamuni Buddha. . . . Then the original American way can be naturally realized.

It seemed to me that Gary's practice might well be "the original American way" I was searching for, or at least an accurate precursor of it. However, the curriculum at Diamond Sangha was not a good fit for me. I appreciated and respected Aitken-roshi but was more engaged with Yamada-roshi's original American way than I was with the Mu koan, the first of the demanding, logic-defying riddles (a mental boot camp) given to young Rinzai-school Zen students to break them out of their small, egocentric understandings.

---

*Robert Aitken, a widely published and respected man, was a very kind and helpful teacher to me. He wrote a number of very useful books, and one in particular, *Taking the Path of Zen*, I continue to recommend and have included in this book's bibliography for its comprehensive how-and-why discussions of Zen practice.

After several years working with Aitken-roshi, and frustrated by
Mu, I (perhaps self-servingly) came to feel that the Diamond Sangha's
stringent emphasis on kensho was trying too hard, turning the event
into performance for a merit badge. Without doubting the efficacy of
koans, the practice was not working for me, and so I returned to San
Francisco and Suzuki-roshi's *shikantaza* (resting in awareness) meditation, where I had confidence in an aphorism about practice he had once
expressed—"When you walk in the fog, it isn't raining, but eventually,
you become soaking wet."

I trusted Suzuki-roshi's "just sitting" and returned to his Soto-
school practice with a new appreciation that awakening would arrive
when the student was ready, just as a ripe apple falls from a tree. It eventually did.

I had initially left Zen Center partially because my personal practice had been initiated and maintained by a materialistic attachment
to the mystical goal of enlightenment. Such attitudes are discouraged
by knowledgeable teachers, because they represent a "gaining" idea,
always associated with egocentric thinking. But that's where I was at
the time, and it continually confounded me that during nearly eight
years in and around Zen Center, I never *once* heard the words *kensho* or *enlightenment* mentioned, let alone any discussion of what they
might mean and how one might achieve or deal with them. Color me
impatient.

I couldn't have been the only person at San Francisco Zen Center
drawn to Buddhist practice by the lure of enlightenment, but the suppression of the subject felt like a taboo. In light of my growing suspicion that more than I could accept of the abbot's behavior derived
from self-serving, I came to believe that such silence offered advantages to him, protecting him from criticism and community pressure to alter some problematic behaviors. After all, if anyone could
be assumed to be enlightened in the Zen community it *must* be the
abbot. Therefore, if the abbot manifested behavior with which students experienced difficulty, the students quite often concluded that

the problem must be *theirs*—and that if they, too, were enlightened, they might consider the situation differently. Being out of touch with one's intuitions or imagining a life different from the one you're leading is an unwieldy perspective from which to consider kindness and compassion.

Writing this more than forty-five years later, I worry that my dissatisfactions on paper may appear to have greater mass and solidity than they did in my daily life at that time. I loved Zen practice and I loved the community at San Francisco Zen Center, and still do. I was taught and inspired by so many people there and made close friendships that continue to this day. I learned more in my eight years at City Center* than perhaps at any comparable period of my life. It's also fair to say that some of my difficulties derived from the fact that I was, and remain, a poor example of a monk.

My adult life has been seasoned by ADD, numerous excesses, and a livelihood carved out within the Babylon of Hollywood. Consequently, my recitation of personal discomforts with San Francisco's strict practice should not be read as criticisms of those who were more disciplined and dedicated to monastic practices than I was.

Still, despite my personal failures, my intuition remained persistent that the exotic *Japanismo*—my nickname for what I perceived to be hagiographic imitations of Japanese culture—might well discomfit other Americans and lead them to ignore or reject the teachings as "foreign" and prohibit wider acceptance.

In the late 1990s, I became reacquainted with Lew Richmond, a senior priest I'd known at San Francisco Zen Center. He had been an ordained disciple of Suzuki-roshi who had left Zen Center in

---

*City Center is the designation most students use to distinguish the San Francisco Zen Center from its other sites at Green Gulch Farm in Marin County and Tassajara Zen Monastery in the mountains near Big Sur. I've learned to be careful in other cities, however, about dropping the "San Francisco" from Zen Center, because Houston, Austin, Chicago, and other cities have Zen Centers, which are not to be demoted by offerring titular authority to my hometown.

disappointment some twenty years earlier during a scandal that had climaxed with the community asking Abbot Baker-roshi to leave. He had an air of nothing-special confidence that attracted me, and in short order I became Lew's student.

Practice with Lew restored my confidence in Zen and inspired me to redouble my efforts. Loosening the Japanese gift wrapping around the Buddha's teachings seemed appropriate to my secular life and served my desire to make Buddha's teachings more appreciable to people for whom Japanese customs (even when replicated by Americans) might be off-putting. I was not rejecting the Japanese roots of my lineage but trying to transplant those roots into American soil, to encourage a vigorous hybrid that someday might be recognized as a true American varietal. Basically, I was seeking an American *vernacular*—the speech of everyday people—for Zen.

The more Lew and I discussed my studies, the more clearly I perceived core similarities among Suzuki-roshi's, Lew's, and Gary Snyder's practices—simplicity, less reliance on elaborate ritual, a marked lack of puffery and hierarchy—for which I coined the phrase "Nothing-Special-Zen." Best of all, I appreciated his lack of any sort of Buddhist persona, the adoption of a persona, studiously designed to appear more "Buddhist" than their everyday behavior.

Yamada-roshi's phrase "original American way" became the koan for my actual life. It simmered on the back burner of my awareness until the superficial distinctions among Suzuki-roshi's, Lew's, and Snyder's practices disappeared in the vast field of Big Mind. One day something blossomed in my own mind-body, and all my intuitions about vernacular Buddhism clarified as the germ of this book.

Today, millions of Americans and Western Europeans strive to model the Buddha's life as their own, guided by his precepts and Eightfold Path. In the midst of this impatient, ambitious, restless, bloody, greedy, entitled, and confusing American culture, we are all feeling our way, and it will take time before the American way clarifies. In the meantime, we have our Buddha-nature and the Buddha's teachings to guide us. Perhaps I don't yet have it quite right, but I feel that I am in good company and we're moving in a good direction. Given another century or two, I have hopes that future expressions of Buddhism may succeed in expressing Yamada-roshi's original American way. I cannot be certain, but I feel that this might have been Suzuki-roshi's deepest intention as well.

8

What Is This Thing We Call the Self?

·····

April 8, 2020

WE ALL FEEL A SENSE OF SELF. Proprioception, awareness of the position and movement of the body, informs us that we are an entity with flesh boundaries, but our awareness extends beyond it somewhat to give us a sense of personal space. We may not like it if people get too close to us before we've assessed their intention. Our impression of uniqueness is reinforced by the mirror. And yet, our awareness itself is curiously complex. Unlike a hand, foot, liver, or spleen, science has never discovered either a location or anything resembling an organ for the self. They have never discovered its color or form. Despite this lack of concrete evidence, most folks remain convinced that "we" reside inside this sack of flesh and "the rest of it" is out there. Quite a puzzle.

Even brief scrutiny will reveal that we are not and have never been as separate from the rest of the Universe as we believe. Believing that the "I" we refer to as our "self" is a discrete, isolated entity is the central delusion of humankind, and the fixity of that conviction leads our species into all sorts of difficulties. Much of Buddhist practice centers around examining what the self actually is—the self that desires enlightenment; the self that seeks to maintain happiness as a permanent condition; the self that feels it's missing out on things; the self that wants to fix, alter, or dispel its moods; the self that we imagine is seeing, hearing, smelling, tasting, and hearing the world we move through.

The Buddha refused to say explicitly whether the self did or did not, or did *and* did not, exist. When Vachagotta the wanderer demanded to know whether a self existed, the Buddha remained silent. In another piece, he cautioned all monks to avoid the dispute, explaining to his disciple Ananda that answering either yes or no would reinforce extreme and erroneous views. He refused to answer questions as to whether the self was or was not "real." He observed, instead, that the Universe is perpetually changing—which is to say, impermanent.

The Buddha was more concerned with people clinging to the idea of a self and fixating on a personal identity as a fundamental problem. He employed the idea of "not-self" as a device that was useful for regarding the "outside" world and acknowledging the vast variety of entities our "self" is attached to and dependent on. Everything we can assert about the self, we can assert about a "not-self" and begin to experience our thoughts and feelings as passing before us on the screen of our awareness, like clouds. We don't need a fixed self to account for reality.

On some level we know this. We can no longer find the child we used to be. Impermanence remains a truth for moods, feelings, impulses, and sensations, as well as the life span of everything from amoebas to mountain ranges. Lines appear on our faces and mottled areas discolor our skin as we age and move inevitably toward no-being. Unless we can discover and ground contentment *within* the kaleidoscopic variety and ceaseless change, with lives, moods, and events ticking on and off multiple times a moment, all our efforts to flee anxiety and discontent will remain estranged from the way the Universe operates.

As you read about Buddhism you may encounter the phrase *not one, not two* as a way of describing the relationship between the mind and body. It is a useful concept for regarding relationships in the material world. We understand that mind and body are not identical, but we can't actually separate them or discern which one is feeding us information or in control. Our self-awareness exists similarly. On the one hand, there is our familiar array of habits, impulses, memories, likes, dislikes, desires, and anxieties we regard as our personality, or "self"; and on the other hand, our body and what Buddhists describe as our true self is not different from the generative energy of the Universe, ceaselessly expressing itself as forms, feelings, impulses, sensations, consciousness, and every nameable thing in what we refer to as reality. Like it or not, we have never existed independently of this larger world, so it is not false to assert that we are a separate reality, but the distortion arises when we consider that is all we are.

Ordinarily, we perceive our colloquial "I" as our personality. It presents as separate and generally more important than everything else. It would conflict with our experience to pretend otherwise. All humans possess a common sense of the body, its capacities and limits; we are familiar with our seeing, hearing, tasting; and we have some self-image and a narrative about our personal history. Arguing that they don't exist would be as foolish as arguing that any and all have ever existed separately from oxygen, water, and sunlight. We all have a sense of the exterior boundary of our bodies—whether it's our flesh or some energy field slightly beyond that. Setting aside certain peak experiences, we usually feel that "I" exists in here and the rest is out there.

This view serves us with efficiency in navigating the material world, as language and naming saves us from constant detailed scrutiny of each object entering our awareness. Once we connect the word *tree* with the leaf and trunk, we don't necessarily need more detail unless our work requires more specificity. However, language also has a shadow side that demands a tax. That tax is its hypnotic ability to trick us into believing we exist independently from everything that does not have our name.

The personality usually responds to this demotion from the dominance of the universal domain by either suffering fear at its own insignificance against the immensity of the world or seeking to bolster itself with various strategies, among which are wealth, fame, status, and political power. Sometimes self-importance (whose evolutionary benefits should be obvious) dominates all our concerns, and narcissism may overvalue our own importance and devalue others. Some people simply take the self as a given and never question it at all, building up a detailed inventory of what they are and are not. It may be useful, but it is not freedom, and the "are not" side of that definition often contains treasure of immense value.

Once we identify and name something, we no longer have to consider it as deeply again, so it affords us efficiency and saves energy. We have identified a few essential characteristics of thousands of things and ideas in the same way, and once we have learned the words for them and their references, we rarely consider the named object beyond their superficial distinctions. We do this with our "self" as well, naming, cataloguing, and simultaneously concretizing as physical an assembly of data points—things we have been told about ourselves; things we have implied about ourselves from the responses of others; habits we've made and observed; self-reflections, and the like—and from that point onward, we may consider the self a more or less known quantity, possessing the characteristic fixity that might correspond to an organ.

This is like assessing ourselves as a "fact," observing ourselves from an imagined *objective* vantage point, as if we were a piece of data and not moving clusters of sensory data, intuitions, memories, experience, and habits (which the ancient Buddhas referred to as skandhas—the impersonal "heaps" of Form, Feeling, Impulse, Sensations, and Consciousness that constitute a human life). This habitual point of view is compounded by a materialistically oriented culture that so often relies on "facts" deduced by scientific observation. A fact in Philadelphia is the same fact in San Diego, and so we often unconsciously adopt a concept of objectivity as a reliable way of understanding ourselves. We believe the world consists of impersonal objects that can somehow be perceived by an imagined person without prejudices, predilections, opinions, wants, and needs. Welcome to Delusionville, or as I once printed on a gift T-shirt in a glaring violation of Buddhist Speech, "Welcome to Dumbf*ckistan."

Applying such an understanding to ourselves amounts to privileging this hypothetical objectivity over our own intuitions and perceptions. At some point in time, we accumulate enough data about our habits and predilections that we cease further exploration, crystallizing the self into a known entity about which we can say with certainty, "I know myself." It is at this point that most growth stops. It's often uttered as a statement of pride and accomplishment, with no recognition of the irony that what is being described is a photograph of moving water and is not the water itself.

Here is the Big Picture: Your and my "I" has never existed in precisely the way we think it does. It has never been independent of water, sunlight, and oxygen. Because our lives have depended on microbes in the soil nourishing the plants and animals we eat, we can assert that "we" do not exist in the way we think we do. We are also dependent on microbes in the soil nourishing the plants and animals we eat. We have also depended equally on pollinating insects and the entire plant and animal kingdoms, which depend in turn on water and sunlight and the Earth's climate, fixed by gravity into orbit at the optimal distance from the sun. If we were closer to the sun, water would burn off and everything we qualify as living would be gone. If we were farther away, water would freeze, with the identical consequence. The Earth is held in its perfect orbit and distance from the sun by all the gravitational forces of the Universe, which, by the way, is also beating our hearts and breathing us. If we need to have faith in something, perhaps that will do. Buddhists refer to this vast, self-organized everything as Big Mind.

Yet with even a brief examination we can see that we are not and have never been *separate* from any of this. Everything is simultaneously unique and distinct (*sabetsu*) and common (*byōdo*). The trick is to be able to see both at once. When we regard our experience relationally, considering all of it, the Big Mind perspective is as equally descriptive as our ego-oriented description. By extending our awareness (via meditation) to include all of our body we can occasionally end the false dichotomy between body and mind. Extending that to include self and other is another way of describing absolute freedom.

One of the benefits of meditation is the softening and sometimes temporary dissolution of fixed boundaries, including our certainties about who we are. What is the self? Try to find it when you meditate. Try to pin down the source from where your internal speech and bizarre little narrative daydreams arise. Meditating allows the apparent boundaries of distinctions to dissolve and the place from which new thoughts and impulses arise to express itself. Big Mind—the awareness of the Universe itself, is large enough to absorb all contradictions, like self and other and being and non-being—this is the main trunk into which our spinal telephone is plugged, the universal source containing infinite possibilities, all questions and answers, all contradictions. When our boundaries are wide open and anything can be included, we really don't know with certainty who's sitting on our cushion or who or what is orchestrating our breathing, and, surprisingly, it is actually more interesting not to know.

What we believe we know is often largely habit, received information, and perhaps a non-skeptical belief in everything we think. Abandoning the idea of a central controller orchestrating everything, we never know what will happen next—when or where the rabbit will leap from the bush, or when we will be surprised by the next revelation of our identity.

It takes some practice to relax expectations of the future and to keep our awareness in the present moment. This is what we do when we meditate. The Japanese call this *shikantaza*—just sitting—and mean it to express having no material ideas about advancement or gain and just being willing to be there, without expectations. Zazen meditation is not to be confused with seeking to evoke some particular or special state of mind. To pursue the idea that we can always be happy is like willing the clouds never to alter their shapes or the ocean to arrest its ceaseless motion.

The point is, can we stay upright? Can we remain firm and composed in the face of the peppered winds afflicting us, and what arises within us as a result? Can we resist the entropic forces of gravity, constantly bearing us toward the earth. Can we resist it with the spirit of our posture? Can we maintain our dignity and dedication to helping others and living a meaningful existence? Because attending our lives— the little wavelets on the boiling ocean of emptiness—bobbing along on our exhales, is like learning to surf, with the added insight that our little wavelet has never not been part of the ocean.

Small mind and Big Mind coexist simultaneously; one we can learn to control, and one we can learn to accept and occasionally access. When we accept the self as an *awareness,* that simple adjustment offers us a bounty of freedom. If we consider it carefully, it implies that our known characteristics, obstacles, and impulses, which we might not appreciate about ourselves—shyness, second-guessing, self-doubt, longing, aggression, habits, and learned responses for which we duck responsibility— they are not permanently fixed anywhere in our bodies or psyches. The self is not like the fixed armature in a clay sculpture with fixed qualities that we might be tempted to assess as wounded, broken, insufficient, or damaged. These are all learned habits and responses held in place by repetition and belief in a fixed self. We are not inexorably bound to them.

I mentioned before that when discussing body and mind, we describe their relationship as "not one, not two." While mind and body are *not* the same thing, neither are they "separate self-entities," a phrase that Thich Nhat Hanh coined in his new translation of the Heart Sutra. Mind and body are one *and* two simultaneously.

Suzuki-roshi once said:

When we breathe, our throat is like a revolving door. We inhale, and we exhale. There's no "I" necessary to that formulation. To say

"I am breathing" the "I" is extra. To say "I am walking" the "I" is extra.

To our "I," every impulse, whim, and desire appear all-important. The "I" identifies with what it thinks and, as a consequence, often believes its mental formulations uncritically. This "I" is not so much the problem as our fixed *attachment* to it and our fascination with its dramas and narratives. We tend to privilege its perspective over all others, which is why our assessments err so often. Whenever we concentrate solely on the self and its perspectives, we are ignoring the rest of the Universe, which remains out of focus, as if we focused on our fingertip held slightly away from our face. The finger is in sharp focus, and everything beyond it is hazy. Our favoring of our own thoughts and beliefs is like this, at the cost of ignorance and delusion.

To be skeptical about who we believe we are is an unusual but useful practice, because when we believe everything we think, moment to moment, without realizing that these thoughts do not require a center, nor continuity, we are whipsawed among identities that change value and valence as rapidly as our thoughts themselves.

During this pandemic, one of the things our nation needs is people with clarity and calm, who keep their heads and assess things objectively and carefully. This is why Dr. Fauci has received such trust and approbation from a large majority of people living on Earth One,* particularly those who remember his heroic efforts during the AIDS crisis delivering experimental medicines to desperately ill people. I find it puzzling to understand why so many might attack and threaten a doctor who has dedicated his life to helping others and hold his word in little repute against that of a man who has paid millions to settle fraud claims, who was tape recorded describing the privileges of being

---

*Earth One was coined by some someone to denote people who believe in fact-based research and science, to distinguish them from those on Earth Two, who appear to be controlled by superstition, belief, and tribal solidarity.

a celebrity, which included grabbing women by their genitals, and who has been sued for sexual assault of women multiple times. What citizens would be comfortable leaving their children with such a person? It is ignorance certainly, but what is being masked by such behavior? What is the fear that's actually driving people to surrender all skepticism and credulity to believe in a gangster with dyed hair?

After only months of beginning meditation and becoming more familiar with the uncensored material arising via my spinal telephone, I was surprised to discover just how dangerous I could be if I was not paying attention. I habitually thought of myself as a good person, but after a few years of remaining attentive to what was rising into my mind and body, I felt as if I should have been moved to the gorilla compound at the zoo. I understood how dangerous I or any other human being could be and that my opinions about myself and my character were not based on much more than wishes and occasional acts of responsibility and kindness. I encountered murderous levels of violence just beneath the surface of my thoughts, which I had labored to ignore or suppress my entire life. It was shocking to discover how primed for aggression I was and how close to the surface floated violent responses to anything I perceived as bullying or aggression toward me or others I cherished. One would think that I might have received a clue had I remembered how, for a good part of the 1960s, I had run around with the Hell's Angels and I and a number of my companions from the Love Generation traveled about armed with pistols.

What compounds our danger to others is buttressing aggressive impulses with the idea that our personal "goodness" somehow inoculates us against error and the consequences of our actions. If I am too readily convinced that I'm a good guy, what is the point of doing any further investigation? The verdict is already in. "I'm okay." Why monitor my impulses or speech or consider the consequences of my actions? I'm a good guy. What could go wrong?

I shudder to remember the nation's Shock and Awe campaign against Iraq during which we gleefully bombed apartment buildings occupied by sleeping men, women, and children in Baghdad in the middle of the night. Why? Because our Republican elites were working on a plan to create a new American century to "re-instill in our foes and friends the fear that attaches to any great power. . . . Only a war against Saddam Hussein will decisively restore the awe that protects American interests abroad and citizens at home."*

Labeling the parents of children murdered by the U.S.-trained Nicaraguan army as communists was supposed to have absolved us of the moral consequences of murdering them.

(I remain amazed at how readily people who profess Abrahamic faiths—Judaism, Christianity, and Islam—will dismiss their Lord's dictates against killing on the slenderest of semantic excuses. Personally, I am unable to discover any sub-clauses or exemptions in the Ten Commandments.)

However, if I have previously decided I'm good, because, for instance, I hold to a belief system that I consider superior to every other, I've made the only moral calculation necessary about myself, my country, and my "side," allowing me limitless options. It's foolproof until you recast the scenario as America being invaded and colonized and consider how we might respond had the Mexican government identified Mafia gangster Joey Gallo as a drug lord threatening their nation and preemptively bombed Queens.

If we cannot say with certainty whether the self does or does not exist, might we not as easily sustain a similar "I don't know" attitude toward our own virtue? The Universe itself is half negative and half positive, and as one of its delegates in the flesh, I'm not cast as either good or bad by nature. My "I" more resembles the empty center of a bamboo tube through which impulses, thoughts, and feelings arise as the by-product of mental and physical processes. I never have encountered a homunculus behind my forehead doing my thinking, seeing, and hearing.

---

*Project for a New American Century fellow Reuel Marc Gerecht, "Why Did We Invade Iraq?" LobeLog Foreign Policy (website). April 28, 2015.

Those impulses, thoughts, and feelings are no more, nor no less *mine* than my breathing and heartbeat. The underlying emotions are universal—love, anger, jealousy, insecurity, and so on. I receive the same quotient of positive and negative thoughts, impulses, sensations, and consciousness as any other human. The *content* of those thoughts and impulses may be related to my personal history, but all humans experience love, anger, envy, and so forth. Those emotions are universal and related to universal circumstances. Pretending that we are immune to half of them places the world at risk, especially now that many more nations spend sizeable fortunes on maintaining their nuclear stockpiles with weapons fifty times more powerful than the bombs that annihilated Hiroshima and burned the shadows of the incinerated into the walls of buildings.

We all know what anger is. We all know what hatred is. We've all known people who have hated haters and failed to perceive any irony in that posture. I've attended "peace meetings" during which people screamed at one another for more than an hour. The mind tricks us all the time. One of the positive consequences of accepting that each of us is fully human is that we can accept personal responsibility to monitor our own shadow states and decide what we allow or refuse to let pass our lips or animate our behavior.

We start by cleaning our internal house, and that internal order can have analogues in physical reality. Once when I was arranging an altar for meditating, my teacher told me: "If you can make one square foot of your house pristine, you can make your entire house pristine." It's true. It would involve going over your house one square foot at a time, but it's possible. Despite failing in the pristine house category, I am normally fairly tidy, and my altars are beautiful. However, I still find it necessary to hire a housekeeper every several weeks to make my home sparkle. I'm trying. I'm continually reorganizing my desktop, kitchen table, and counters to make them as orderly as my altar. I know it's possible because I have managed the four square feet of my altars well, but keeping track of where I put that damn jar lid, spatula, or the scissors I had in my hand a moment ago eludes me. (So, I might add, does saving all beings, but I don't quit.)

If we doubt what one human can achieve in a lifetime, remember Martin Luther King Jr., the Dalai Lama, Bishop Desmond Tutu, Franklin D. Roosevelt, Michelangelo, Bernini, James Baldwin, Nelson Mandela, or Gregory Joseph Boyle, the Catholic priest in LA who built Homeboy Industries to offer employment and attitudinal change to former gang members. The world is filled with examples of human greatness.

Many people want to meditate as an antidote to where "ill-being" (Thich Nhat Han's substitution of *suffering*) afflicts them. We push away uncomfortable feelings about being different, lonely, estranged from others, in search of wellness and happiness, but the Universe doesn't work that way. Our true option as adults is to learn to accept both as expressions of the same miraculous force sustaining us.

Meditation helps us to perceive the insubstantial nature of things, including mental images, which makes it easier to observe them without flinching. That is only a half-step away from containing them. It becomes easier to remember that *any* feeling indicates that we are alive. If we can stop owning them as "ours" (which means attaching them to an idea of self) and suspend our judgment as to whether they are good or bad, our intuitions will guide us toward appropriate responses.

This is especially true when we communicate with others who perceive the world differently than we do. If we own all the good in an argument, the only place left for others to inhabit (for us) is the evil corner, and who wants to rest there? Judging others as evil actually reduces our own options. It indicates that we have been suckered into believing only the bright side of ourselves and ignoring our shadow sides. Such judgment is based on our assumption of a fixed, permanent self and easily identifiable options for reliably distinguishing good from evil.

Buddhists may criticize the *behavior* of others, not their essence. We understand that their essence is the same as ours, which is the essence of the Universe itself. That person's genesis is the same as yours and mine. They are expressions of Emptiness, neither precisely being nor non-being—just as we are.

When I am stressed by a dispute with someone, I try to consider what experiences this person may have had that made them think and feel so differently from me. Taking it further, and actually questioning them calmly, I practice my friend Brent Becvar's admonition and ask myself: Are there *any* circumstances under which I could imagine myself behaving as they do? If my answer is yes, I'm reminded that they are human. If my answer is no, I haven't considered the question deeply enough.

Until we can feel and/or touch the heart of another person, we will never understand them, and neither of us will ever change. If they do not change their thinking and beliefs, they will continue as they always have, and that is true for us as well. So while we may condemn their thoughts or actions, we are not actually effecting any change in them if we cannot come into some relationship with them. When martial artists practice Judo, it is not the biggest, strongest contender who wins, but the fall usually goes to the most conscious.

Without some contact there is no possibility of influencing another person. If you have a relationship with someone, even if you don't agree with the person, because you're in relationship, that person will respond very differently when they feel as if they are not being judged.

While distinctions between self and other appear inflexible and permanent, from the Big Mind perspective they are both the temporary expression of Buddha-nature, changing as we watch. The belief that we/they are permanent is the central delusion consequent to regarding the world only through our ego. It's not to say that we *don't* exist; that would be foolish. Neither is it to say that our existence is an illusion and the real truth is the emptiness behind it. It is to understand that we are not the solid entity we believe ourselves to be, and neither is anything else. Yes, Form is Emptiness and Emptiness is Form, but Dogen amended that to include Form is also Form and Emptiness is Emptiness. That is not to say that either is real, or doesn't really exist.

A dream exists, particularly while we're experiencing it, yet we can no more grasp it than we can grasp anything in the world. That is not the same thing as asserting that it's all false.

To realize this fully is to experience the world, if only for moments, from a vantage point other than the ego's. Such a state is usually identified as kensho—awakening. It's in this human realm between birth and death where we can achieve enlightenment, but whether we do or do not achieve it—and there are many credible teachers who insist it will take care of itself—we still need to practice and encourage ourselves to delve deeply and stay focused. Either before, after, or alongside it, the Buddha pointed out to us that enlightenment is our natural default position, only we don't realize it because of the distractions of our evolutionary heritage of greed, hatred (anger), and delusion. When they arise in the life of an enlightened person, they are mental/physical phenomena that are observed but not identified with. When they arise in an ordinary person, the person may say, "I'm angry," indicating that the entire self has been captured by the emotion.

Even after enlightenment we must return to our quotidian daily life, because this is our fate while we possess a body. We still need to remind ourselves to be helpful and kind to others and to practice an enlightened life—which means not to be distracted from intending helpfulness and compassion and resisting the tricks of our self-centered ego's thinking and emotions, believing everything we think or feel.

9

Form
and Ceremony

·····

May 13, 2020

I'D LIKE TO DISCUSS WHY ZEN FOLKS pay such attention to form and ceremony. I know a number of people who consider themselves friends of Buddhism but resist practicing it because they are overwhelmed or intimidated by its formal aspects. They usually offer some declaration like, "I'm not into organized religion," or "I don't need all the extra stuff." Such remarks suggest that there is something inherently superfluous with people organizing to achieve an objective. Taken literally, that could eliminate society itself, government, the army, or any corporate structures. It may be that problems with other people might dilute their ideas about spiritual integrity. It's never stated, but to me such remarks imply a fear that these folks feel unprepared to handle the difficulties that zazen is completely appropriate for addressing.

Imagine entering a disorganized hospital or DMV office. Imagine a basketball game without rules, or city streets without stop signs or traffic lights. Imagine flying in a plane in which the pilots can't be bothered to follow the safety checklist protocols before taking off. Organization is the method humans have devised to secure predictable outcomes. Reliable guidelines allow dependability—planning as an antidote to

102

chaos. Without rules and norms, we might feel free, but we are living by whim and not by vow.

There have been many times when I have been frustrated by some difficulty in my sangha or larger community and quipped, "The problem with Buddhism is that it's got people in it." That's what people usually mean when they say, "I'm not into organized religion." They mean, "I find it difficult to get along with people whose ideas of spirituality are not identical to mine."

What problems in the world do such folks imagine their spirituality will solve if it cannot weather personal frictions and disagreements? Doesn't such a posture secretly imply, "I'm in this by myself, and if I can only get myself straight, I won't care what other people do." This is another of the various restatements of a belief in a separate, isolated existence that lies in residence within us but is never interrogated or tested for truth. Before we address that assumption, however, let's look more deeply at just what kind of spiritual practice belief in the Four Noble Truths and the Eightfold Path might be.

First and foremost, Buddha is not a god. It's important to understand that he was an ordinary (if privileged) mortal. The wisdom he offers is in complete concord with personal integrity and the ways in which the Universe operates. It is less a sense of following edicts and commandments than it is discovering the order of things within ourselves. As such, what one discovers includes Buddha's and our own wisdom.

When Buddhists bow to a statue of Buddha, they are not worshipping the representation of an ancient dead man from Nepal but instead are expressing gratitude for his teaching and are trying to meet his wisdom with our own, *expressed in physical form.*

The "I" who is not into organized religion, the "I" who does not want to follow a schedule or act in harmony with others, the "I" who argues or is easily offended is isolating itself to protect the partiality to their personal point of view, shrinking their own nature into something they consider more manageable. This misses the point that the "I" who defends their doing exactly as they choose is the same "I" seeking spiritual relief from their problems. This is analogous to someone whose car has an unreliable engine and brakes, which they address by painting it a different color.

What is organized religion in the context of this conversation?

First and foremost, it is a community of individuals organized around expressing core beliefs and practices they are convinced improve their life. Usually such membership is deeply concerned with ironing out tangles and avoiding the snares of ordinary life. They are usually concerned with aiding others. Because its construction is a product of human agency, it, by definition, will possess every problem one might find in any other institution and the world itself. This often discourages people from practice, *and yet, that is precisely the point*. A religious community, as an integral part of a non-dual Universe, is never going to be pure. Furthermore, ideas about purity (outside of a scientific context) are another restatement of the ego's comparisons of what it prefers and what it dislikes. It is not in harmony with what *is* but with what it *wishes the world to be*. This is a recipe for difficulty. A spiritual community is a smaller, more manageable piece of the world, which seeks to operate by trusting that its members are all committed to a common goal. The rules and norms they adopt make it easier for members to practice and also make it a safe place to examine conflicts and problems.

Anything organized with humans will suffer frayed edges—conflicts, status concerns, difficulties with hierarchy, authority, jealousy, envy, and competitiveness. It's going to possess all the messy stuff of the world because it *is* the world and created by human agency. Even a dedicated convert hoping to escape the world's snares will be disappointed, because every choice we make arouses the entire world *within* us. We never escape the shadow sides of creation or our own nature. This is why some mechanism to slow down and identify them as they arise is so critical.

When I first arrived at San Francisco Zen Center, my first Buddhist community, I immediately perceived that it had a certain number of jerks in it. (I overlooked the fact that I was one of them.) I questioned the utility of Zen practice if, after thirty years of practice, so-and-so was still practicing and still a jerk. Eventually I came to understand that (unlike me) they had come to understand and be compassionate toward themselves while remaining, by and large, dedicated to polishing their flaws. The difference between us was that they understood that they had problems and had joined a monastic community to work on them. I thought I was polishing up my innate enlightenment with a few tweaks and they were the problem.

Our negative stuff may be disguised, or subtle, but believe me, it's there. If you can't see it, you're not looking. The jerk you see in me is you, only you don't understand that you're holding the mirror. If the perception of problems and contradictions is your excuse for avoiding an organized practice, you are protecting your own shortcomings from objective review and dismissing the degree to which problems in an intentional community are more under control and thus less harmful than they are, say, in Washington, D.C.

The late Katagiri-roshi was a Japanese Zen teacher who came to America to help Suzuki-roshi and later founded a Zen center outside of Minneapolis named Hokyoji. He once observed that the rigors of a formal practice were like putting your life into a bamboo tube. *"Even if you're crazy,"* he said, *"the craziness is in the tube, too, so it's all right."* Accepting the limits of the tube makes it possible to contain that craziness, anxiety, or fear. The tube is like nirodha, the Third Noble Truth of containment. In a monastery, the container is the relentless schedule and occupation with forms and norms. Outside the monastery most people seek to escape the limits of form, dressing as they please and seeking freedom helter-skelter as they can. In a monastery, everyone adheres to the same rigorous schedule, and everyone dresses identically. You might think that people's individuality would be repressed in such circumstances, but the opposite is true. You can still immediately identify people by the shape of their head or feet. The uniqueness is baked in. Outside, where each of us is trying to be unique, we resemble a crowd.

When we meditate, we sit with all beings. Zazen is actually a ceremony, and, like all ceremonies, it changes us. Whether or not we are aware of it, we live every moment with all beings, connected to the living and (theoretically nonliving) by infinite umbilical cords. Being conscious of our dependence on not-self sources (all together now . . . oxygen, sunlight, microbes in the soil, etc.) is an inducement to express that consciousness *physically* as well as mentally: caring for all beings by being mindful of our speech and behavior; deciding what we allow to pass through our lips and what we don't. Buddhists use the word *practice* to describe this effort because humans are all fallible and fumble. We make mistakes in the same way that we lose track of our breathing while meditating or get swept away by fantasies. Only it is much easier to notice against the spare, formal background of monastic life. This is one of the reasons that teachers tell us that it is easier to live in a monastery than in the world, and that even after many years practicing inside, we must have even more years in the world to become balanced with its relentlessness and diversity.

Our vows help us to remain steadfast, through our disappointment, boredom, setbacks, and loss of inspiration, all of which happen only to the living—in other words—to all of us. Vows assist us in trying, again and again, to bring our minds back into harmonious relationship with "all of it." Particularly in dangerous and tumultuous times where threats, disorder, and bad-faith players are aided by sophisticated media, the world requires people who remain calm and see clearly and who will not lose their heads. We might say that such people "see things as it is."

When people who share common values come together to express those values in their everyday lives, a magnification of those personal efforts occurs between the two parts: the *coming* together and expressing one's values by *doing things* together. The "together" part is what Buddhists refer to as the sangha.

The Three Treasures of Buddhism are Buddha (the teacher), dharma (the teachings), and sangha, the community of people following the Buddha's way. Gary Snyder reminds us that wilderness is an alternate way of naming this and is the multidimensional truth of existence:

> The wild is everywhere: ineradicable populations of fungi, moss, mold, yeasts, and such that surround and inhabit us. Deer mice on the back porch, deer bounding across the freeway, pigeons in the park, spiders in the corners. There were crickets in the paint locker of the Sappa Creek oil tanker, as I worked as a wiper in the engine room out in mid-Pacific, cleaning brushes. Exquisite complex beings in their energy webs inhabiting the fertile corners of the urban world in accord with the rules of wild systems, the visible hardy stalks and stems of vacant lots and railroads, the persistent raccoon squads, bacteria in the loam and in our yogurt.

To remind us that we ourselves are wild to our deepest levels, he continues:

> Our bodies are wild. The involuntary quick turn of the head at a shout, the vertigo at looking off a precipice, the heart-in-the-throat in a moment of danger, the catch of the breath, the quiet moments relaxing, staring, reflecting—all universal responses of this mammal body. . . . To speak of wilderness is to speak of wholeness.*

It's our fellow practitioners (sangha) who will call us on our "stuff" and protect us from self-centeredness, keeping us honest. They will alert us when we drift off plumb. It is as important to spend time with committed peers as it is to spend time on our meditation pillow.

People who insist that they do not like organized religion are, whether or not they realize it, breaking spiritual practice (and the Universe) into a hierarchy. They want "the most important" stuff for themselves (how they determine that remains a question open only to them) and consider what is difficult, boring, or does not interest

---

*Gary Snyder, *The Practice of the Wild: Essays* (Berkeley: Counterpoint, 2020).

them as being extra. I have friends who have spent thousands of dollars exploring Egypt, crawling into the pyramids to be bathed by their vibrations. I have others who travel to Peru to take ayahuasca with shamans, and others who microdose LSD at the office, seeking a creative edge, but none sit alone with themselves without distraction on a daily basis. When Buddha vowed to save all beings, I doubt that he considered running them through the pyramids in small batches. The Quick Fix is always wishful thinking of the lazy.

Unlike democracy, the practices of Buddhism have been refined over millennia by thousands of minds impersonally regarding the practice from enlightened perspectives. One need not like someone to bow to them and treat them with respect. One does not have to like or condone a person's behavior to entertain and answer their arguments and assertions. If you cannot do that, how do you intend to save all beings or save the planet from the consequences of human self-centeredness and greed?

Nothing prevents you from staying up late every night and sleeping late every day, doing whatever you like (until your money runs out or your friends or family object). You might consider living like that as personal freedom, but it's actually just the path of least resistance— life by whim. This is one of the reasons that it is often difficult for extremely wealthy people to be successful in psychotherapy or practice. True freedom is learning to keep the mind free and poised *within* the chafing limits of human life. Freedom is being unafraid of one's own mind, unafraid of commitment, and unafraid of the boundaryless.

I worked with a psychiatrist for some time who had worked at Yale University. He told me that psychiatric practice with the wealthy and entitled was extremely difficult, because when things got tough and commitment to the work became important, "a wonderful opportunity for a safari or some opportunity they 'could not pass up' arises, and they're gone."

This may be why Buddhist theory stresses that it is only from the human realm of struggle and suffering that people can be enlightened.

Dwellers in the heavenly realms, for instance (think of the uber-rich and A-list movie stars), where everything is beautiful, precious, and perfect, often remain fixated on the fear of losing it, which inhibits their possibilities of freedom.

The only way that we learn to recognize the insubstantiality of our own thoughts and beliefs, the impermanence of our body, the fact that there is absolutely nothing in the Universe (except the Universe) to depend on, and learn to find joy in that reality, requires boundaries. It means we subject ourselves to voluntary limitation so that we are not distracted in our pursuits of vexing problems. Those boundaries can't be simply of our own choosing, or we would just be reinforcing the preferences of our personalities.

If you could meditate any way that you wanted, disregarding posture, continually adjusting yourself for your comfort, scratching every itch, you would be sacrificing every standard by which to measure your own progress. If there is a "correct" form, everyone has the same impersonal standard to judge themselves against. Eventually, you will be unable to help finding your own way, but that is only accomplished by honing your edges against the whetstone of the given forms.

A ceremony is the physicalizing of an intention expressed as action. As my friend, the writer David Harris, expressed it in part 3 of this book, "Values that are not embodied in behavior do not exist."

Learning such things changes you. When I became a priest, I had already been practicing nearly forty years. When my teacher asked me to submit to a three-year priest's training regimen, I demurred, explaining, "I'm never going to be a priest." He was unfazed by my refusal and said simply, "Just try this training and see what you get from it."

The training turned out to be inspiring. I became so impressed by the caliber of my classmates and what they had accomplished that I was finally moved to up my game. At the training regimen's end, I asked my teacher if he would ordain me as a priest, and he agreed, smiling as if he'd anticipated my request.

Ordination required a lot of effort. I had to sew a *rakusu,* a small cloth bib, which is a miniature copy of the priests' formal robe, the *okesa*. The rakusu is small enough to wear while working and stands in for the okesa, which is nearly the size of a double-bed bedsheet and is worn over a priest's other garments on ceremonial occasions. An okesa (which I also had to sew) is impossible to wear while performing physical work. The sewing required precise and meticulous (measured to the millimeter) folding, ironing, measuring, and pinning edges before stitching them together, reciting a little prayer with each stitch. It took me a year to complete. When I was finally ordained and ceremonially received my new rakusu, okesa, and monk's bowls, I was somewhat numb from the effort and expectations that had led me to that moment. I was not at all sure that I felt particularly changed.

About six months after the ceremony, I began to settle into my priest's identity and more fully appreciate the calling and feel capable of honoring the commitment I'd made. The implications of it began to permeate my psyche, particularly when I began officiating weddings and funerals and learning what holding ceremonial space implied. Most surprising was precisely what my teacher had predicted: the lineage I was now a part of began to speak through me, and I would hear myself making observations and confidently answering questions I had not been previously aware of knowing.

I particularly enjoy officiating at weddings—a ceremony that, while it is familiar to all of us, we rarely consider in its deepest implications. *Wedding* (from the same root as the word *weld*) merges two worlds and braids of DNA, combining them to create a previously unknown entity. Ancient lineages will meet and generate children. The families (in this modern age) may have barely known each other but now arrive to bear witness to this joining, and this witnessing is a critical element of the wedding ceremony's power.

A marriage used to be referred to as "plighting one's troth," or pledging one's truth. The pledge was certified by placing one's body in bond. Default could be a capital offense. This ancient recognition that a marriage is an act of high seriousness is one reason they are always witnessed.

In this casual age where sweatpants are fashion statements and pretending to be "regular" is a cultural trope, we might wonder why a couple couldn't just go into the living room and inform their parents that they are "hooking up." Others insist that they do not need papers or "the state involved in our personal life" (a similar trope to not liking organized religion), but they rarely explain what that "need" is for and what it accomplishes.

Ceremonial commitments alter us in unforeseen ways. Taking vows before witnesses charges them with high seriousness. *Husband* and *wife* are new identities requiring new demands and adjustments. Likewise, *parent* is an identity with new requirements, expectations, and demands. The dressing up, the presentation of the bride and groom as objects of beauty and value are heightened and ritualized not simply because they're going to have children and genes are going to be recombinated, but because this melding of *families and lineage* creates an entirely unique organism composed of the present and historical membership of both families. This is literally starting the world anew, fresh and unsoiled. The intentions of the bride and groom are expressed and sealed by vows, and witnessed to distinguish them from promises.

A vow is quite different from a promise. Promises are easy to break—cross your fingers behind your back. *A vow is a commitment made with the totality of your being.* It is a statement of intention and determination, superseding facts and probability. For this reason, they always require witnesses, because in a marriage not only are the bride and groom being joined, they are also melding their larger communities. They are forging a community, like the armorer's folding and refolding of steel and iron together to produce Damascus steel, known for its exceptional sharpness and utility due to the fusion of the levels of metal. The bride is now a wife. This signals that male members must treat her with circumspection and refrain from overly familiar behavior.

The same vows alter the groom's relationship to women community members, and by participating in the ceremony, witnesses pledge themselves to assist the marriage and foster community stability, with appropriate behavior, honest counsel, and understanding. Taking these vows publicly, before witnesses, is what makes them so binding; consequently, witnesses are critical.

The same altered relationships pertain to the bride and groom. When I perform weddings, I place a single pillar candle on the altar, framed by tapers on either side. The tapers are lit before the service begins, the pillar is not. Before the bride and groom recite their vows, they light the central pillar from the individual tapers each holds. I've explained that the unlit pillar represents the marriage itself. Because their vows will be stated not only to one another but also to the marriage itself, after lighting the pillar together, bride and groom replace their lit tapers on either side of it, signifying that in this marriage neither husband nor wife should have to extinguish their own authenticity.

I don't sacrifice my left hand (my dominant hand) when I temporarily subordinate it under my right in the mudra (hand position) during meditation. I am willingly subordinating my active side with my passive side, in the same way healthy relationships swap dominance. It's often done instinctively as an act of affection, but doing it consciously can be an act of liberation or repair.

Ceremonies change people by moving them physically through certain levels of awareness and understanding, without which everything in life remains casual and in perpetual flux. If everything is casual, everything remains completely mutable, making it more difficult to maintain fixed intention. Yes, we understand formlessness, but we express it in the world of form, where we live, and to do that we use other forms. "How are you?" is a form, a hug is a form, shaking hands, Thanksgiving dinner, with all its preparations, expectations and things going wrong is a form, too.

If you live together because you "don't need a piece of paper" and you have a bad argument, it's natural to think, "I don't have to put up with this!" But if you are married, if you have been through such a ceremonial public commitment, with witnesses and the public recitation of vows, if you have legally registered as a couple and hold common property and wealth, and perhaps children in common, the form itself tends to support thinking, "I *do* have to put up with this. This is my life, and if it is not working, I need to change somehow." Thoughts such as these give us the impetus to maintain determination to see things anew, to change old behavior and assumptions that can founder open, loving relationships.

Such inducements make us dig deeper and try harder. It expands our perimeters. Of course, it doesn't always work, and it will not protect us from poor choices or choices made in the service of unexplored needs.

I've been divorced twice, and each were excruciatingly painful events in my life. My first marriage was a formal Buddhist ceremony in a Buddhist temple in front of eighty chanting black-robed monks. I took these vows publicly and took them seriously. One of the most difficult thing I ever had to do was admit to the revered widow of the Zen master, a woman I referred to as "mother" (*Okusan* in Japanese), that I had failed my marriage vows and was going to be divorced.

Anyone who's ever been through a divorce will tell you it's like being carved up by dull knives. Part of what is so difficult—beyond the minutia of distributing shared assets, precious objects, and mementos, the enduring difficulties of the children and visiting schedules, working out holidays (double that if there's a pet to be shared)—is the fact that we are severing and fracturing these ties in our larger community as well. We are breaking promises made with the totality of our being, as free and responsible adults, publicly admitting our failure. Severing these vows exacts a penalty, and it's steep. For the first year after my first divorce I felt as if I had lost my luck in life and all sense of direction. Whether or not you were "in the right" or wronged, or simply unable to accommodate what the other needed, you will suffer, and your children will suffer for that inability.

After divorce, mutual friends will tend to side with either the bride or groom. Friendships are lost, networks and relationships readjusted, close friendships may become impossible to maintain. I can say now, after two deep dives into the issue, that, besides love and attraction (which initiated the marriage), each of my marriages was driven by invisible and unresolved issues with my childhood family. That's hard to face; to understand that you've in some manner recapitulated the worst parts of your relationships with your family, which hurt and troubled you the most. Very little will knock you off your "adult" pedestal as brutally as coming to terms with your lifetime of personal, unresolved "stuff." And yet, nine years after my second divorce I'm marrying again. Trying to do better again is practice.

Today I'm inviting you to rethink any negative ideas about forms and ceremonies. Try this for the benefits they offer, to soften your attitudes and regard to reconsider them less subjectively, less attached to a personal point of view. The more appropriate concerns include: What am I delivering myself to? What am I helping to create here? What is my intention?

I'd like to ask you to consider the word *intention* itself; to ask yourself what your deepest intention, your *fundamental* intention might be, not simply in terms of your marriage, but for your personal life. A fundamental intention is one we follow almost without thinking, "with every breath." If you discover that, and stay in harmony with it, generally things will go well for you. It is what Carlos Castaneda's Don Juan called "following a path with a heart." If we don't follow our deepest intentions, we become like leaves blown by the wind, unable to draw boundaries and exert ourselves fully. You may not have considered it before, but try it now. See if you can identify what it is that you are primarily "doing" all the time. What wish or intention resides deep within you always, simmering on the back burner of your thoughts? If we behave harmoniously with that fundamental intention, our life will be harmonious. If we don't, things can be rough.

10

Emptiness and the Heart Sutra

• • • • •

May 20, 2020

THE MAN WE CALL THE BUDDHA (the Awakened One) was named Siddhartha Gautama about three thousand years ago.

Gautama's father was a ruler of a large tribe called the Shakyas, and Gautama was raised in the warrior/prince caste and trained to be a ruler and warrior. His father, like most parents, went to great lengths to ensure that his son had the best possible life. In Gautama's case, because he lived on thousands of acres of forests and streams and places to play, his father was able to ensure that his son never left the boundaries of the family's estate. Consequently, as legend goes, he was spared introduction to the world's suffering—sickness, old age, and death.

One day, after he'd been married and had children, enjoyed his concubines, hunting and martial arts, he demanded to accompany his chariot driver outside the palace walls and into a nearby village. It was there that the young prince came upon a very old, disfigured woman in rags, hobbling along on a cane. He was shocked. He'd never before seen anything unsightly, jarring, or not beautiful. Later that day, he encountered dead bodies stacked in the streets and others bathed in melted butter and burned on piles of logs, surrounded by weeping mourners. In the course of a single day, he witnessed multiple examples of illness, old age, suffering, and grief, and they affected him to the degree that he became determined to understand how and why such conditions existed.

Gautama's obsession with this question increased to the point that one night he stole away from the palace, leaving his wife and children to be cared for there, and joined a group of penniless religious ascetics in the forest to find an answer this question.

Gautama lived, practiced, and studied with these men for six years, punishing his body and ignoring the material world in an attempt to break through into what he imagined was a pure, spiritual awareness. Like theirs, his body became emaciated and skeletal; sculptures representing him at this time depict him as a virtual skeleton in rags.

One day, legend informs us, he fainted from malnutrition. He was discovered lying in a ditch along the road by a milkmaid who was delivering an offering to the local temple. She took pity on Gautama, helped him back to his seat, and offered him the warm, fresh milk mixed with rice she was carrying to the temple. Her gesture was so selfless and sincere that it moved Gautama deeply, and, combined with the energy he received from her food, he could continue his practice.

With newly renewed strength, Gautama amplified his effort and vowed to meditate in the shade of an enormous Bodhi tree, where he'd taken shelter. Bodhi trees are curious because they send roots downward from their branches into the earth, and these branches eventually thicken into columns. Such trees afforded shelter to numerous mendicants. Gautama sat in such a place, vowing not to move until he attained enlightenment.

For later generations, his decision to nourish his body has served to warn young seekers not to privilege spirit over flesh but instead to care for the body as the precious and rare gift it is. Ancient histories describe the last night of Gautama's old life, with numerous phantoms and temptations arising before his eyes, challenging his determination. Mara, the great temptress, sometimes presented as the Lord of Death and at other times as the embodiment of all sensual pleasure, materialized every conceivable allurement or terror in an attempt to make Gautama cease his search for enlightenment.

Gautama never wavered, and at dawn—some say the same day, others three days later, and still other assert forty-five days later—as the morning star rose, he had his enlightened awakening and became the Buddha. He had understood the myriad connections between everything he had considered his life and that which apparently existed outside of it. He had penetrated the subjects of *emptiness, interdependence,* and *transience* as core universal truths. He had tracked suffering to its root and now understood the nature of suffering and the causes and workings of karma. He understood that while sickness, old age, and death are unavoidable, there are practical steps one can take in life to liberate oneself from the sufferring they cause. The core of this new understanding was Emptiness.

Buddha explained the way the world actually is (as opposed to how we conceive it) as *dependent origination.* Just to remind the reader, this means that every solitary existence depends on everything else for its existence. The apparent separation of self and other—our default reality—is based on the illusion that "we" are inside and everything else is outside. But the self we refer to as "I" and "me" has no physical existence. We cannot find it. It doesn't have a shape, a color, or a location. It is boundaryless and might best be described as an *awareness.*

Buddhist theory posits the self as a mass or aggregate of multiple awarenesses, with eyes, ears, nose, tongue, body, and mind each possessing their own, organized and overseen by the mind.

If we don't realize that and consider ourselves a boundaried entity that is always being described by ourself to ourself or by others to us, over time that made-up identity begins to add layers of narrative and description to itself and eventually develops a kind of solidity we now consider as fact. For all its usefulness, like language itself, it taxes us.

Because the 10,000 things (remember the Chinese expression for the world's infinite forms on page 54?) are actually composed of one another, it follows that there is no core, separate identifier—no "tree

identity" to be found in the cells of a tree. There is no "bark" identifying bark other than its constituent parts—leaves, bark, pith, sap, roots,
and cellulose.

The situation is the same for our self within the sack of flesh that
temporarily shelters our awareness. We have names for these things certainly, and the words *I* and *me* are invaluable conveniences, but Buddha
made a distinction between the map (the name) and the territory itself.

This affliction of human beings appears to be a by-product of one
of its greatest strengths: language. The word *tree* serves a useful purpose of rapid identification and association, but it also creates a delusion
that the existence of the tree is an event distinct from everything that is
"not-tree." This is what Buddha refers to as delusion. They are partially
true but express only half of reality. He had seen through the assumptions of his vain and alluring ego and its self-importance and insistence
that it possesses an independent existence. In so doing, he had become
immune to its foibles and tricks.

In Zen literature this awakening experience is often shorthanded
as "forgetting the self." Buddha had perceived that the fundamental
nature of the Universe and the nature of his own mind are identical—a
luminous awareness.

I said earlier that Emptiness is a core foundation of Buddhist practice, and Suzuki-roshi expressed that in this way: "It is vitally important
to believe in absolutely nothing." All forms, colors, sounds, smells, and
tastes emanate from this vitality, constantly transmuting itself into the
myriad visible forms of the world. It is an observable act of faith for
Buddhists to believe that one's original self and the Buddha's are the
same, and those original selves are not different from the vast mind of
the Universe itself. It is a faith that allows us to intend ourselves toward
something we cannot express in language, cannot know except in small
glimpses, and, for the most part, have never previously experienced.
However, bolstered by the 3,000-year-old record, plentiful traditional
lore, and the care and attentiveness of millennia of skillful and attentive teachers, these teachings and awakenings have been certified and

reaffirmed from person to person up to and including the present day.

Ancient Buddhist Chan master Yongming (904–975 CE) said, *"Faith without understanding increases ignorance; understanding without faith increases subjective opinions."** This is why Zen folks don't consider Zen a religion, though there are some sects of Buddhism that do. For Zen people the Buddha was, most importantly, a normal man, fully human and not a miraculous figure. He solved a problem that has plagued humanity since the imagined Garden of Eden, when Adam and Eve were punished for disobeying God. Their disobedience split the Universe into Good and Evil, sacrificing its original primal wholeness for a world filled with contradictions and opposing forces to be negotiated.

And what is Keizan's understanding?

According to Keizan, "The substance of true awareness is neither more nor less in ordinary people, students of fully awakened beings. It is beginningless and endless, and it is never given by another."† For a number of days (forty-nine we are told), the Buddha worried that his insight and its implications were too subtle and difficult for ordinary people to understand. He meditated on this, and my personal conclusion is that his compassion for human suffering was so great that he resolved to try to teach what he had learned, perhaps assuming that he might help *some* people.

It was faith in this that allowed me to transcend the sense of loss after my own kensho when I perceived Emptiness for myself. I understood that even Buddhism, in which I'd placed great desperate faith and dedication to as a source of sanity, was empty.

What saved me from surrendering to despair was realizing that the

---

*Yung-ming was an important Chan master who synthesized all systems of Buddhism— particularly Pure Land and Ch'an (the Chinese precursor to Zen) thought—in theory, and, more importantly, united all approaches of Buddhist disciplines in practice. See Heng-ching Shih, "Yung-ming's Syncretism of Pure Land and Ch'an," *Journal of the International Association of Buddhist Studies* 10, no. 1 (1987): 117–34.

†See *Transmission of the Light*, translated by Thomas Cleary (Boston: Shambhala, 2002).

Buddha himself must have understood that as well, but in that moment, as the expression of his true compassion for others, decided to try to be helpful.

Buddha's first public utterance was made on the occasion of his return to his fellow ascetics and concerned the Four Noble Truths and the Eightfold Path. Upon his return, some of his old friends initially judged him harshly for forsaking his vows and taking nourishment. However, he was so self-evidently transformed that his old companions prostrated themselves before him and became his first students.

Fast-forward 500 years of transmitting the Buddha's insight from teacher to student. The main sect of Buddhism for that first 500 years were referred to as the *Sarvāstivādins*. Because the Buddha had organized his understanding so systematically, they believed that the world was ultimately knowable. Building on his teachings, discussing and refining them for 500 years, early Buddhists compiled an encyclopedic system of thought to account for the world's phenomena that did not require the existence of an ego to perceive it. This encyclopedia, known as the *Abhidharma*, is a fascinating collection of philosophical thought.

A leading scholar of this school, named Shariputra, dedicated himself to systematizing and making mnemonic lists about points of dharma. His system of interlocking dharmas—the five skandhas, the twelve abodes of sensation, the eighteen elements of perception, and twelve links of dependent origination—was a vast and original undertaking, a magnificent intellectual edifice that held sway over Buddhist thinking for centuries. Today we refer to it as the school of the elders, *Theravadins,* because their primary concern was *self*-enlightenment, and they believed that only the dedication and austerities of a monk's practice could lead to enlightenment.

More recently and less judgmentally, they are referred to as the Fundamental Vehicle, as their practices are foundational to all schools of Buddhism. They are also referred to as the Hinayana school and concentrate on subtle distinctions between "Desire Zen" (desire for enlightenment or gaining wisdom) and "Pure Zen" (practice with no idea of gaining)—Buddha's practice. Suzuki-roshi uses these distinctions to argue that

> it is not correct to say that Zen Buddhism was established only after Bodhidharma came from the West. Although there was not a specific Zen school by that name, Zen ideas were clearly pointed out in the Hinayana way. If we miss this point the Zen school will become [only] one of the many schools of Buddhism. Every school should be only Buddhism.*

Around the first century BCE, a more expansive, inclusive understanding began to evolve in Buddhist thought, which became known as the Mahayana school. *Mahayana* means "great vehicle" because adherents aspired for enlightenment for *all* sentient beings. They reasoned that if all phenomena are expressions of Emptiness (Buddha-nature), nothing exists outside of it, so why should anyone be exempt? Why should knowledge of the way things are be the province of only a select few? The Buddha accepted all castes and genders in his practice; why, they argued, should his successors do less and ban women, Dalits (Untouchable caste), and Hindus?

On a Chinese stele dated to 660 CE, the Heart Sutra, the earliest known text of this Mahayana school, was carved. It is framed as a dialogue between Sariputra, one of the leading scholars of the earlier Hinayana school, and the Buddha who speaks in the incarnation of Avalokitesvara (Ah-velow-Keet-esh-vara)—the Buddha as Compassion. He/she is correcting Sariputra for his conceptual errors.

Around five hundred years after the Buddha's death, his followers, who became known as the Mahayana, critiqued the earlier school understanding (Hinayana) from the perspective of the universality of

---

*"Buddhism is very philosophical, and sometimes intellectual and logical." Shunryu Suzuki transcript, One-Day Sesshin lectures, November 1965. Available online at ShunryuSuzuki.com.

mind itself. The Heart Sutra is purported to be the Buddha's own words but actually appeared long after his death. It is perhaps the most condensed version of Buddha's teachings, chanted daily in most Mahayana Buddhist temples.

In Sanskrit it is called the "Maha Prajna Paramita Hridaya Sutra," the Great Understanding of Highest Wisdom. The word *prajna* means "wisdom," but it's a compound, where *pra* indicates "before," and *jna* indicates "knowing," thereby referring to *the knowledge you have before you know anything*. Suzuki-roshi referred to this state as "Beginner's Mind."

I'm going to share the Heart Sutra here, but there are a few things I have to explain so that you can make sense of it. It's cast as a little dramatic play that begins with the Buddha as Avalokitesvara sitting in deep meditation. The first word of this sutra is the name of the person speaking—Avalokitesvara—sometimes known as Kwan Yin, sometimes as Kanzeon. Statues of her in her feminine aspect are usually depicted in a long flowing gown, holding one hand with palm facing out to protect people against anger, fear, and delusion and clutching a small vase of wisdom water. She is a bodhisattva (one who is so dedicated to save all beings that they vow to be the last enlightened). She hears the suffering of the world and responds. To many she reminds them of the Virgin Mary, regarded by many Christians as the great heart of warmth and compassion, perhaps more approachable than Jesus himself.

Sometimes we see Buddhas represented with hundreds of arms, which are a visual expression of their tireless efforts to help all beings. The bodhisattva was a stunning evolution of human archetypes. Perhaps you have been involved at some time with a group effort where people were seeking a high goal in common for all the noble reasons one might imagine only to see those efforts fall apart. Even in a monastery competition, personal preferences, jealousy, and ambition can seep in and, sometimes, camouflaged by the allure of "perfect wisdom," self-interest can warp personal and collective behavior.

People may justify spiritual ambition by thinking, "If I can just get enlightened, then I can help everyone." Before we know it, such a person (which is each of us) is too obsessed with their personal goal to allow space for selfless human interactions and kindness. We've all observed how such thinking plays out in the world of politics in the past several years.

The bodhisattva vow actually short-circuits such selfishness by vowing to be the *last* beings to be enlightened; willingly remaining behind to help everyone else across first.

The sutra begins:

> *Avalokitesvara Bodhisattva when practicing deeply the*
> *Prajnaparamita (highest, perfect meditation),*
> *Perceived that all five skandhas in their own-being are*
> *empty.**

The word *skandha* is related to the trunk of a tree, because the early understanding (expressed by Shariputra, whom Avalokitesvara is criticizing in the Heart Sutra) was that eyes, ears, nose, mouth, impulse, and sensation were each supported by a "trunk" of consciousness. Avalokitesvara takes such scholarship to task, explaining that these skandhas are empty of any fixed permanent self because they don't exist as fixed entities but rather as part of the infinite formulations of the Universe's essential energy and are inseparable from it.

Avalokitesvara continues:

> *Oh, Shariputra, form does not differ from emptiness.*
> *Emptiness does not differ from form.*

---

*In most translations, this line includes the phrase "and was saved from all suffering," a much later Chinese addition, which as I explained earlier, suggests that after enlightenment dukkha ceases to exist—a misunderstanding that has sent many Western Buddhists off in an unfortunate direction. It's explored in greater depth later, but for now, consider that when we save someone from drowning, we don't drain the ocean, we save them from the effects of the ocean.

> *That which is form is emptiness.*
> *That which is emptiness, form.*
> *The same is true of feelings, perceptions,*
> *impulses, and consciousness.*

According to Shariputra's systems, a human being consists of these five skandhas (heaps or clusters): form, feeling, impulses, sensations, and consciousness—each with its own awareness.

> *Shariputra, all dharmas are marked with emptiness.*

Dharma means individual things, but it also means "truth" or the "suchness" of things.

> *They do not appear or disappear, are not tainted nor*
> *pure, do not increase or decrease.*

Consider the ocean generating millions of little wavelets dappling its surface. Each wavelet could represent a nameable object or perception. Each appears to be discrete. Each rises into form for a while and then settles back into the ocean. We call things "in form" living, and when they return to formlessness we call it dying. However, we and the little wavelets forget that they have never, for one moment, ever been separate from the vast ocean (Formlessness/Emptiness). To say "appear" or "disappear" or "begins" or "ends" is regarding only that which has form but ignores the vastness generating it all and of which each supposedly separate thing is composed.

Avalokitesvara continues describing Emptiness and its implications. Everything is expressed in negatives because Avalokitesvara is systematically obliterating the armatures of Shariputra's belief that intellectual study could lead to enough knowledge to decode the essential mystery of reality.

Therefore, in Emptiness, there is no form, no feeling, no
*   perceptions, no impulses, no consciousness.*
No eyes, no ears, no nose, no tongue, no body, no mind;
No color, no sound, no smell, no taste, no touch, no
*   object of mind.*
No realm of eyes until no realm of mind-consciousness.
No ignorance and also no extinction of it;
until no old age and death and also no extinction of it;
No Being, No non-being.*
No suffering, no origination, no stopping, no path,
no cognition, also no attainment.

Centuries later Dogen-Zenji, the man who brought Chinese Chan Buddhism (Zen in Japanese) to Japan, offered a corrective clarification: *"Form is form, and emptiness is emptiness."* Form and Emptiness are neither a dualism nor a contradiction. "Sun-faced Buddha, Moon-faced Buddha" are different expressions of Buddha-nature, like waves and water or the "shit-smeared stick," which an ancient Zen master offered as an answer to a student's question: "What is Buddha?"

Emptiness is the womb of all Forms, but neither exists independently enough to grasp. Everything is always present. Each of us is born with Buddha-nature. That nature is obscured by attachments to negative thoughts and impulses, which misunderstand it as "separate self-entities."

But even these supposed errors of understanding serve us. If there was no anger at the fruits of ignorance, how would we stiffen our resolve to win enlightenment, to save all beings? If there was no greed,

---

*The revered Vietnamese Zen master Thich Nhat Han added the phrases *No Being, No non-being* to this list, to help people not implying that *everything* is a delusion. He is reminding us not to misread form and emptiness as a dichotomy, and assume that Emptiness is the underlying *truth* and Form only the secondary expression of it, or worse, that your physical body does not exist.

why would we search for wisdom. If there was no delusion, how could
we spin the lovely fantasies about the Buddha and what enlightenment
must be like? Everything has multiple faces, like coins spinning on our
tabletop.

> With nothing to attain, the Bodhisattva depends on
> Prajnaparamita. And the mind is no hindrance.
> Without any hindrance, no fears exist.
> Far apart from every perverted view, they dwell in
>   nirvana.
> In the three worlds, all Buddhas depend on
>   Prajnaparamita.
>
> Therefore, know the Prajnaparamita is the great
>   transcendent
> mantra, Is the great, bright mantra, Is the utmost
>   mantra,
> The supreme mantra, which is able to relieve all
>   suffering and is
> true, not false. So, proclaim the Prajnaparamita
>   mantra.
> Proclaim the mantra which says:
> Gaté, gaté, paragaté, parasamgaté.
> Bodhi. Svaha!

Gaté means "gone." Paragaté means "to the other shore," parasamgaté
indicates "gone beyond beyond"—beyond all formulations and concep-
tions. Bodhi means "awakened." Svaha exclaims "done," "accomplished."

This is the most famous sutra in all of Buddhism, expressing the
core truth of emptiness—Gone, gone, gone beyond, gone beyond beyond.
Bodhi (Awake). Svaha!

It's my feeling that the mantra, rather than being a miraculous
utterance, is a mnemonic device to retrieve and remember the entire

Heart Sutra. It also leads me to believe that at the time and place of its creation there were probably many mantras competing for dominance.

Buddhists often express three ways to consider wisdom. The first is **mundane wisdom**—everyday wisdom—which (according to Buddhist philosophy) has everything backward, viewing the impermanent as permanent, including the self, and imagining it hitchhiking from body to body or residing permanently in heaven. It sees the impure as pure. It believes that what has no self has a self.

Most people appear to believe that we possess a permanent self corresponding to an organ. People often say, "I know who I am." If you know who you are, it means you are no longer in the process of becoming. It means you have defined yourself and are now acting out a more or less fixed idea of who you are, or assuming that your habitual responses *are* you. That is the fundamental mistake that Buddha addressed by explaining dependent origination. Given the absolute intertwining of creation, how can there be a permanent, identifiable self, separate from the rest of it. It would make the self the only thing in the universe that does not change. Perhaps we might consider our awareness like the blank luminous screen in a movie theater. Our internal images and narratives play across the surface, but those images, narratives and the screen itself are all ineffable awareness.

The next description is **metaphysical wisdom.** Metaphysical wisdom views what appears to be permanent as impermanent, what appears to be pure as impure, and what appears to have a self as not having a self. It's an advancement. People who study "the mysteries" receive a more sophisticated and more nuanced understanding that is closer to the way things are but also results in attachment to views, ideas, concepts, and knowledge derived from the mystery traditions. Metaphysical wisdom leads many people off the path, because when searching for teachers, we usually seek them outside of the ordinary, as if they were members of an enlightened or "special" realm only the wise inhabit, one that can be identified by visible signs—long beards, robes, fetching smiles, and occult symbols.

There are numerous transcendental charlatans—people we expect to be more perfect than they are—flytraps for the unwary. They may possess some insight—the most alluring do—and may puzzle you with impenetrable utterances, but they're not special beings, and they are certainly not different from you and me. Very often, the projection of special powers we attach to a teacher camouflages our own attachment to power and dominance.

There is only this reality in which even a housefly is a mystery beyond understanding. Any single thing the eye rests on is an impenetrable miracle, so searching for a special state of mind in which the weather is always sunny is dressing reality in a fool's cap. Suzuki-roshi urges us to just "say 'Yes' to everything." It never fails to amaze me how often people find teachers who make them pay, in one coin or another, for their own birthright.

The third mode of understanding is known as **transcendent wisdom,** where immersion in deep meditation (*shikantaza*), the primary practice of the Zen sect of Buddhism, softens our views, ideas, concepts, and knowledge of the world. Transcendent wisdom regards all things mundane or metaphysical, both sides of the spectrum, as neither permanent nor impermanent. Both are incomprehensible and beyond description, as the Heart Sutra reminds us: "No old age and death, and also no extinction of it."

Buddha never stated that the self was real, or false. He said it wasn't a fixed, stand-alone event. The transcendent perspective sees objects and events as neither pure nor impure, neither having nor not having a self, free from the constraints and implications of language. The Great Matter is all inconceivable. When an ancient Zen student was once challenged by his teacher to demonstrate his understanding, he responded, "If I speak, I am a liar. If I don't speak, I'm a coward."

I said before that language, for all its gifts, exacts a use tax by reifying (making an abstract idea "real") what it names. Several consequences flow from that, as I've mentioned earlier. However, it's worth reiterating habituation to the idea of fixed identities implied by naming renders it unnecessary to reconsider each person we meet as a fresh event in a fresh moment or to observe ourselves in that manner.

"Oh, yeah," we might say, "I get that guy. Carhartts, a four-wheel pickup, and rifle rack. A Trump voter." Or "Yeah, I get it—a Yuppie—L.L.Bean, a Tesla, and a Labradoodle. A Liberal." A stopped clock is right twice a day. Sometimes such intuitive snap judgments are correct, but they often fail to consider realms of contradictory data—Hell's Angels' Christmas drives, long-haired highway road crews, or the mob of "patriots" storming the Capitol on January 6, 2021.

Reductive judgments like these are direct consequences of conflating a name and the concepts we hold about it. We can't get on every day without them, but remembering the inherent tendency of language (and symbols) to fracture reality is a useful aid in developing a softer, more fluid understanding when we speak, remembering that the map is not the terrain.

I remember once watching a video clip of a woman attending a Trump rally who was wearing a T-shirt that stated, "I voted for Hillary." She was walking a large Golden Labrador, and everyone who approached her was so mesmerized by her dog they smiled and chatted about their own dogs convivially. Not one person alluded to what was written on her T-shirt. Life's not simple and often depends on what we decide to concentrate on.

This mind we have, its essential awareness, is identical to Buddha's. It is the Universe itself. The human realm is the only realm from which we can be enlightened, and it's the realm where we struggle, live and die, fall ill, and blunder. Nothing will exempt us from consequences in that world, and Buddha's teaching, among other things, is how to exist in it with dignity, calm, and an open and compassionate heart.

11

Enlightenment: Seeing the Unseen

.....

May 27, 2020

I FIRST READ ABOUT ZEN BUDDHISM when I was about fourteen years old, in a book titled *The Three Pillars of Zen*, by Philip Kapleau. In that book, enlightenment—seeing into one's own nature—was described (and extolled) in a somewhat romanticized manner perfect for an overweight, awkward fourteen-year-old who couldn't speak to girls without embarrassing himself, was uninterested in athletics, liked the cows better than the cowboys, and was unable to mimic the self-assured nonchalance of his more poised classmates. Reading Kapleau's book, I developed the idea that enlightenment would be the solution to all my problems by making superhuman levels of awareness and physical skills available to me.

I began an obsessive course of reading about Zen and before long was anesthetizing my friends by quoting Zen aphorisms and koans as if I understood them, practicing idiosyncratic forms of speech filled with cryptic, mystical-sounding utterances. I mean, how should a friend respond when he asks you what's for lunch and you answer, "The crow with no beak eats only no food." Somebody should have slapped me. You can imagine how well remarks of that sort were received by my peers.

Sixty years later, after nearly fifty years of practicing Zen and knocking about various Zen centers and communities, I've learned that many people initially attracted to Zen practice were drawn by precisely that same wish or promise of enlightenment that had motivated me. It's a bit like beauty in men and women—it may not sustain, but it draws you in for a closer look.

During my years of study at San Francisco Zen Center, I was disheartened to observe that no one ever discussed enlightenment and that it was virtually never mentioned as an aspect of Soto school practice. On the contrary, at Aitken-roshi's Diamond Sangha, a Rinzai school practice, some years later it seemed that all anyone talked about was kensho, or cracking the Mu koan. It felt like trying too hard. I wasn't good at it, and to this day I prefer koans that arrive from one's life and have no existing answers, so I eventually returned to Suzuki-roshi's Soto-style practice of San Francisco Zen Center.

I eventually learned that there are plausible reasons for both forms of practice. The idea of "gaining" something by practice, and reifying enlightenment into an achievable goal, what Mel Weitsman-roshi from Berkeley Zen Center (through which my lineage runs) referred to as "materialistic practice," is a subtle and serious antagonist of progress and understanding. An enlightenment experience may or may not occur, and its absence is hardly a report card on one's spiritual development. Hakuin Zenji declared the Eightfold Path itself enlightenment, and certainly practicing the Eightfold Path diligently puts your feet in the footprints of enlightened masters. However, searching for some imagined mental state that is not your own becomes a detriment to every other state in one's life. It initiates a discrepancy between two imagined states—who you believe yourself to be and an imagined, idealized state you'd like to attain. It's kind of like talking to the television when it's off. Some sects of Zen, particularly the Rinzai school, consider kensho as the beginning of viable practice, and I understand why. Aitken-roshi's practice was secular. People had jobs and responsibilities and carved out time to attend sesshin's and went hell-for-leather searching for what they imagined they wanted. Enlightenment has not been so exalted in the Soto school where my lineage first evolved. My teacher, who ordained and transmitted me, put the matter to rest succinctly when he said, "If you're not kind and helpful to others, who cares what kind of spiritual experiences you've had?"

Grasping the *idea* of enlightenment is a problem. If we approach meditation with the idea that our self is an imperfect identity snarled and tangled with problems and dangle enlightenment before ourselves like a destination we do not already occupy, it will be difficult to merge the two. Self and enlightenment as differentiated somewhat oppositional entities have been made the premise of your search. Such ideas can run around inside our skulls like gerbils on separate exercise wheels. We go around and around, unaware that we have already conceived of them as sequestered in different places.

I'd like to meander through this subject a bit in an attempt to connect the trunk of enlightenment to its fruit—the Buddha's Eightfold Path, his road map of an enlightened life. I think a closer look may well explain why so many ancient teachers considered this path—marga in the Buddha's Four Noble Truths—enlightenment itself.

It is true that sometimes in periods of intense meditation our attention can be focused unwaveringly and exhaustively enough that the ego temporarily surrenders its dominance. It is important to understand that the surrender is not permanent. Whatever your experience, you will eventually return to "normal." In his book *Changing Your Mind,* author Michael Pollan cites the research about a part of the brain known as the Default Mode Network, which is tasked with keeping our sense of ordinary reality in charge. Psychedelics and meditation will loosen those connection in creative ways, but our "default" consciousness is normal. We will possess self-awareness as an organism as long as we have a body. But in the same way that a short distance that takes you around a corner offers a radically different perspective, one does not return from such experiences unchanged. To be clear, one should not try to fix such awakenings permanently or regard them as merit badges. Accept that they indicate that your practice is on a good path, and let them enter and exit as they will.

I've observed a number of Zen groups where students have *assumed* their teacher's enlightenment and then construed that as evidence of their inhabiting a different realm of consciousness that implies infallibility. Zen communities who have fallen prey to such error can be identified by the inappropriate sexual contacts between teachers and students, substance abuse, and fiscal improprieties that have plagued their communities. Where such assumptions are prevalent and students have some problem with the senior teacher's behavior, the onus is improperly on them to adjust to the teacher. The teacher may have impeccable qualities and still remain unevenly developed in others. In such cases where the students are forced to adjust, they are being forced to override their common sense and forget the Buddha's admonition that

> if anyone should speak in disparagement of me or of my teaching or of our community, please do not be angry, resentful, or upset by it. To become upset in that way would only be a hindrance to you. For if when others criticize me you become angry or upset, you will be unable to judge clearly whether what they are saying is true or false.*

It is delusional to consider enlightenment a barrier to be hurdled, imagining that once on the other side we will live a carefree life, but it is a compelling delusion that endures.

The cable channels are filled with stories of "enlightened beings" disguising narcissism as wisdom; owning fourteen Rolls Royces; pursuing

---

*From the Tevijja Sutra, in *The Long Discourses of the Buddha: A Translation of the Dīgha Nikāya,* by Maurice Walshe (Boston: Wisdom Publications, 1995). Available at deeghanikaya.wordpress.com.

endless sexual encounters; attended by servants and wealthy patrons. Roughly translated, their common patter on the subject is that "freedom means can do whatever you want, when you're enlightened and no longer attached to the delusional values ensnaring the 'little people.'" (Rationales like this are the coming attractions for a community circular firing squad.) What they say about absolute freedom is true, but they are ignoring or ignorant of the fact that enlightenment does not absolve people of the consequences of cause and effect.

There is a famous story concerning an eleventh century Japanese Zen master named Baizhang that makes this point. One day after his normal lecture, Master Baizhang observed an old man who had attended many of his lectures previously. He usually left immediately afterward, but this day he was lingering to speak with Baizhang. In conversation the old man confessed that he spent the past five centuries condemned to live as a fox for telling a student once that an enlightened person is free from cause and effect. He begs Baizhang to clarify the matter for him so that he can be freed, and Baizhang warns him never to ignore cause and effect. The monk thanks Baizhang and informs him that he is now free of the curse. He requests a Buddhist funeral, and leaves. Baizhang notifies the head monk to prepare for a funeral. The monk is confused because no one has been sick and as far as he knows no one has died. Later that day, Baizhang is walking in the woods with his students and they find at the base of a large rock, a dead fox, which he cremates with traditional Buddhist service.

Even if you experience kensho, it's going to consume only a small part of your life. After that, you'll return to the not-so-ordinary world you've been overlooking, and while you've received a "letter from Emptiness," it may require multiple readings of it before its contents are fully absorbed. As the story alerts us, even a Zen master is still subject to the laws of the Universe.

During that kensho when "I" temporarily disappears or feels as porous as a colander, you may clarify the interdependence of objects, ideas, feelings. Everything but *you* will remain. The experience will be deeper than any possible description. Consequently, when someone once asked Suzuki-roshi about enlightenment, he responded, "You might not like it."

My reaction to a powerful kensho experience during a sesshin was a sudden implosion of critical doubt and anxiety. My first thought upon "returning" to my self, after being presented indisputable evidence of Emptiness, was, literally, "Oh my God, what am I going to do now?!"

I had labored for more than forty years, building a scaffolding of Buddhism to protect me from sliding back into addiction and chaos and the perils of previously untamed impulses and compulsions I'd given free rein to during my years in the counter-culture. I had faithfully pursued the beacon of enlightenment in the hopes of securing reliable techniques to build dependable boundaries to protect myself from myself. I wanted to protect other people, particularly my children, from them as well, but now I understood indisputably that the world and *all* my ideas about it, including Buddhism, were as impermanent and insubstantial as soap bubbles; relative only to one another. There was nothing in this world I could permanently secure. It was a shocking revelation.

As I continued sitting that night and my world reassembled itself familiarly, I realized that Buddha himself, a human like me, must have experienced a similar doubt. And yet, far from disabling him, he returned to inculcate a life of teaching dedicated to helping others. When we come back from such an experience, the "self" reasserts its prominence. We still have a body to care for and numerous responsibilities. From that time on, however, we will perceive it as a less reliable guide and privilege it less. The ego has critical functions to perform for us, but the distinction that makes a difference is that we have seen beyond its parameters and limited panoply of choices—disliking, liking, or neutrality. From that point on existence resonates on more nuanced and expansive frequencies.

Teachers remind us that enlightenment should not be a goal or overriding concern, not only because of the implied dualism we create by reifying it, but because such a single-minded pursuit will also distract us from attending to the needs of others and the world around us. People sometimes disguise their personal ambition for enlightenment by claiming that their pursuit is temporary; once enlightened, they promise they will save all beings. It is the bodhisattva's selfless vow that puts the lie to that test. However this conceit is sliced and diced, it remains spiritual narcissism. Overemphasizing spiritual experiences of any kind can also heighten one's sense of a superior self, separate and apart from others. It can make us less willing to listen and be sensitive to their concerns.

Refining our understanding of the Eightfold Path, developing intimacy with Buddhist Livelihood, Awareness, Effort, and so on, and considering the precepts when we make decisions and choices will help us keep our life grounded, wholesome, compassionate, and helpful. When our practice is sound and grounded, enlightenment will arrive when we are ripe, without seeking or effort. We will notice that post-enlightenment we must continue to contend with the problems we confronted previously. However, we'll also perceive that they now exist in a much more spacious field in which we can discover many more alternatives for dealing with them.

There is an ancient Japanese poem about observing a portion of the moon glimmering from behind clouds. In the same way that partial view suggests the moon's entirety, the shine on a leaf can trigger an impression of the entire Universe for us. Dogen reminded us in his thirteenth-century Shobogenzo how the distance between the Earth and the moon can be reflected in a drop of dew. A bird's cry or the plunk of a stone thrown in the river were the kind of ordinary events Suzuki-roshi referred to as "letters from emptiness." Normally we fail to perceive such letters or immediately translate them into previously known experiences. After some deep experiences however, we *know* indisputably from where they were delivered.

I had a rough time with my father when I was growing up. He

was a dangerous man with an explosive temper, harnessed to a boxer's discipline* and black-belt level jiu-jitsu training. His intelligence was formidable and gained him admittance to MIT at fifteen. Looking back from old age, I can see now how complex and gifted a man he was: principled, charming, and often capable of great generosity. He was respected and exorbitantly successful; a generous man who sent the children of a number of friends, employees, and at least one friend of mine through college. However, especially for me in childhood, for all his gifts and abilities he was extremely impatient, given to violent rages, and obsessed with being "the best"—whatever that may have meant to him in the moment.

His childhood had been traumatic and violent. His father killed his horse with a hammer in front of him when he was seven and later that same year subsequently chased him up three flights of stairs and was in the process of squeezing him through a third story circular attic window for laughing when his father stepped on a rake and smacked his own face painfully. Luckily my grandmother knocked him unconscious with a heavy metal lamp before he succeeded or I would not be writing this book. When he was fourteen, skating with his identical twin brother Wally, Wally fell through the ice and was swept downstream and drowned.

God knows what personal terrors he held at bay, and though I had no idea at the time, I suspect also that he wrestled with a deep fear that my difficulties with mathematics and word problems indicated some mental insufficiency and was not aggressive enough to defend myself against the teeth and claws of his world.

Night after night he would enter my bedroom to "supervise" my homework and invariably end up screaming in frustration at my mathematical confusion: "How can you be so effing *stupid*? You *can't* be this effing stupid!" he would shout until my mother, attracted by the uproar,

---

*In college he had been the sparring partner for Philadelphia Jack O'Brian, world light heavyweight champion.

would enter my room to defend me. The two would stand nose to nose on either side of me, shouting at one another, while I sat below, brain-dead and doodling and feeling at fault for their upset. Many years later, discussing these events with my younger sister, who was exempt from such scenes because she was quicker than I and our dad found her fear-less response to his temper amusing and admirable, observed, "In our house, it was better to be a thief than to be stupid."

Even after I left home at eighteen, I struggled with the suffocat-ing sensation that my mind remained trapped in a closet with my father's overwhelming force. I could never win enough psychic space to breathe deeply or think clearly about anything without slashing my way through the tangle of his judgments. I certainly don't use his behavior as a justification of my own failings, but today I can under-stand more clearly the numbing allure of the heroin I employed for self-comfort.

Now, after many years of counseling and therapy and nearly fifty years of zazen and study, offered the grace of distance and time, it's eas-ier to recall many of the useful things my father taught me; the protec-tive shelter he offered me to mature in and the teachers and mentors in my life—many his close friends—he made available. It sometimes feels that on some level he understood that his personal problems diminished his skills as a father and sought to provide me the company of adults who nurtured and mentored me where he could not.

Today those memories are harmless, in many ways simply part of the world's variety. Once we become intimate with our difficulties and pains, our personal problems assume the same kind of insubstantiality as everything else. While they may still possess something of their old tang and flavor, we are no longer condemned to regard them as tangible, solid obstacles that can overwhelm us. We can learn to trust our abil-ity, nurtured by nirodha (containment) to hold their explosive force in check and survive.

Dependent origination posits relationships in a Universe without requiring an ego or a self to witness them. Both the self*ish* and the self*less* view are equally real—each is a correlate of the other. In the context of this discussion, wisdom might be described as oscillating between the two—selfish and selfless—allowing each to highlight the shadows of the other so that we travel less blind to the shadows of our own thoughts and interior language.

An egocentric point of view excludes, ignores, or subjugates the vast objective networks and systems to which we are connected, reducing the immensity of the Universe to frames of reference we like, dislike, or remain neutral about. It is akin to trying to pour a quart of water into a pint jar.

The holistic view, is not a panacea, either. In the first place it is unknowable except in small parts and bears its own freight of problems, making it deceptively easy to overlook the value of any singular existence—human, animal, plant, habitat, or, for that matter, entire species—and sacrificing them to the Big Picture. Autocrats like Stalin and Mao Zedong constructed grand social designs based on rigid ideologies that caused the deaths of 40 to 50 million people when grand agricultural schemes failed. As humans, Americans are not exempt from such blindness, and we must include the genocidal consequences of the European occupation of this continent, which camouflaged its ethnic cleansing under the banners of god and "civilization" which must be included in the karma of our sins of commission. The four-century holocaust of slavery and its antecedents must be included as well. Our own Big Vision boys—the McNamaras, Rumsfelds, and Cheneys—who led us into wars that killed millions and wasted our own blood and treasure find it all too easy to forget that *each* trampled existence is an irreplaceable, unique entity.

Each view—the singular and the holistic—may serve as a corrective to the other. From the big picture, the eradication of a tiny bog turtle, or red-cockaded woodpecker, or Bartram's hairstreak butterfly may mean nothing compared to the anthropocentric conveniences and services of a shopping mall, housing development, or hospital, but that is a one-sided view. They meant something to Nature or they would not have existed as part and parcel of the web of creation. By considering each species as a sacred, unduplicatable expression of the Universe, we can adjust our actions to align more appropriately with the processes of the Universe itself. It is not to suggest that we *never* build anything in the habitat of an endangered species, pure water, wetlands, or wilderness but that we include them as stakeholders when we consider the alternatives and ways in which we might mitigate the damage we cause.

12

Believing in Nothing

·····

June 10, 2020

I WANT TO SHARE A QUOTE from *Zen Mind, Beginner's Mind,* my favorite Zen book by Shunryu Suzuki-roshi. This quote is from a chapter titled "Believing in Nothing":

> This is a very important point. No matter what God or doctrine you believe in, if you become attached to it, your belief will be based on a self-centered idea.

In the full text, he adds an important distinction:

> It's absolutely necessary for everyone to believe in nothing. But I don't mean "void-ness"—there IS something. There is something. But that "something" is always prepared for taking some particular form. It has some rules or theory or truth in its activity. We call that "Buddha Nature."

When I let my imagination play with the idea, Buddha-nature appears as a kind of pregnant energy, ceaselessly expressing itself as form, perhaps in the way in which clouds transform as we watch them. When this energy is expressed as a person, we call it "Buddha." When we think of it as the ultimate truth of our phenomenal Universe, we call it "dharma." And, when we accept this truth and attempt to express it in our life with others, we refer to it as "sangha." Even though three apparently distinct expressions—Buddha, dharma, and sangha—exist, it's all one thing, in the same way that ocean, wavelets, rain, steam, and fog are all one thing. Emptiness is always ready to assume form, color, and duration. Buddhist teaching is philosophical and logical (which is one reason many people appreciate it), but in the final analysis it is deeper than both—it is a practice for the radical transformation of what we used to consider the private property of the self.

Without understanding this, no religion or practice will help us. It's fine to have religion, but if we understand that religion (like everything else) is *itself* an expression of this primordial, pregnant energy, our thoughts and ideas about things become less constrained, our judgments and distinctions become less absolute, because we perceive the common source. Our beliefs are contributors to the infinity of possibilities available in any moment but not necessarily privileged among them. We don't insist on them being the *only* truth.

Suzuki-roshi reminds us that such acceptance is a way of continually saying "Yes" to the Universe, accepting that what arises from Emptiness is an expression of the Universe itself and that no matter how odd or aberrant they may appear to us, they are following some law and the consequences of previous acts.

To accept does not mean to condone. To accept that weeds are Buddha-nature and understand that they have an equal claim to existence and operate for their own being as we do doesn't mean that we allow them to choke out our food. Understanding that hatred is a part of our human nature does not mean that we give it free rein, any more than we allow an infant's tantrums or impetuousness to place the child in danger.

If we understand that malignant, jealous, envious thoughts are included within the wildness of Buddha-nature, we can be more compassionate toward them when they arise in ourselves and others and monitor them without inflicting the extra judgment of ourselves or others as "bad" people. We don't risk much in accepting such thoughts or impulses when we have mindfulness and meditation practices to determine what we let past our teeth or activate our muscles.

This morning, waking from a dream, still in half sleep, dream residue of myself in a yellow T-shirt with black letters across the chest declaring me "Batshit Crazy" made me wake up laughing. As I rolled out of bed to brush my teeth, I thought, "Maybe I should wear such a shirt during my dharma talks." We can understand our personalities and fallibilities and foibles with humor instead of self-judgment and disgust—which lessens their solidity and significance.

Meditation allows the mind to be the mind and the body to be the body. The brain is a gland generating thoughts and images. We are not obligated to believe them or believe that each is an omen freighted with significance. We meditate in stillness, and the thoughts and emotions that arise (samudaya) will not harm anyone while we remain in meditation. They do not signal that we are deranged if our thoughts are wild. If we don't act on them, we can allow them free rein in zazen, grow increasingly intimate with them, and eventually, once we've gained confidence that they will not leak or control us, they will cease to bother us. Remember the phrase from the Heart Sutra? *Without any hindrances, no fears exist.*

Suzuki-roshi used to say, "Don't invite your thoughts for tea." In zazen posture, we can leave our thoughts alone until we have some need to consciously engage the mind and organize them in a productive direction. There's no need to block them from entering our awareness, but we don't have to invite them to tea. In this way, we can have confidence to observe, study, and behave appropriately toward any phenomena without unbalancing ourselves with too much judgment and second-guessing. We can do this at any time, on or off our cushions.

Only a person who has reduced their needs has the bandwidth to open themselves entirely to the world. I certainly don't claim perfection at this, but it's a goal I'm working toward. Only a person who perceives in each and every manifestation of Emptiness the miracle of its presence can sit stolidly and unshaken before whatever presents itself.

When we sit zazen, as our thoughts slow and as the mind clears its agendas, we somehow merge with Emptiness. This may be another way of saying that our personality becomes porous and Emptiness seeps in. This does not happen immediately. Perhaps, at first, we become aware of how distracted and unfocused we are, how much chatter exists in our minds, and how busy and restless it is. But, when we quiet the body and diminish stimulation to the mind, when our breathing becomes tranquil and unforced, and when our stomach and face muscles relax, awareness can intimate the vastness in the deep oceans of consciousness or the still, reflective surface of a lake on a windless day.

Thich Nhat Hanh suggests we practice maintaining a half-smile, imitating the Buddha's, while we meditate. Not only does it relax the forty-three muscles in the face, but it also induces the kind of equanimity and serenity that comes from deep acceptance. The mind slows down. Eventually, we become intimate with Emptiness.

I've already mentioned that we should not seek any particular experience or state of mind when we meditate. If we merely accept what arises as an emanation of the Universe, with its own logic and history, that has a deeply restorative effect, infusing our ordinary reality with clarity, spaciousness, and calm. Suzuki-roshi once observed, "To have a headache will be all right, because you are healthy enough to have a headache. When you are too sick, your head stops hurting and then you are really in trouble."

People tend to begin Zen meditation in search of some heightened event or state of mind preferable to what they're currently experiencing. They want something better than their normal existence. I certainly began my practice in hot pursuit of my imagined ecstasies of enlightenment. But normal existence—everyday, quotidian reality—is the miracle itself! That's where it is, *just as it is,* and the regard of every experience as a miraculous, unrepeatable expression is the true savor of everyday life.

Even the experience of fear or revulsion reminds us that we are alive.

Everyone I've ever met who knew Suzuki-roshi agrees that when they met him, he was present and intimate to an unforgettable degree. His behavior admitted no distinctions of rank or wealth, Buddhist or non-Buddhist. Universally, people describe him by saying, "I had never met anyone like that before." It's my deepest belief that he could be "with" people to this degree because he knew in his bone marrow that we are all poignantly temporary, conjoined in a common source, and that each instant of life is too precious to categorize or submit to hierarchical comparisons.

I encourage this same simple practice of daily zazen, allowing our small mind to calm itself, exerting the discipline and intention to sit upright and still and observe what occurs within our mind-body in each moment. We're not trying to turn the mind off or change it. The thinking mind has a job to do, it is not an aberration of nature, nor is it the ripest fruit. If a thought arises, leave it alone. If you don't like it, examine why and how your body responds to that thought or feeling. Do this dispassionately, as you would appraise a pair of shoes or a dress you were considering purchasing. *Why* does it bother you? Does it generate a feeling you're uncomfortable with? Why? Where in the body is that? What memories does it dislodge? It won't hang around forever, you can take it. Don't be distracted. Don't fidget. As Kobun-roshi once said, "If the body moves, the mind moves."

Absolute freedom is available to us. This is what nirvana really implies. In the very next instant we are totally free to do something we have never done before. That freedom can also involve surrendering to forms or social norms, or not, but you have the space and ability in which to do that.

The more unstable and difficult things become in the world, the more necessary it is to have people available who see clearly, operate fearlessly, and are not preoccupied or deluded by self-centered thinking. The state of our current world might be inducement enough to try this practice.

13

The Three Treasures: Buddha, Dharma, and Sangha

·····

August 5, 2020

THIS MORNING I'M SITTING IN FRONT of very sophisticated computers, cameras, a microphone, and amplifier, supplying me with gigabytes of information I don't need—my frames per second in kilobytes, for instance—and yet, I can't manage to find what I actually require: changing the size of my image on the monitor.

A teacher would be a good idea for anyone who wants to learn something practical like this, something concrete—Photoshop, for instance, or Zoom, since that's how I often communicate with students. As far as computers go, or retouching a photograph, we may not be too concerned about a teacher's personality or ethics. We simply require them to know their subject and be able to communicate the information we need in a manner we can understand and utilize. Being pleasant or easy to get along with would be an added benefit, but basically we are looking for help within very specific parameters. Because of these limited

146

parameters, we consider teachers for subjects like these quite differently from spiritual teachers.

I'd like to discuss this today, because in the course of my practice and work I've witnessed numerous relationships between students and teachers go off the rails. Sometimes the students had unrealistic expectations of what a teacher could provide. I have moved to promote students before they were ready, or before I knew them well enough to intuit subtle difficulties they had. Other times, practice has been derailed by the malfeasance of the teacher: theft, alcoholism, or sexual impropriety. Of course, these derelictions are always aided by the credulity of students, who somewhere along the way missed or forgot the ancient edict, *Put no head above your own.*

When we suffer a malaise for which spiritual practice might be remedial, first and foremost we should clarify our intentions and goals. Some people want to stop relentless negative thoughts. Some people want a life of unending bliss and joy. Some people want to learn how to get out of their own way, to cease badgering themselves with second-guessing and shoulda-woulda-coulda concerns. Some people have read widely on various esoteric religions and have preconceived or received ideas about what wisdom must look and feel like. Others have identified only an unfocused desire for *something,* without being able to declare precisely what that might be.

If we were studying cooking, we might think that what we need to learn from a teacher are recipes and techniques—how to make a béchamel sauce or prepare a perfect omelet. However, it might turn out that what a good teacher really teaches us, no matter the discipline, is how to slow down, settle into the body and nervous system, open oneself to tastes and impressions, pay scrupulous attention to the vegetables and herbs considered for use, and be ready to change plans according to altered circumstances.

A teacher who insisted that we come shopping with them or browse an art book or reconsider how we organize our twenty-four hours a day; a teacher who did not run the student through a list of specific recipes and give inside tips on what brand of butter is best, might be mistaken for a poor teacher. In such a case, the student's assumptions or fixed ideas could very well be obscuring their learning.

Suzuki-roshi's concepts of "Not Knowing" and "Beginner's Mind" reveal their usefulness and profundity in precisely this area. In spiritual dimensions, our body, if we slowed down enough to tune in to its hundreds of thousands of years of accumulated wisdom, probably already knows everything we might need to learn. That's probably true, but the problem is that *I* don't know that—meaning my *idea* of who I am doesn't know that.

The universal human attributes we all contain, a perception of unity and the wholeness of creation—the larger truth that contains all contradictions—is omnipresent and an integral part of the human inheritance passed along the generations. It remains clouded by unresolved attachments to greed, anger, and delusion—the fealty we offer our small mind—the parameters of our personality. Suzuki-roshi often said, "You are perfect just the way you are, and you could use a little work." Both are true.

The innate quality of mind, our vibrant, empty awareness, is unsullied, wide open, and as generous as the sky. It excludes nothing and admits everything. It admits what we like. It admits what we don't like. It admits everything. This is the big picture humans are struggling to navigate, but our compass will have to require something more profound than our intelligence to navigate it. We will have to use our deepest feelings and intuitions.

Accepting is acknowledging that everything that exists arrived in our reality with an inheritance from prior circumstances and an innate logic or it would not be here. The *why* of any particular event, person, species, or circumstance may be beyond our understanding, but it is not too difficult to understand that everything, form and formless, has a history, a long tail to which it is connected and that its existence in this moment is the nose of that enormous dragon. If we don't like it, it is not necessary to posit abstract judgments about it, like evil. Evil does not exist as an identifiable entity in isolation from a host of other values and concerns. Our judgment and use of the word effectively disguises how, under the right influences, any of us might behave similarly. Those connections are vast and subtle and more profound than like and dislike. We have it within the authority of our instincts and intuitions to discriminate from moment to moment, far more accurately than any definition of good or evil offers us.

Tenshin Reb Anderson, one of the most senior teachers at San Francisco Zen Center and one of my earliest Zen friends, explained to me once why he lived with a painting that he did not particularly like by explaining, *"Even if you don't like it, it's still your taste."* I was a new student then, and his response stymied me for weeks until something popped open and I thought, "Of course!" Liking and not-liking are the opposite ends of the same seesaw. What you don't like indicates your taste as clearly as what you do like. All that's different is that you might enjoy one experience more than the other.

Very often, when people seek spiritual practice, they don't have a clear idea of what they're looking for. Usually, they are plagued by an impenetrable dilemma or just want to feel better. They may be struggling with grief or loss, plagued by old and unconscious impulses. If they knew what to do, they would do it. Because the consideration of spiritual practice takes place within the context of everything we previously have known (none of which has solved our problem), it is not illogical to search for help outside one's normal boundaries, especially if those domains make radical promises of eternal peace, joy, and unequivocal love. *It is perilously easy to become fascinated and enamored by the gift wrapping of other cultures and their wisdom traditions.* Therein lies the rub. Every non-native spiritual practice is the result of a kind of friction between the transcendental insights from one culture seeking to translate themselves into another's vernacular. The gist of the work my sangha and I have been exploring the past several years is how to honor the gift, without confusing it with the gift wrapping. Zen, for example, is a Japanese expression of Chinese Buddhism, Shintoism (the indigenous nature-worshipping religion of Japan), and Japanese culture. It has remodeled and changed some aspects of Buddhism to make it comprehensible within the mores and values of their own culture, but it is still Buddhism at its core.

There's a Sanskrit term, *upaya,* which signifies "skillful means." It reminds people that even if you can see the solution to someone else's problem, you can't simply declare the answer and expect it to be useful. It's necessary to communicate the answer in a manner and mode that the student understands. I've seen many teachers during my years of Zen practice, and most by far were honorable people earnestly trying to be helpful. It is not as simple as suggesting that the power hunters among them were simple frauds. Most were complex, highly but *unevenly* developed people, and it is not a contradiction to say that an alcoholic or a thief (and there have been acclaimed Zen masters in both categories) can teach you something you needed to know. What they could *not* teach you is how to *behave.* It is the rare man or woman in whose life we can observe an evenness of attention paid to every detail.

It was precisely this quality that first attracted me to Gary Snyder. I'll never forget my first encounter with his workshop. In it was mounted next to nearly every tool the appropriate tool for repairing or tuning it. I'll never forget my first visit to his home, a rustic but elegant fusion of a Japanese farmhouse, Native American dwelling, and country house made of local timber, unconnected to the grid, offering everything his family of four needed without pretension or show.

Lessons can be positive or negative. Chogyam Trungpa, an influential transmitted Tibetan teacher who came to America, was a notorious drinker and smoker, yet he inspired thousands of people, developed a university, and adored Suzuki-roshi to the point of reverence. When a friend of mine left Zen Center after Suzuki-roshi died and went to study with Trungpa at his center in Colorado, Trungpa told him: "Just do what Suzuki-roshi taught you."

It is also true that Trungpa's *chosen disciple* slept with sangha members when he knew he had AIDS. Do we imagine that those he infected cared overmuch about his teaching after that? I think we have the right to high expectations of spiritual teachers, and one of those expectations might be that they respect social norms and common decency, for if not, what are they doing but teaching personal release absent the moral and ethical matrix of the Buddha's life? How could they transmit the skillful use and recognition of them in aiding others?

Life is not simple, and people who may appear unqualified to a new student can be great teachers, even if some of their deepest lessons are negative. The problem can be that if a student believes themself to be truly deficient in something, they may fixate on receiving what they believe they need, overriding their common sense and skepticism, and become vulnerable to manipulation. If you would not accept a particular behavior from a lover or mate, there is no reason to accept it from a Zen teacher. In both cases, it would be wise to interrogate that decision to learn exactly why you won't tolerate it.

But—and this should always be considered—our ideas of what we want may also be deluded. Most people come to Buddhism because of some intractable problem in their lives. It requires incentive to subject ourselves to the discipline and restraints of Zen practice, and suffering is usually a very effective incentive. However, people may also arrive at a practice with their own developed ideas about the remedy they require, which may be unsupportable, ineffective, or contrary to the way the Universe works.

If we become too fixed on a preexisting idea, we may overlook any number of opportunities that failed to arrive dressed in the costumes and mannerisms we demanded. Before drafting a personal shopping list of tools to modify our personality, it might be wise to first take a thorough inventory of what life feels like in this very moment. There may be much we wish to maintain (let's start with pulse and breath), especially if our self-criticism goes beyond comparing ourselves against imagined ideals.

To the degree that we may believe we are deficient in something; to the degree we overlook that we are an unrepeatable experience generated by the same forces that produced hummingbirds and leopards; to that degree we may abandon our senses, intuition, and the fruits of common observation we are vulnerable to our own ignorance. One of the things a good teacher does is assure you that you're also okay. That you are a part of the Universe, and as Suzuki-roshi repeatedly said, "You're perfect just the way you are . . . and you could use a little work."

This is why I've never been attracted to the guru tradition. Perhaps it's my experiences growing up in a culture organized around the procurement of personal wealth, power, and status. I'll admit my reluctance to give the bequest of my being to another human who demands I dismiss my own intuitions and insights. Ram Dass (Richard Alpert) became a beloved and respected teacher in his own right, but he selected his teacher in India by giving him LSD and observing that it appeared to make no change in his behavior. So he made the assumption that his teacher lived in a kind of permanent LSD state. Ram Dass got lucky. His teacher could have been a criminal sociopath who had learned the equivalent of defeating a lie-detector test. Passing through an LSD trip while giving no evidence of internal disturbance, wonder, or off-plumb behavior, appears to me, snapshot evidence, but there's no arguing with success. I knew and admired Ram Dass as I got to know him, and he visited San Francisco Zen Center often and would confess his doubts and uncertainties to Roshi Baker. He certainly grew into an admirable teacher and human being under his guru's tutelage.

Usually it requires time before we can safely bet on the character and proclivities of a teacher. It is only prudent to withhold committing until we've developed some basis of trust other than their charisma, ability to attract many students, or their ability to handle heavy chemicals. Just saying.

This is not an unexamined prejudice. I fully appreciate why there are certain teaching traditions that seek to weaken the ego by demanding fealty to a teacher who might serve as a reliable guide to one's fallibilities and errors. In those traditions a student humbly obeys the guru because they believe that the guru is a perfected and infallible being, and the student knows they themselves are not. The abandonment of their small self is a prophylactic they hope might insure them against remaining in their current state of uncertainty.

They may be correct, but I prefer the posture of not being lonesome for heroes. If we are patient and study people carefully—put our cow in a big field, as Suzuki-roshi advised, we will always know where it is and how it will behave. We will fare better and make fewer mistakes in our expectations and assessments of others if we observe them when they are left to their own devices. Then, we will know them more intimately and be able to predict how they will behave in different circumstances. If you have made the decision to seek a teacher, give yourself the grace to study them carefully, or on a trial basis for at least a year, before committing or writing a big check.

In Zen tradition, our teachers are not regarded like gurus. They are more like wise uncles and aunts who have been out along the path ahead of us and can serve as reliable guides. They've been through the rigors of our training, and particularly in secular practice have wrestled with many of the same problems that all living beings have. They are available when we need counsel and are otherwise there to help us. We are not there to help them other than by being the best students we can be, but if we are diligent and act wholeheartedly, it will be inevitable that we will be helping our teachers as well. We are certainly not there to be snared by the teacher's delusions or to be their uncompensated laborers.

There can be a high price for disconnects between self-perception and our perceptions of your teacher. One dangerous blind spot in the one-on-one student-teacher relationship is the confusion of the deep intimacy of Zen with sexual intimacy. A friend of mine once observed, "There's no stopping testosterone," and history would probably judge him correct.

I was shocked, meeting and speaking with Buddhist monks in Lhasa, Tibet, and discovering that in the temples many sought comfort and protection from older teachers through sexual relationships that very carefully threaded Buddhist prohibitions and precepts. However, I'm pretty certain no one's mother would have approved.

In the 1960s and 1970s, a number of male Asian teachers arrived in America and Europe. Many were honorable missionaries, and few were hoping to take advantage of opportunities offered by the inchoate spirituality that Western youth were exploring. In most cases these were principled and highly developed people. However, a number of them misread the American zeitgeist, and some teachers (both Asian and American) responded to the explorations in sexual liberation coursing through Western culture with variants of *Oh, this person is an adult and if they want to sleep with me, that's okay.* This appeared to be especially true for teachers who arrived here from cultures with no deep histories of Puritanism. Whether it was honest confusion, predation, or students seeking to raise their status by being lovers of the teacher and therefore first among equals, those relationships were, in every case I heard of, disasters, destructive of community goodwill and corrosive of community trust.

At the very least, those teachers ignored or overlooked the power and status differentials that accrue to teachers in relationships. In some instances this led to secret, long-term affairs that caused great confusion and damage to the sanghas. Teachers are human! Full stop. The teacher might have been lonely or overwhelmed or dazzled by the adulation and respect they discovered in a new country. Sexual intimacy may be a perk they claimed as way of reward for decades of work. Teachers have absconded with funds or used their power to benefit themselves in other ways. Long-term students have gone off the rails, stealing monastery money for drugs.

The problem with Buddhism is that it has people in it.

Just as harmful but less overt, student-teacher affairs may create cliques of favorites within the sangha and neglect treating each student with equal cordiality and concern.

For those students who project a teacher as lovely, kind, and worthy, I can only hope they are lucky enough to be studying with a gem. But such glittering projections are perilously close to romance—and if it is a romance it will certainly end in loss, and that loss may generate such hurt and disappointment that the relationship between the teacher and student is broken, or worse, the student abandons their practice. In any case, the sangha is damaged by the loss and consequent distrust directly related to the indulgence of the teacher.

Whether it is a spasm of affection that got out of hand or whether it is an unpolished aspect of the teacher's character, it is the teacher's job to protect the students by being alert to such sudden eruptions. Any teacher worth their robes should understand that confusing a student with a sexual affair is not modeling the Buddha's behavior. It will imperil and certainly confuse other students to the detriment of their practice. The teacher's behavior will reverberate throughout the sangha, damaging credibility and belief. Even if a sexual event doesn't take place, the secrecy and imbalances of a private romance will be destructive.

Consider the teacher-student relationship as a form, like zazen posture or a mudra. (And remember that they are forms designed to help us.) Forms are not imbued with authority. They are guidelines to help us self-correct our practice. And the form of the teacher-student relationship must be observed by both sides. These are not exotic observations.

When famous quarterback Tom Brady underinflated a football by several pounds to gain the advantage of an easier grip, there was tumult in the world of sports when the knowledge became public. People understood intuitively that without rules and norms, there is no game of football. In the same way, violations of rules and norms during the administration of President Trump threatened the "game" of America.

Japanese culture is extraordinarily sensitive to nuance and detail, but they are also an emotional people who keep a close check on their expressions of feeling. *American* Zen practices, indelibly molded by imitating the forms of our honored Japanese founder and teachers, have, to my way of thinking, also piggybacked some aspects of Japanese culture that resonate with American culture in unwholesome ways. In particular I am thinking of the hierarchical and autocratic values in Japanese culture (including Buddhism) that evolved under the watchful power of royal permission. When translated into American idioms, these hierarchical practices can too easily morph into status differentials and class distinctions as well as authoritarianism.

Like students, teachers will have some highly evolved characteristics and some that remain unpolished. Within a temple where the teacher is granted an authority bordering on infallibility and often allowed or expected to be the standard for every aspect of community life, the fact of their "uneven development" can be considered off-limits for discussion. The consequence of this lapse may extend the teacher's most enlightened attributes to shelter their entire personality, disguising their clay feet. Such errors will definitely snare the unwary.

We don't help ourselves or our sangha by believing that "this teacher is obviously enlightened and I don't know anything!" To do so abandons our own Buddha-nature. It is simply not true. The student who believes that they have a need to begin studying may not have trained themselves to the degree the teacher has, but that does not mean they should surrender their common sense, their intuition, or their skepticism. They should not forget that their awareness is no different from the teacher's or Buddha's.

Awareness is not a personal property. Plants and trees can transmit the dharma. Insects obviously have awareness, and it may be that human receptors and scales are too insensitive or idea-dependent to measure what boulders and mountains might sense. For this reason, students (and teachers) should be consistent about checking themselves, perennially on guard for when we are being stubborn or sticking too rigidly to our own way. A good teacher will create a climate encouraging students to speak frankly and fearlessly with any and all concerns they may have about sangha life or the teacher-student relationship. He or she may offer advice, but the student is not obligated to accept it.

We have a right to expect some things from a teacher. First, that they model uprightness, transparency, and honesty. We should expect that the teacher will see us as an absolute expression of the Universe and also perceive our singularity to be worthy of the same respect we offer them—as worthy of respect as a Buddha, a dolphin, or a hummingbird.

We might expect a level of humility as a signal that within the sangha, aside from actual practice instruction, a rough democracy prevails. If the student-teacher relationship advances to a more rigorous level, students should understand that within the parameters of ferreting out blind spots and fixed attitudes, a teacher may be strict or even appear severe, but such attitudes should not extend beyond *dokusan* (practice instruction). A teacher may insist on observing certain forms *because they are trying to help us* resist laziness and bad habits. This is a natural part of the teaching relationship but is never a demand that the student surrender their dignity or their status as an equal among the sangha. For those students having difficulty accepting discipline or advice, they might do well to remember that the part of them resisting is the same part causing them difficulties.

Our deepest intuitions should orient us as to whether the teacher's demands are selfless or tainted by personal predilections for power. If the student suspects that might be the case, a frank discussion is in order. If the student remains unwilling to accept their teacher's explanation or perspective, after thorough examination as to whether the student's own shadows are coloring the interchange, it might be best to work with another teacher or senior student in that sangha. It is not written anywhere that only the student must change their behavior when difficulties arise.

The teachers that the Buddha stressed, are our circle of fellows— the sangha itself—and sitting. And by sitting I mean regular sittings on some schedule that the student commits to, and occasional sesshins (multiple days of numerous periods of zazen). It is difficult to find opportunities for extended periods of sitting, because they require much organization and many helpers, but there is no better way to deepen your practice. The breakthroughs that occur during sesshin are fixed and reinforced by our regular periods of meditation. If there's a shared commitment to working on ourselves and living with a common intention to model the Buddha's teaching, there is no substitute for sitting sesshins, working with a sangha, and a regular practice.

It's important to observe that in secular practice daily sitting might not always be possible. In that case, the student should make a schedule for a particular period of time and try to hold to it. At the end of that time, the schedule can be reviewed and altered so that it works for your life, but it's important to make and try to keep a commitment.

To transform our lives we need a teacher, dharma, *and* a community of practitioners we respect and trust. It could be a Buddhist teacher, rabbi, minister, or imam. It could be a sewing teacher. It could be a cooking teacher. It could be an aunt or uncle, but it should be someone whom we firmly believe is an exemplary person doing their best to help us.

Perhaps our most important teacher is the sangha, the community of fellow practitioners who have made a common commitment to Buddhist thought and practice and with whom we are deeply intimate. The intimacy that develops within those relationships, the constant scrutiny, will bring things to our attention that we might otherwise overlook. Within that context deep transformation is possible, but we have to be careful. We have to stay checked in. It is easy to slide off the mark, and no one will notice that slide more readily than fellow sangha members. If we listen humbly to criticism we will receive invaluable insights into our own behavior, which we might otherwise never observe.

The relationship between you and your teacher is—at the end of the day—*intimacy*. What we are really learning, absorbing, and assimilating is the teacher's *mind*. No matter the subject. You might love them or you might not like them personally. The mind is ungraspable, but we can still become intimate with their way.

Teachers don't necessarily have to be exemplary people, but it helps. Personally, I would have difficulty following someone who violated the Buddhist precepts. *We* have to be alert, checking the teacher's pronouncements and behavior against our own intuitions and feelings. *We* have to decide where we draw the lines we will not cross in the relationship. If we don't, the teacher may draw the line for us for their own personal benefit. The deepest implications of Emptiness are that *there is nothing for us to rely on and nothing we can consider permanent.* Please remember that.

Sustained practice together allows us to untangle the little curlicues, back eddies, and snares of our mind. It will help us accept "things as it is." The more we become intimate with our own mental formulations and the more we recognize them, the more easily we can understand them in others. Our narratives of childhood and the recitations of our traumas at a certain point become boring tropes, and eventually we just let them go. If we find that we can't, we should seek therapeutic help, because zazen is not a panacea.

Zazen is the practice of expressing our spirit in our life, in each moment.

A good Zen teacher will teach us how to sit. They will maintain a space for our inquiry. Zazen will train the mind and body to fully experience the present. It's like housebreaking a puppy. It requires constancy and repetition. When our mind wanders, we bring it back. Our mind wanders, we bring it back. We *think* about the past or the future, and when engaging in the thought may useful, we linger with those thoughts, otherwise, we let them go, return to our breath, posture, and mudra. Getting angry with ourselves for our mind wandering is extra. Eventually we settle in—settle the self on the self—and that practice pays off in an expanded sense of spaciousness, ease, and subtle inputs from all of it "out there."

One final thought: Most American practice of Buddhism is secular, performed by people with jobs and families. Despite my gratitude and appreciation for the Japanese culture and aesthetic of Zen, I sometimes wonder if we are not at times confusing the gift with the gift wrapping.

I love the tatami mats in my little zendo because they are part and parcel of my earliest introduction to Zen, but as far as I know they are not made in America, and they were expensive. We have our own

American standards of beautiful floors, and I've visited scores of lovely, makeshift zendos in old houses using polished wooden floors as their substrate. The mats under our cushions will protect our ankles and knees from hard wood. Japanese clothing is comfortable, but we also have dark, comfortable clothing appropriate for the zendo. I sometimes worry that our Japanese names and customs will forever translate our practice as "foreign" to most Americans, and we will miss opportunities to share dharma with them for that reason.

Suzuki-roshi taught us Buddhism as he learned it, but he appeared to be anticipating an American varietal. If we imitate Japanese cultural forms too rigidly we may find that the authoritarianism and hierarchy (highly developed in Japan) may morph with our native varieties in ways that make questioning authority, and democratic relationships, more difficult. I have to wonder if a teacher supported by autocratic norms is not more of a danger than a gift. Time will tell, but I am curious about the changes that America will make in our practice and look forward to their helping integrate Buddhism to the widest possible audience.

14

The Role of Faith in Buddhist Practice

·····

March 17, 2021

MANY BUDDHIST PRACTITIONERS DON'T CONSIDER faith as a part of their practice. When questioned about this, one of my old compadres commented, "I don't need faith in Buddhism. Buddhism is very clear. It's very rational. It tells me what to do, and I get the results that I want, and that's that."

I think he could be speaking for many Westerners who may have been attracted to Buddhism for its practicality and appeal to reason. Normally, we think of faith in the Abrahamic religions—Judaism, Islam, or Christianity—as the arbiter of loyalty to the tradition. Faith has us commit to statements of fact and miracles that we can't certify for ourselves. Common to all is a belief that God is one entity, eternal, all-knowing, and powerful, and his creation is something separate from his existence. In America, God is always referred to with masculine pronouns. Followers generally believe that God exists outside of space and time and therefore is never subject to any of the laws and rules governing his creation.

Faith in a prophet or faith in the Father, Son, and Holy Ghost; the burning bush; or other unverifiable events is often regarded as evidence of devotion and sincerity—calibrated as a different way of knowing, and many people are able to sustain religious faith even in conflict.

There are also schools of Buddhism that are primarily faith based, practice such as reciting the names of Buddha or chanting *Nam Myoho Renge Kyo* (based on the Lotus Sutra—*Nam* means "ultimate truth," *Myoho* refers to the Mystic Law, *Renge* is the Lotus Flower, and *Kyo* refers to scriptures). Millions of Buddhists ascribe to these faith-based practices, which are quite different from Zen. But even in Zen when we sew our rakusus and robes we dedicate a prayer with each stitch, *Namu butsu kyo* (I take refuge in Buddha), which could be regarded as an act of faith that "someone" is listening.

In Buddhist epistemology, there are five faculties known as *indriyani,* derived from Indra, Hindu King of the Gods. The indriyani are the "top dog" faculties—Faith, Energy, Mindfulness, Concentration, and Wisdom. You could think of Faith in this context as confidence, Mindfulness as attentiveness, and Wisdom as discernment.

Each of these faculties regulates an opposing force. Faith counters doubt. Without some faith, doubt may cripple us; at an early point in my Zen training, I could not perceive the relationship between the two. At that time, I was in turmoil and sought advice from my friend Tenshin Reb Anderson, already a transmitted disciple in Suzuki-roshi's lineage and one of my first dharma friends. As we walked together, I was confessing trouble in my marriage and feeling besieged by doubts about my capacities and worth.

He responded by saying something that at first mystified me. He said, "Can you see that great doubt is the flip side of great faith?" My response was a blunt *"No,"* so he explained that the depth of my doubts *implied* a faith in very high standards of what a person might be. My doubts were measuring myself against my highest ideal of what a person could be. It was a revelatory act of mental jiujitsu that stopped me in my tracks. Mentally stilled for the moment, I was able to fully appreciate what he said next.

Think of it like a coin, with one side faith and the other doubt. If you concentrate only on the doubt it will cripple your confidence and make you unable to act. If you just consider the faith side, you will never press yourself with the tough questions required to grow. The trick is to roll the coin on its edge as you proceed. The doubt will raise questions that vex you, but the faith will help you press on, believing that somehow, some way, if you persevere, you'll be able to vanquish the problems afflicting you, one by one.

That advice still floats among the highest percentiles of significant advice I've ever received and opened my "practice eye" perhaps for the first time.

Energy is the faculty we employ to overcome laziness. Stillness of mind supports deep concentration, which supports wisdom and discernment. Discernment is important because our normal monkey mind doesn't ordinarily know what it wants. Traditionally, it's represented clambering around a huge tree adorned with the world's bright and shiny temptations, picking and choosing restlessly. Discernment, or wisdom, is our ability to choose wisely, to select what in Castaneda's Don Juan's terms is "a path with a heart"—a path that will repay our efforts in contentment and spiritual nutrition.

A common misconception about Buddhist practice is that it will *end* suffering. In my experience that's not precisely true. As I've said earlier, enlightenment is not a fence that we hurdle and discover ourselves in a perpetually blissful Buddhist Disneyland. The Heart Sutra states that while in deep meditation, Avalokitesvara (Buddha in the form of compassion) "perceived that all five skandhas* in their own being are empty and was *saved* from all suffering."

When we save someone from drowning we do not drain the ocean. To be saved from suffering cannot mean the annihilation of suffering

---

*In early Buddhist philosophy, the five skandhas (heaps) were the constituent parts of a person—form, feeling, perception, impulse, and consciousness. Despite having names signifying they are different from one another, each, by virtue of being composed of multiple, non-self elements, is empty of any identifying essence, of self.

but instead something closer to being *saved from the effects of suffering*, from attachments to our thoughts, impulses, and desires, and the imagining of fixed, permanent self being afflicted. After enlightenment, one does not take up residence in a Universe where negativity and shadows have been eliminated. By realizing that afflictions, in their own right, are as empty and transitory as the self being stressed by them are Buddha-nature themselves, practitioners understand they can be contained, withstood, by the force of spirit and intention, analyzed for the parts of which they are constructed, and then allowed to disappear. Practitioners become aware that they have the power and courage to marshal the energy of what assails them and transform it into a dignified and helpful existence.

There are many forms of suffering—anxiety, tension, stress, grief, fear, loss, frustration, and the like. Buddhist practice is not a cure-all. As long as we have a body and nervous system we will suffer some types of anxiety. But understanding their evanescence and perceiving them as energy rather than "the slings and arrows of misfortune" leaves us free to transmute them. Understanding that at root such afflictions are expressions of the Universe, like weather, lowers our levels of distortion and fear.

What the Buddha taught us is how to engage with our suffering, and by engaging how to transform it into a dignified, noble, compassionate life. He was not addressing the suffering of drowning or being caught in an earthquake. Those are phenomena that we can't do anything about and, at the worst, can prepare ourselves to die calmly. Even in such circumstances, however, we can at least deal with the mental components of such afflictions.

Dukkha is a truth of the world that will never disappear. It's going to arise in every life somewhere. If it means anything, the word *truth* means "real." Buddha appends it with the word *noble*—dignified, worthy of respect, reminding us that we are not neurotic or spiritually undeveloped if we suffer. It is nothing to be ashamed of, and there is no need to pretend that one is experiencing constant gaiety or soporific calmness to signal one's spiritual development. Buddhist practice and meditation, and the five faculties—faith, energy, concentration, mindfulness, and wisdom—give us the tools to deconstruct dukkha, experience its insubstantiality, and repurpose its energy.

The difference between faith as Buddhists describe it and the faith that most people attribute to deeply held religious beliefs is that Buddhists use the term to describe a *confidence* developed from experience and the efficacy of helpful teachings that do not require any idea of divine intervention.

For this reason, there are some who define Buddhism as agnostic (a person who claims neither faith nor disbelief in god), but I believe they miss the point. Abrahamic religions cleave the world in two—there is a god of good, and a god of evil (Satan). Because Buddha-nature is the Universe itself, there is no way to separate a god from his or her works. If Emptiness itself is sacred, so, too, are its emanations. We could say, therefore, that Buddhists believe "the whole thing" is sacred, but they might use the word *prajna*.

Judy Lieff wrote a nice article in *Lion's Roar* magazine, describing prajna as "a Sanskrit word literally meaning 'best knowledge,' or 'best knowing.' Prajna is a natural bubbling up of curiosity, doubt, and inquisitiveness. It is precise, but at the same time it is playful. The awakening of prajna applies to all aspects of life, down to the tiniest details."*

When discussing faith, we are also referring to the history of enlightened beings that preceded us and left us the footprints of their explorations in the form of texts, instruction, and lore that we can follow. That faith is bolstered by the observation of our teachers and exemplary students of dharma and the lives they lead. It includes the record of their achievement as observed and commented on by other teachers, historians, and even emperors. It is a faith buttressed by experience. It is not a faith that contradicts facts.

When we follow the Buddhist precepts, when we follow the

---

*Lion's Roar Magazine, May 5, 2002.

Eightfold Path, when we meditate, we receive immediate benefits of focus, mindfulness, clarity, and engagement with our intuitions. We develop discernment and, most importantly, through repetitive practice, we absorb wisdom.

These qualities are a part of our common genetic heritage. Buddhism will not deliver us to a world where coyotes never eat bunnies, or where human beings are never cruel to one another or grasping for power and status. But by the time we have discovered that our world includes all of it, that there is no pure place to stand outside it, we will also have developed our personal toolkits to deal with it. Instead of feeling victimized, or fearful, our experience of what we have, by then, received from this practice will function as an internal stabilizing gyroscope.

Faith pierces doubt. The coin is tipped on edge. Energy controls laziness. I'm lazy. Trust me. I know that about myself. I still struggle with getting up to sit zazen as soon as my alarm goes off, when I would much rather lie in bed with my dogs or read for an hour before starting my day. There are times I would rather play my guitar and sing instead of dealing with students. What allows me to overcome my inertia (most of the time) is the energy derived from serving that which is larger than my personality.

I want to share another quote with you from Thich Nhat Hanh, from his book *The Heart of the Buddha's Teaching*. Thich Nhat Hanh was one of the leaders of Buddhist resistance during the Vietnamese-American War. His name was on the death lists of nearly all combatant forces because of his unswerving dedication to Buddhism, which often led him to ignore political realities such as his refusal to consider others as his enemies. He was reviled as a Communist by the Diem government because of his peace activism and as a reactionary by the victorious North Vietnamese government for his enduring efforts to aid the boat people fleeing Vietnam who were dying at sea in extraordinary numbers from the predations of pirates and the dangers of the oceans. He was quite diminutive, very quiet, and almost delicate, yet virtually every power structure contending in Vietnam wanted to kill or jail him. He was very gentle and soft-spoken, but also as sharp and supple as fine steel. This is what he says about faith:

> The first of the five faculties or bases . . . sometimes translated as "powers" is faith. When we have great faith, a great energy in us is unleashed. If our faith is in something that is unreliable or false, not informed by insight, sooner or later it will lead us to a state of doubt and suspicion. But, when our faith is made of insight and understanding, we'll touch the things that are good and beautiful and reliable. Faith is the confidence we receive when we put into practice a teaching which helps us overcome difficulties and obtain some transformation. It's like the confidence a farmer has in his way of growing crops. It's not some belief in some set of ideas or dogmas.

It's important to understand that for Thich Nhat Hanh, faith does not stand in opposition to facts. It is not belief in a set of ideas or dogma but instead observation of facts manifest in a life informed by "insight and understanding." Faith must be grounded in understanding. The small mind of our personality is perennially charmed by its own thoughts. We tend to believe everything we think. It's hard to explain how subtle and tricky we can be with ourselves and the degree to which we believe our inner voices without ever interrogating them to certify whether they are reliable.

When understanding is grounded in insight, we can see through the ego and its limited vocabulary of like, dislike, and neutral. When we can step aside and interrogate ourselves honestly, we can understand perceive how insistent we can be seeking our own way.

I have a black cat named Duke who moved in to live with me from a neighbor's house, despite my two dogs. He's fearless and extremely clever. I don't blame him for his nature, and while I don't appreciate his solemnly delivered gifts of occasional small birds and mice, some still living, which I ferret away to freedom, I understand that's his nature. I don't blame my own nature, either, for pursuing what it wants or avoiding what it dislikes. That's the nature of my ego, my small mind. But, I also understand that it is not always a reliable partner, and, furthermore, that it's just a tiny part of who I am.

Faith is not separate from insight. It's not separate from intellect, but intellect alone will never get us across the finish line to a peaceful, compassionate life. We need the power of faith, in this case, as expressed by the three thousand-year lineage of human beings who have preserved Buddha's wisdom, expressed their confidence in it by dedicating (and re-dedicating) their lives to it, burning themselves alive for it, teaching, refining the teaching, sharing it (many times at great sacrifice) to model the life of a Buddha in their own lives. This is not to suggest that faith means that we will never doubt or correct our path; never have "bad" days when everything seems meaningless.

Yesterday, on my way to visit a friend, late for an appointment, I was stuck in a long line of traffic, alternating passage through a one-lane bridge. Cars from each lane were passing one after the other, it was a hot day, I was running late, and it took a long time for my turn to come around. As the car on the other side entered the bridge, suddenly another car from the same side peeled off and followed him closely across the bridge, breaking the voluntary order of one-at-a-time. As he passed, I raised my middle finger and said, "Fuck you" aloud. It was shocking. The first time in many years that I've so completely lost track of myself like that, and therefore a humbling reminder that our work at self-development is never finished. Flipping someone the finger is not so far removed from pulling a trigger, and who knows what the consequences might have been if the driver had compounded my lack of control with his own.

The faith that we practice in Zen is that the nature of our *true self*—our fundamental nature (not our personality)—is Buddha; the fundamental energy and luminous awareness of the entire Universe. That energy is without beginning and end. It is impersonal, not something that we own and can control. Therefore, the awareness we refer to casually as "I" is the same "I" that Buddha possessed. It's the same "I" that you and all the Great Beings of Buddhist history, the bodhisattvas, the Compassion Beings continue to possess. When we understand that, they still live in this present moment!

If I believe I'm a different, lesser being than they, I have killed them and reduced them to symbols. It's only necessary to understand that our intrinsic self is the Buddha and possesses what it needs. It's not to be sought elsewhere. No teacher can give it to you. You have always had it. Fundamentally, it is not even separate from our personality, but it is occluded to our perception because our mind is too busy trying to satisfy the wants and needs of the ego and is obscured by negative energies that prevent us from seeing through the scrim of our negative energies fascinating us with their hypnotic fixity.

When we bow to a statue of Buddha, we are *not* bowing to a god but to wisdom. It is also our own wisdom, which is not different from the wisdom of the Universe. When we practice the Eightfold Path and precepts, we are modeling Buddha's enlightened life. We can discover this for ourselves. We can meditate and see for ourselves. Wisdom is our birthright. We can practice paying careful attention to our inner and outer realities. When we have an impulse to do something, we can examine it *in the light of the precepts* and determine for ourselves the most helpful way to respond to it. We don't have to believe everything we think.

An ancient Zen master named Yongming (904–975) once declared, "Faith without understanding increases ignorance." Much contention surrounded Yongming, particularly in the Rinzai sects in Japan. During the Song period in ancient China, two interpretations of Buddhism rose to particular prominence, Chan (the precursor of Zen) and Pure Land (a practice where people strove to be reborn in a land under Buddhist influence). Pure Land was widely popular among the poor and non-elites, and perhaps for this reason Yongming became closely connected to both groups—which aroused much controversy among those trying to "place him" squarely in one context or another.

I appreciate his Mahayana understanding and sometimes struggle to reconcile my faith-based impulses and Zen practices. Understanding without faith creates subjective opinions. Without faith in Big Mind and Emptiness, the largest common denominator, nothing is available to help us perceive the limited nature of our personal reality. I feel, as I imagine Yongming did, that in a world of infinite interconnections, it doesn't matter where you start—you arrive at the same irreducible truth.

When faith and understanding are combined, the Buddhist path clarifies rapidly, aiding us in choosing wisely. Buddha repeatedly says *follow your own understanding, investigate what I'm saying. See if it's true.* Examination and understanding are not antipodal to faith. They do not exist at the expense of faith. Buddha is urging us to align our understanding and our faith.

I want to stress one more point. Nothing I have said is intended to suggest any requirement that one is expected to become a Buddhist or change their religion to benefit from Buddha's teaching. There is nothing in his teachings that are inimical to any faith-based *practice* founded on love and mutual respect. There may be conflicts at the level of dogma, but they are inherently superficial against the immensity of Buddha-nature. His Holiness the Dalai Lama has said that there is no need to change your religion. Just practice kindness, because kindness is the deepest expression of interdependence—what Thich Nhat Hanh referred to as "inter-being." And the inter-being of miraculous unrepeatable experiences generates the deep love that the Buddha described as *bodhicitta* (bo-dee-chee-ta)—the desire to save all beings.

Kindness saves us from devaluing *any* particular expression of the Universe. A housefly or spider is a mystery beyond our calculation. How much more so a human being? We are produced by that which produced our enemies. It's our task on Earth to consider that, and deal with the understanding that, on some level, it's all "us."

15

On Time:
Host and Guest

.....

January 6, 2021

NORMALLY, WE THINK ABOUT TIME running as an unbroken continuum from the past through the present to the future. We say "time passing," but we never really clarify exactly *what* we believe time is passing, or what might be standing outside of time.

Either way, the implication is that we are losing ground to an implacable, immutable force, a perfect belief to generate stress. In both cases the supposition is that we are somehow one entity and time is another. It is an easy delusion to maintain because we have a word for time, which, in the same way that we have words for everything, suggests that it exists as a boundaried, isolated, entity.

That's just how our minds think about it. For those of us who grew up with analogue watches, time, like the solar system, is a circular, recurring pattern. From the perspective of zazen, however, time might be the interval between two chimes. We sit, focusing awareness on our exhale, and as we relax and internal dialogue quiets down, so does time. From this place, time actually appears to unroll from the present moment backward, like a spool of black thread disappearing into a bottle of black ink. There's only this present moment in which we and everything else coexist; the moment when we experience everything and when the seeds for the next moment sprout and grow. The future is simply an idea, an apprehension, an expectation, but it doesn't exist until we reach it, and when we do, every item and entity in it will have sprouted from the seeds of the present moment immediately before.

The present moment has an inception, a fullness, and then a decline, like fall and winter or winter and spring. Another moment is arising on it as a foundation, and yet each has its inception, fullness, and decline. Normally Zen folks don't overthink the nature of time (or death or rebirth), but do not separate it from objects, either. We might say we are time, each of us, each entity expressing time at its own rate and frequencies.

My teacher Lewis Richmond has a lovely way of thinking about time in both a horizontal and vertical dimension. Horizontal time represents our ideas of the past present and future. The past is clearly marked and delineated, the future is bit fuzzy because it hasn't occurred yet. The past is the realm of memory, and the future is the realm of hopes and fears. We all know this. His metaphor for the vertical dimension is very useful. That's where we exist when we sit—our back is vertical (vertical) time. Nothing moves but our breath, on the inhale and exhale. It doesn't go anywhere, anticpate anything, it just *is*. This is the realm of zazen.

In Zen monasteries time is marked with the han, a heavy wooden block suspended from a thick rope and struck by a wooden mallet. The han is run in several cycles, giving students time to change out of workclothes and into their robes and to appear in the zendo before the "roll-down" signaling the beginning of zazen. Kuden Paul Boyle of the Chapel Hill Zen Center reminds us that

> when the Han begins to sound, it reminds us to let go of our conceptions of "I, me, and mine." To let go of finishing my cup of tea or coffee, or that moment of my quiet time on the back porch.

The practice of time is quite strict and impersonal in a monastic setting. It is often troublesome for new students to fulfill each of their responsibilities and deadlines as they move through the course of a day. The observation of a strict schedule is part of learning how to control the twenty-four hours and master time without stress and how to distinguish one's personal sense of time from our common time as a community.

We don't describe autumn as "early winter" or consider summer as "late spring." Each has its characteristics of beginning, fullness, and decline—a life span that sets the stage for the following moment's inception. Looking beyond this moment, everything is hopes, wishes, apprehensions, or curiosity. Looking behind this moment, everything is memory. For Zen practitioners, the present moment is the object of our attention.

No matter where, when, or how one discovers their practice, our life is time, and time includes all the various parts—the blooming, the leaves coming, the leaves falling, the bees arriving, the birds arriving. Time is not outside of this. These phenomena are not painted on time like the logo on a delivery van. The time of a bee is different from the time of a person, but they are both time.

Observing time as running past us is to see ourselves outside of time—another trick of the small mind to establish awareness as a personal, fixed, permanent entity, thus disguising the subject of our own impermanence. We are time. And like everything else, we have an initiation, a fullness of expression, and a passing away. If we can't really say who lives, we can't really say who dies, can we?

Death is also a moment, or perhaps a hinge. I think that when we use the word *dying* we often imagine a vital essence in the body leaking away. But death, like life, has an initiation, a fullness, and a passing. That's the nature of this world. There are lots of theories about what occurs next, but no one really knows, and for this reason Zen practitioners tend to concentrate on the present moment.

I have met Tibetan *tulkus* (supposedly reincarnated holders of specific lineage, empowered and trained from a very early age) in both Tibet and the United States. Their tradition fully embraces reincarnation, and I discussed the subject candidly with the tulkus I met.* They were all good-humored and shy in their common response, which was to smile and say, "I have no idea. This is what I was told."

Whenever I encounter people telling me about their past lives (they were almost always more elevated than they are currently, or suffered trauma that conveniently "explains" their problematic behavior in the present.) To me, such descriptions sound like fanciful extensions of the ego and creating narratives out of images generated by the mind. It is convenient to assert a view of past lives—as explanations for current problems in this one—but it is really an *assertion* and not a provable premise, and it is most certainly received wisdom. Even supposed memories of past lives occur in the present moment and form, where they could as easily have been logged in the unconscious, which does not recognize time.

Where my own mind settles on the question is that it appears contradictory to assert dependent origination and reincarnation in the same system of thought. But does it matter? Life transcends all beliefs about it, and so I don't argue about the subject.

Time flows. Yes, it does, but it doesn't mean it goes from here to there. Neither does it mean that it is the mind moving and not something outside of it. We can be pretty certain that *something* is moving even if we can't say exactly what. Perhaps it's simply the mind stream. We can certainly experience vast cycles flowing. It requires 365 days for the Earth to orbit the sun. Our year is the tick of a very different clock. It's not the breakdown of the twelve hours into seconds and minutes, which is the way we've internalized ideas of time. You, your very own self, are time, and there is a great relief and empowerment that derives from exploring this fact.

---

*According to Tibetan tradition, the bodhisattva vow to save all beings is so concrete that practitioners have chosen to be reborn, so as to continue their work. This is not a Zen practice or belief, and one can study Buddhism equally well without being committed to the idea of rebirth.

My computer screen tells me it is 10:21 a.m. as I write, but it tells me nothing about the fog-shrouded pasture beyond my window, jeweled drops of water adorning the grass glimmering before the Mayacamas range in the Russian River drainage of Northern California in the section of Sonoma County that the current inhabitants refer to as Westcounty. I don't know what the previous inhabitants, the Pomo, Miwok, Wappo, and Kashiya people, called this place, but I know that they were here and that they had their own understandings of time, their own calendar and way of recording events.

Here's a Dogen quote on time I particularly like:

> Time is not separate from you. And as you are present, time does not go away. Don't think that time merely flies away. Don't see flying away as the only function of time. If time only flew away, we would be separated from time. The reason that you don't clearly understand the time-being . . .

Dogen uses the phrase "time-being" (*Uji*) in a startling way. Normally, Westerners say "the time being" indicating the temporary, as in, "We can let this alone for the time being." Dogen means *literally* "time is its own being," its own entity, which he clarifies by continuing:

> The reason that you do not clearly understand the time-being, is that you think of time only as passing. But it doesn't pass, and it doesn't arrive. It's moving at different speeds in different places. Everything is a moment in time.

We're as empty as bamboo tubes, and what's inside the tube is awareness and the tube itself is awareness. We are aware of a body. We are aware of form, feeling, impulses, sensations, consciousness, and we know them when we experience them, or more accurately, they recognize themselves. Perception is the fundamental ground of mind and it is not a personal possession.

To be able to slip our personality, render it permeable, or let it rest for a moment is one of the skills zazen facilitates, and it produces a visceral alteration of perspectives on everything that touches "our" perception, including time. If body and mind fall away even for a few moments, we remember the experience as a touchstone and reference point.

Because the mind is always moving, awareness binds our thoughts and engages our feelings. It grabs on to our stuffy nose or the weird look that somebody gave us across a restaurant. It occupies itself with every possible combination and permutation of experience. As long as it is engaged and supported by our personal narratives, likes, and dislikes, our personal dramas, it commands us hypnotically to stay within its purview, preventing us from perceiving reality outside its strictures.

Once mind slows down, once we stop wiggling, and moving, and deny it the stimulus of impulse and sensation; once we concentrate on our breath and our attention becomes increasingly one-pointed, the mind has nothing to interact with *except* itself. When that occurs, the movie screen *behind* the projected images, awareness itself, is revealed.

It is important to understand that our basic nature is enlightened. The mind of Buddha, the Big Mind of the Universe and our own, at their root, are identical. We have always possessed it. No one gave me my awareness, and no one can give it to you. We earn it. The best a teacher can do is to help us see the nature of our own mind—which is to say, help us clarify and render transparent our human negativities and impediments to wisdom, our evolutionary inheritance of greed, anger, and delusion. A skillful teacher helps us to discover what has never been there.

In the classic *Ten Guidelines for Zen Schools,* a celebrated ninth-century Zen master named Fayan wrote,

When the founder of Zen (Bodhidharma) came from India to China, it was not because there was something to transmit; he just pointed directly to people's minds, so that they could see their essence and realize enlightenment—how could there be any sectarian styles to value?

In Keizan's *Transmission of the Light,* it is described as "the subtlety that cannot be passed on even from father to son." Once we have personally perceived everything as its own unit of time, perceived for ourselves the interdependence and uniqueness of things, we return to the starlight of our familiar miraculous world with traces of that experience and a heightened sensitivity to it. After that, when we see a flower, we see the birds that scattered the seeds, see the sunlight, water, and soil, the oxygen and microbes, the rain and sun that nurtured them, we remain in a different relationship with the 10,000 things and no longer identify ourselves simply as the isolated personality with which we are overfamiliar. Once we see for ourselves, we can never be deceived. We won't have to come and listen to people like me chatter, devour spiritual books, take advice from the dead, or rub crystals over our chakras to achieve some imaginary state of grace.

A venerated tenth-generation Soto master named Hongzhi devised a concise and useful metaphor for the relationship between body and awareness, emphasizing the equal contribution of both: "If the host (Awareness) does not know there is a guest (the Body), there is no way to respond to the world; if a guest does not know there is a host, there is no vision beyond material sense."

Hongzhi alerts us that *if the host doesn't know there's a guest,* all the objects of the senses, the infinite varieties of Emptiness manifested as Form, remain imperceivable. *If the guest doesn't understand that there is a host,* there can be no experience of transcendent awareness. Material reality is reduced to nothing but meat and potatoes, and there's no bandwidth for any spiritual dimension. How else do we translate sense impressions of our Universe *but* with our sack of skin and its senses?

Your "I" is not a personal possession, nor is it trademarked to you (hence my skepticism about the body-hopping of reincarnation). The guest—the *sack of skin*—is the temporary raiment of awareness, which *does* arrive and depart. The host is not a prize to be possessed, and the guest is not a contestant on Buddhist Jeopardy who can win it.

The ancient Zen ancestors—both men and women—understood the metaphor, referring to awareness as the host because it is always home. The guest—the one who stays awhile before leaving—is the body, this sack of skin. In other words, to experience and navigate the world of form we require a form, and consequently we will be always subject to the limitations of that form. There's no way around that. However, if our understanding simultaneously includes the boundless freedom of Emptiness, which includes life and death, "there is no hindrance," as the Heart Sutra reminds us. *Form is Emptiness, Emptiness is no other than Form.* This is the host/guest boogie-woogie.

Returning to the subject of time and quoting Dogen again, *the way the self arrays itself is the form of the entire world.* The word *array* means "to display a variety of objects," and it usually has a positive connotation. We lay out an array of desirable jewelry or chocolates to entice or please others. Dogen uses the word *self.* "The way the self arrays itself," which can mean "displays" itself or "attires" itself or "garbs" itself, "is the form of the entire world." That array is our awareness. Turn in a slow circle with your eyes open. Our awareness forms the center of the circle, like the sharp point on a compass, and "the form of the entire world" is itself a moment in time expressed as a vast array. When we observe hills and clouds and trees, birds, traffic, high-tension wires—they are the array of the self, meaningless without the awareness of observation. The world is what our awareness is interdependent with and supported by. We are not separate. The knower is not independent of the known.

Our awareness accepts everything. It's not like *we* are "in here" and it's all "out there." That way of perceiving is a surrender to habitual ideas of a fixed, independent, and permanent self floating around inside the body.

Dogen is discussing creation, which includes the self. Suzuki-roshi used the metaphor of an empty screen in the movie theater, reflecting whatever is projected on it. In that metaphor, it's fair to ask, What is the projector? It's creation itself—Buddha Mind, Big Mind, the mind of the Universe. Both the screen and the projections are different forms of awareness. Time is not different than Big Mind expressing itself. (Remember the Old English Dictionary reminds us that *expressing* also means "to press, squeeze, or wring out.") So, Form and Emptiness are literal expressions of one another.

It's impossible for us to understand the scale of the Universe, but we can experience it when we drop our petty judgments and the convenient little human-scale rulers we carry in our minds. Suspend for the moment what we like, don't like, and are neutral about—the three judgments our small mind is capable of. We sit to let those small rulers fall away. And because we are not here alone, because we share this time with everything, because we are actually made of everything, we try to treat it all well. Which is why we practice the precepts. Why we practice the Eightfold Path. To create a world of harmony and serenity. We *have* to try because some inner impulse has demanded of us that we do.

As I've grown older, I find myself often speaking with people who have recently experienced a death of someone close to them. I was on the phone this morning with someone who had just lost their brother. Every guest eventually leaves, but we don't want to become so preoccupied with the departures that we ruin the visit. The old masters remind us that life is life. It's *not* a preparation for death. Death is its own moment. Our efforts to understand it are time. Our thoughts about our efforts are time. Who is there who believes they exist outside of time? This is what Buddhists study and consider, practicing daily "quieting" of the self and its incessant demands so that the mind can range free.

16

Fuketsu's
Speck of Dust

·····

From a Suzuki-roshi
Dharma Talk, July 26, 1971

TODAY, INSTEAD OF MY OWN NOTES, I'm discussing a transcript from a dharma talk that Suzuki-roshi gave in 1971 on a koan entitled "Fuketsu's speck of dust." It's one I'm particularly partial to, because it doesn't matter if you are a Buddhist or not to appreciate its depth and grasp. For people unfamiliar with the word *koan,* they're a kind of logic-defying riddle used primarily in Rinzai-Zen practice but also in Soto school. They cannot be answered by logic alone and force the student to explore every possible meaning of the question. Most people have heard the phrase, What's the sound of one hand clapping? That will give you an idea of a koan, but one can often think of difficult problems in one's personal life as a koan, to be sat with and slowly penetrated. The student goes before the teacher, sometimes for years, to present his understanding until he gets a nod from the teacher that his understanding is correct.

I'm partial to Fuketsu's koan because it provokes thought about actual difficulties we encounter (or suffer the consequences of) as we live in the world every day. It is the riddle of being human. It goes like this:

There was a famous teacher named Fuketsu who was the fourth disciple of Zen master Rinzai. Rinzai, along with Dogen, had been one of the two major teachers from the two largest schools of Zen practice—Soto and Rinzai schools—in the twelfth century. One day in a dharma talk, Fuketsu said:

> If one particle of dust is raised (if you pick up one particle of dust),
> the state will come into being.
>   If no particle of dust is raised, the state will perish.

When he died, his disciple, Hsueh-toh, gave an appreciatory verse, and said:

> *Let the elders knit their brows as they will.*
> *For a moment, let the state be established.*
> *Where are the wise statesmen, the veteran generals?*
> *The cool breeze blows, I nod to myself.*

Whether we are lay practitioners or priests, whether we are Buddhists, whether we are spiritual, whether we are secular, the task we are faced with is to allow ourselves to be instructed by Big Mind, not the whims and impulses, the comings and goings of our personality or the mental pets and slogans of the moment.

We are all deluded, Buddhists as well as everyone else, deluded by our attachment to and fascination with our small minds. But the practice of meditation, finding the spaces between our thoughts, sinking into them deeply, allows us to escape their hypnotic clutch to appreciate things as it is.

When you begin to practice this way, it's at first a very exhilarating experience. We feel like we are including everything—our parents, our teachers, the altar, the incense, the birds, the trees. It's heady; a real high. If we continue this practice, the state normalizes, and we don't have to think about Big Mind so much, because it has become a more familiar geography.

If we are picking and choosing, we are doing this within the realm of personal preference, not Big Mind. Big Mind is normal. Big Mind is the way things are, like the Big Picture. That is what we are trying to be receptive to and instructed by, and usually our most reliable guide in this endeavor is our intuition.

The reason that we sit zazen, the reason that we have these Zen practice centers, the reason that we have Buddha statues and forms in our practice is so we can be reminded to refer to this Big Mind moment by moment. We can be ourselves.

Picking up a speck of dust means the undertaking of any task— creating a Zen temple, saving the whales, building a political movement, or protecting civil rights. Next to the immensity of the Universe, such activities are "a speck of dust."

Now, there are people who are not moved to pick up a speck of dust, who can see the suffering of the world and remain unmoved by it. For those people, nothing happens. But, if you are one of those people impelled to "do" something, it is important to understand that Fuketsu uses a "speck of dust" to refer to any willful human undertaking.

Usually we begin good works full of anticipation and positivity, in some manner feeling protected by our good intentnions. Fuketsu reminds us that when we pick up the speck of dust, it is important, *critically important, to be aware that we are actually picking up the entire world:* birth and death, good and evil, generosity and cupidity, selflessness and egoism. We do not get to choose selectively and pick only the parts of reality we favor. As a consequence, we mustn't be blinded by the glow of the good we believe we're doing and trust that it will shed no unintended consequences. For every good thing that we think we are doing, we also are perpetuating a number of negative consequences. There is no way around it.

The moment we begin to act, we begin generating karma, and not only good karma. Everything we do will have a shadow. Consequently, it is important to act, without considering permanence. We are not building a Zen center for the centuries, because we don't know what will be needed in the centuries. We can only know what is needed now, during our lifetimes. If everybody dwelled in Big Mind, we wouldn't need a Zen center. If everyone was wearing priest's robes, we wouldn't need to wear priest's robes. So we are responding to a particular situation as best we can, perhaps in the only way we know, in the midst of delusion, with deluded responses, but *trying our best* because we need to do something.

A speck of dust is just a little thing. When Fuketsu said it, he meant something like building a monastery or building a practice center. Compared with the immensity of Buddha Mind, such tasks are still just little things. So it's important not to attach too much importance to it, or too much certainty. The best we can do is to be wide awake to every ramification we can consider.

The most important thing to understand is that when we pick up the dust, when we act, we are effectuating the entire world of contradictions, of duality, and acting within delusion, and there's no way to avoid it. How to operate in this world and accomplish something worthy while admitting that we are simultaneously creating an antagonistic reality at the same time is the great koan of human undertakings.

We can pick up the dust. We can start to practice Zen. We can begin to save the last whale, creek, or canyon; fight global warming. We can start to do anything, and we will inevitably generate negative karma and negative consequences, as well as the positive ones we are concentrating on. *But if we don't pick up the dust, nothing at all happens.* That is the conundrum.

The purpose of this Buddhist practice is not to create more Buddhism in the world. Buddhists do not simply dive into real-world circumstances with a fixed goal and permanent strategy. The goal may be "Saving all Beings," but the execution must be refined and rethought moment by moment to make sure we remain on track. The point of this practice is for us to become ourselves, to model the life of a Buddha, and to help others. Dogen said, "To study the self is to forget the self. To forget the self is to be actualized by myriad things."

Another way of saying this is that we allow ourselves to be *implied* by the entire world. The five skandhas are interacting with it, but that's not necessarily a personal activity. To surrender the self is to surrender to all instruction by Big Mind. If Big Mind (or our intuitions) tells us to do something, we do it. If it doesn't, we don't do anything.

We call this the "Genjo koan." This is everyone's koan to solve one way or another. The actual koan of our lives. How do we live? How do we minimize harm? How do we support life and positivity? How do we minimize negativity?

The goal of Buddhism is to realize that your teacher is already within you. If you don't have a teacher, you can (if you're sufficiently trained) follow your own way, which is the best way. You may need a teacher to reach that point, but it is important not to be confused about where the source of wisdom resides. Each of our spinal telephones is plugged into the trunkline of the Universe.

We don't become a teacher to be a teacher. We teach to help people become themselves. When they become themselves, they don't need us, and that's the best case. And if everyone were to become their true selves—which is to say, expressing Big Mind—we wouldn't need all these practices, and religions and spiritual practices.

The most important point is to always try to do something from a Big Mind perspective, and to do it as purely as you can. We take this practice on because we have an intuition that there's something besides our small mind concerns and preoccupations, something that will put us more in consort and concord with the Universe. That's why we meditate. We meditate to find those spaces between our ideas and delusions where we can hear our intuitions speak, to slow down our body and allow ourselves to detach from the hypnotic attraction of our own thoughts and impulses.

When Chinese Chan master Hsueh-tou (980–1052) (pronounced "Setcho" in Japanese) said, "Old men will be unable to relax their eyebrows as they would otherwise. Oh they'll say, 'Silly boy, starting a Zen center. Oh, you guys. What are you undertaking?' Zen master Hsueh-tou said this because the old men already understand that for every good deed, you will unleash five or ten or twenty bad deeds. But if we are built a certain way, we don't have a choice. Something moves us to pick up the dust. We either pick up the dust or not, or leave everything exactly the way it is.

Suzuki-roshi reminds us in his talk on Fuketsu that it is good to fulfill our responsibilities—for me to be a teacher, or you to be a priest, or you to be a lay student or follow whatever your practice is. To do your job. To do your work in the world. But if there is a trace of self, of a gaining idea, or self-aggrandizement, Dogen affirms that we are as far off the mark as between heaven and earth.

It's like looking at a huge carpet and fastening on one little part of the pattern. You can watch the stars all you want, but it is part of the whole carpet. What we want to do is be in relationship with the entire carpet.

Even when we have a "good" practice, that can be an enemy of Buddhism. That means we've already got some idea of good and bad. We're judging ourselves as if from the outside, as if we were facts. That's not why we are studying. Remember Dogen's admonition: *To study the self is to forget the self.* We have to observe the self to wake up to discover how it enchants, tricks, and fascinates us. We have to observe it to recognize it in its guises and all its beguilements, its forms, its self-importance, and then we forget it. When we sit zazen and our attention has shifted to our posture, mudra, and breath, we allow the mind to be the mind, and, without trying, we see its characteristics.

Suzuki-roshi clarifies this:

We should not be proud of our faculties, or our personality, or our bright smart minds. When you have a good practice, that is also the enemy of Buddhism. You should not pursue the Buddha Way for the sake of change, or for your own personal interest. You shouldn't seek advantage in your everyday life. Whether people like what you do or not, if it is necessary, you should do it. And it is necessary if you feel your instructions come from Big Mind. If you pick up a speck of dust, people may not like it. But you should understand that it is just a tentative beginning.

Those of us impelled to be helpful or innovative do what we have to do, because otherwise we do nothing but allow the world's suffering to continue. If we don't pick up the speck of dust, don't try to help other people, we don't practice compassion. We don't practice mindfulness. We don't revere the animals caught in snares and traps and killed for furs, ivory or folk-medicine cures. We don't respect the clean air and the water. If you are on one side of that divide, it scours the heart to comprehend the amount and degree of suffering in the world. On the other side, there's Diet Coke, luxury vacations, and antidotes to boredom. My example is unfairly skewed against people who do not make attempts to be helpful. If no-dust folks were all "just being" I could comfort myself that they are like Zen students, but they're not. The people who don't care about others certainly care about themselves and their level of consumption, and material absorption in this country and Western Europe certainly makes life difficult for others. Such people exist in poor countries and poverty as well. I could argue that struggles to survive might diminish the bandwidth they have available to consider others, but I've traveled extensively in the Third World and seen as many acts of kindness and compassion there as in my own country. So, I'm forced to conclude that Nature made humans in a variety of sub-species, and they're all equal as her children, in her eyes. But I'm also sure that crows prefer the company of crows, and so my small mind picks a side to favor, because even doing nothing is a choice, which is the core of my argument for action.

Those who must pick up the speck of dust need to remember that their action also bears delusion within it because it is often so fraught with expectations and blindness to its shadows. No one is protected from unintended or negative consequences due to the imagined purity of their intentions. When they pick up the speck of dust they pick up the entire world, and so we pick it up *tentatively*. Everything begins with an impulse—to build this temple, or food bank, or hospital, or sangha of people to meditate and talk.

We don't know how long it will last. We don't know how long it will be necessary, but we move forward with the sensitivity of a fox, stopping often to sense the air and see if anything has changed, to see if our idea is still appropriate in a slightly altered environment. Knowing this, we can sense the folly of bragging and saying, "It'll be simple." If we are cautious and listen well, test the wind for trouble and remain constant about checking strategies against prevailing conditions, we stand a better chance of diminishing unanticipated consequences. Finally, let's never forget to query, "Are we doing good? Are we helping others? Am I being smart about my plan? Am I being good? Am I helping anyone?"

Fuketsu's speck of dust reminds us that we establish Buddha's way with defilement. Defilement arises with our decision to establish Buddha's way. And when we do this, it's still delusion. Knowing it's delusion, staying detached from winning or losing, but choosing, doing something is the bodhisattva's way, because the bodhisattva is an enlightened being responding to the suffering of the world and who will not sit by and do nothing. Anyway, that's the team I choose to play for.

We are trying to bring Buddha to life, by modeling Buddha's behavior. Our original teacher left us an instruction manual—the precepts, the Eight-Fold Path—and reminded us that we have never been separated from all-of-it except by our ideas. The entire Universe is supporting us, and if we relinquish fealty to our personal ideas and identity, we are leaving space to remain open to the instructions of Big Mind.

When Hsueh-tou said, *Who will live and die with you?*, he lifted up his staff, performed an act. That was his piece of dust, his teaching. He wasn't trying to enlist an army or make more Buddhists. He was trying to make the point that you are a unique expression of the Universe and are free to act. Now do something. You'll know what to do.

We have this short expanse of time during which we're afforded this sack of flesh and awareness. And if we hear the cries of the world and are moved and must do something, then we do it. But we know that we are also creating a mess. So we do it delicately, carefully. We don't take overmuch pride in the magnificence of the edifice, the greatness of our practice, how good we are at all of this, because for everything we do, we are just creating destruction as well. We build a hospital; you've wiped out the area where 100,000 creatures lived.

Suzuki-roshi has a beautiful little statement about this:

> Even in Tassajara, we're eating eggs, you know. They are living beings. Eggs are not dead. Each grain is a living being. You are killing them. But you have to eat them, knowing they are not dead.

We don't have a choice. We cannot help but destroy life. Life eats itself, that's the way things are. We can do what we must because we have chosen fealty to Big Mind. However, Big Mind also reminds us of the sacred obligation to cherish what we use, and so we say grace to express that cherishing and our gratitude for doing what we must and never forget our tender feelings for those beings that sustain us. I won't press the point, but consider this quote in terms of the current debate about abortion. Every cell in a fetus is alive . . . and yet!

Small mind will say, "Oh no. The Buddhist precepts say I can't take life." Big Mind says, "Sometimes it's okay. This is the way it is. Be grateful. Be tender. Be tentative. Have rituals of apology. Have rituals of sensitivity. Acknowledge the lives you are forced to take."

The Genjo koan affirms the proposition—Yes, it's a life, and there are many circumstances where we take life, in which we must do so to foster some other goal. We can't make hard and fast rules. Even our Buddhist vows remain wedded to circumstance. So let's move with tenderness. Let's move with respect. Let's move as if we could be wrong.

We don't know what will happen in the future so we are concerned about this moment. How fully can we be open to this moment? How carefully can we navigate this moment to minimize harm? How aware can we be in this moment?

Whether we are happy is important, but we will be happy if we are following a good path. If our bodies are healthy, and even if they're not, we'll be happy to be alive to sense our illness.

But here is an important caveat from Suzuki-roshi:

> If you think you can do this without any training, if you can have that kind of life without any training, that's a big mistake. You don't know what you are doing. When you say that you don't need Buddhism, you are either a great fool or a very selfish person! I'd rather you be a great fool than a selfish person.

Even though Buddha spoke about freedom, Buddha's idea of freedom, Big Mind, does not mean doing whatever you want, whenever you want to. So, we require training to see clearly and objectively. We need training to diminish our selfishness so that we can exist with others. We need this training to understand what Nature actually is. Not our little nature, not the biases of our personality, but Buddha Mind itself. Gary Snyder's great poem "This Tokyo" begins this way:

> *Peace, war, religion,*
> *Revolution will not help.*
> *This horror seeds in the agile*
> *Thumb and greedy little brain*
> *That learned to catch bananas*
> *with a stick.*
> *The millions of us worthless*
> *To each other or the world*
> *Or selves, the sufferers of the real*
> *Or of the mind . . .* *

---

*Gary Snyder, "This Tokyo," *The New American Poetry*, ed. Donald Allen. (New York: Grove Press 21st printing).

So, when we realize our nature, it can be a big problem. You are going to disappoint people. You are going to make people unhappy. But, for someone to say that all you have to do is follow your own nature, those people don't understand Nature.

We are never separate from the Universe. It's our only reliable guide. Unless we are supported by some truth and follow that truth, we can never be free. That's the rub of being a human.

So, Buddhists have discovered, tentatively, temporarily, that Buddha's truth seems to do less harm and produce more beneficial results than following our own whims for a fat and fancy independent existence. We are not traveling blindly. We follow this path fully understanding that we are eating living beings. That we are killing other creatures to build our temples and houses, the garages for our cars. But we are doing our best to follow a high ideal in a conflicted world, as do any of the world's sincere spiritual practitioners. Trying to stay awake. Not pretending we are good. Not pretending we are better. Not pretending we are pure or have some pure place to stand outside the rest of it. We are doing our best. But there is one piece of the Buddhist puzzle that is not shared by the rest of the world's religions. It's the part of Buddhism that is not a religion but rather a detailed analysis of reality. That part, really an insight, but an insight that takes us around a corner—that the self does not exist in the way we believe it does. God is not different than Her works.

And so, we sit zazen, and we sit zazen, and we sit zazen. Whether we are bored. Whether we are happy. Whether we are unhappy. Because in between discomforts, in between those breaks in our thinking, the world intrudes like a whispering tsunami, drowning language, concepts, and ideas in the great, unified, blissful . . . ? The world enfolds and instructs us.

PART III

⊙ ⊙ ⊙

ENGAGED WITH VERNACULAR ZEN

Introduction to Part III
·····
Flashing in the Dark

I'D LIKE TO BEGIN THIS SECTION of the book by sharing two quotes from Suzuki-roshi selected from *Zen Mind, Beginner's Mind*, both from a dharma talk titled "Constancy."

> Cultivate your own spirit—meaning—Don't search outside of yourself. Cultivate your own spirit, clean and weed your own garden. . . .
> It is quite usual for us to gather pieces of information from various sources thinking in this way to increase our knowledge. Actually, following this way we end up not knowing anything at all.

I plead guilty. Observing my own mind sometimes evokes an image of a gerbil family loosed in a cage of weasels. Both my sister and I probably suffered from ADD long before it was diagnosed and treated as a "condition." We both loved to read widely, to absorb information, then collate and cross-index various sources in interesting ways. I have the kind of mind that if I were forced to stand in the corner as a punishment, I would find something interesting in the wallpaper. Intriguing as the world may be to me, there is a downside to this ceaseless acquisitiveness, which Suzuki-roshi is trying to warn us about, what Sojun Weitzman-roshi referred to as materialistic, or "gaining," goals. It is greed.

Sometimes, in my daily rounds, I'm moving so rapidly that I have set a glass down on the counter, turned toward my next task (confident that the final drop of an inch or so to the countertop was assured), only to learn with the shock of shattering glass that I'd opened my hand as I turned toward my next task while inadvertently pulling the glass past the edge of the counter. I wish I could say that such things have only happened once in my life. When I am not scrupulous in following my activities all the way to their conclusion, I will set things aside, including critical tools, without noticing precisely where. Moments later I'll discover myself wandering around the house looking for "something," no longer able to always remember the object I'm seeking.

This habit was brought to my attention like a slap when I was staring blankly into my open refrigerator one day, scanning the condiments and jams, moving the almond milk and orange juice to see behind them before realizing that I was searching for my fountain pen. As idiotic as it is, it was useful noticing the problem and keeping it available on a back burner of my awareness so that I can work on it. *Changing* habits requires the same constancy it required to create them. It is not necessarily wisdom, but we might call it a precursor.

There are occupations—for instance, defusing bombs—where the accumulation of knowledge is critical, but when we are not at work, we should not forget to clear our minds and let them settle to reawaken with everything freshened. The second quote by Suzuki expands on "knowing."

When you know everything, you are like a dark sky. Sometimes a flash [of lightning] will break through. . . . After it passes, you forget all about it, and there is no residue, only the dark sky. The sky is never surprised when a thunderbolt breaks through. . . . When we have emptiness, we are always prepared for watching the flashing. . . .

If you want to appreciate something fully, you should accept it like lightning flashing in the utter darkness of the sky. It is not necessary to compare, to judge, evaluate. People who know, even if only intuitively, the state of emptiness, always have open the possibility of accepting things as they are. . . . Even if the flashing of enlightenment comes, our practice forgets all about it. Then it is ready for another enlightenment.

If the mind is preoccupied with anxiety, desires, fantasies, daydreams, or too much to do, it does not remain open in the moment. In such a state, we are actually obscuring a great deal of information, by concentrating solely on what we want.

I want to talk a little further about Emptiness because it is such a core understanding of Buddhism, and further discussion might prove useful. Let's begin at the simplest explanation of Emptiness—dependent origination. We've discussed this before, but the deepest implication of dependent origination is that if something is made of other unrelated elements, we can't possibly say that it has an independent existence. Independent of what? Sunlight, water, and oxygen? I don't think so. We consider our awareness "ours" and the locus of our self, but if the guest (the body) was not nourished and fed by non-self substances, there would be no platform for the awareness to function.

When we look deeply, a blade of grass *is* the entire world. It is not a symbol or metaphor for it, but an actual, tangible expression of the mutuality of all things.

Because the blade of grass and all existence are *inter*dependent, we can say that they don't exist in an independent, singular manner as the name suggests. It does not mean that each individuated expression of Emptiness is not unique. Each is an unrepeatable experience, just as each snowflake is unique. But the "thing," the object or person we feel so certain we are observing as an isolated fact is not what we unquestioningly believe it to be. That is only the visible half of its reality. The absolute truth of its reality is that it (we) are a part of everything—inseparable from all it without possessing a separate reality. Water, oxygen, bees, plants, other people do not just sustain our existence, they *are* our existence.

Despite our deepest convictions to the contrary, our life-long narrative about our solitary personal existence, for instance, cannot be proved. Search as you like, you will not find any fixed entity of self within you, like an organ that could be identified as your "self." Your "I" has no location, no color, no form. We're clusters of awareness: form, feeling, sensation, impulses, and consciousness coexisting in a dynamic interface. Each of our organs *is* awareness—eyes, ears, nose, tongue, body, and mind translating outer and inner worlds into dimensions predicated on perception itself as ground zero. Mouth (or eye or hand) is *x* distance from strawberry is a translation of proprioception into language, the "I" (or me or mine) is extra. Buddha never suggested that Self and Other did not exist as practical matters. He would never answer the question as to whether or not the Self was a *fiction*, and an expression of Universal energy—Buddha-nature—and an indivisible part of the total fabric of that Universe.

If what we describe as a self is not discrete, with an isolated perimeter, then neither are the 10,000 things we call the world. No matter how precisely we might dissect an apple, we will never discover the core of appleness within it. Our self is not independent of our sense organs, our pulse, hormones, air, soil, and water. We call the apparent solidity of the self an illusion, not because it won't be obliterated if we ram our car into a brick wall at high speed, but because all those separate descriptions and definitions, the independent names for the 10,000 things, have, to some degree, Balkanized reality into jigsaw puzzle pieces, disguising the original unity from our observation. Our quotidian reality is so engrossing and compelling we forget the innumberable umbilical cords (Thich Nhat Han's term) connecting us to the world. So, we set sail every day on tumultuous, ever-changing oceans without the requisite ballast of realizing that we are also constituted of many things that do not die—the buzz of bees, the croak of frogs, water, air, and the like.

Believing that *we* are inside our bodies, virtually never changing, and the rest-of-it is outside, changing all the time, is the common delusion of humankind, the root of continuing difficulties, which

Buddha clarified and explained nearly three thousand years ago.

Modern science acknowledges and studies Buddha-nature by another name, which they indicate as the *background energy* in the Universe. Physicist Richard Feynman, a patriarchal figure in contemporary science, identified forms of energy in the Universe—including kinetic, magnetic, chemical, nuclear, gravitational, thermal, sound waves, and potential energy—but apparently (unless I simply haven't studied deeply enough) did not make the imaginative leap to it being a formless common denominator of existence.

Martha Rogers (1914–1994) was a nurse-scientist who advanced the Theory of Unitary Human Beings,* closing in on a very Buddhist concept.

> Human beings do not have an energy field, they *are* an energy field. [Emphasis mine] More importantly, energy fields do not have parts. For example, a magnetic field or a gravitational field, which are physical fields, cannot be divided into parts. Nor do they have boundaries. Because energy fields have no parts, they are considered irreducible. Irreducible means that it is indivisible. Furthermore, parts do not explain anything about the nature of a whole. The meaning of the term unitary is irreducible and without parts. Human beings are irreducible wholes who are more and different from the sum of their parts.

Modern string theory has been proposed as a "theory of everything" to replace the standard physics model, which apparently can explain everything but gravity. String theory posits that beneath atoms, electrons, and quarks are tiny one-dimensional strings that become atoms, electrons, and quarks depending on their vibrational frequency. Ms. Rogers's statement sounds like a scientific metaphor of nature—3,000 years after Buddha. Her explanation is missing only the implications of an ethical framework implied by interdependence. This is what sets Buddha's obser-

---

*Martha Rogers, *An Introduction to the Theoretical Basis of Nursing* (Philadelphia: F. A. Davis Co., January 1, 1970).

vations apart from science and theory. There is a fundamental, underlying energy, and that energy is not separate from that which it manifests.

Emptiness is only accessible to us through its manifested forms. We know this energy is formless because there's practically no form it cannot become. The myriad things of the world—our thoughts, sensations, impulses, consciousness, the jillions of insect species, the multiple forms of birds, snakes, spiders, black holes, supernovas, and negative energy—all of these are expressions of emptiness.

We should not make the mistake of considering formless energy as the *true* underlying reality and all its formations as illusory projections. Buddha never said or implied that. The Heart Sutra informs us that *Form is Emptiness, Emptiness is Form.* Eleven centuries later the towering Japanese Zen master Dogen reminded us that *Form is also Form* and *Emptiness is Emptiness.* Without Dogen's refinement—"Form is Form, Emptiness is also Emptiness"—we would be creating another dualistic opposition that appears to deny the reality of both: "Form is Emptiness, Emptiness is Form, Form is not different from Emptiness." They are and are not precisely the same nor are they precisely different.

When we meditate, sitting still and concentrated on our posture, the mind, deprived of stimulation, calms itself. We can't force it to be still, nor should we try. Unfortunately, many people believe stopping the mind to be the goal of meditation and give up meditating when they repeatedly fail to do that. Stopping the mind does not mean stopping the *activity* of mind. It is more accurate to say stopping one's engagement with it. You may have periods of sitting where your interior devolves into something like the test patterns on TV, engaging fantasies may rise and fall, but if awareness is dedicated to your posture, mudra, and breath, the mind cannot run away with you. It's like a motor idling, and your preoccupation with posture and breath is like the clutch preventing it from engaging the energy of the engine. That's when my mind is most like the sky, but even that temporary blankness is not the utterly transparent, *knowing* quality of my true mind.

The sky is extraordinarily generous. It accepts everything. Trees impinge on it. Birds, mountain peaks, bats, contrails, all coexist in the sky without tension or rebuff. Sky remains unperturbed. That is one way to consider *things as it is*—beyond like and dislike. It doesn't mean that we ignore the communication of our intuitions, but it does mean that we assume some dominance over our standing, walking, and sitting. Suzuki-roshi referred to this dominance as "being the boss of everything."

It's not necessary to be paying attention all the time. Hypervigilance is exhausting and presents its own difficulties. I spent a good part of 1988 studying knife fighting for a film I was preparing to make in Brazil. It was very intense, but fun. One of the indelible lessons of a Filipino teacher I worked with (a dazzling master of the butterfly knife) was not to fixate on the other guy's knife but to expand my field of vision to include all of my opponent, explaining, "If you pay too much attention to the right hand, you'll miss what's in the left."

That observation has been reinforced sitting zazen. My eyes are open but looking at nothing, I see everything without looking. An empty mind admits everything. A mind that's full of chatter has much less bandwidth available for the unexpected. As someone once quipped to me when I was mourning the loss of a girlfriend, "The empty bowl gets filled, buddy." Shakespeare expressed this lesson in another way in *Hamlet*. In the first third of the play Hamlet is trying to think everything out. In the second third, he becomes a man of action, killing Polonius, Rosencrantz, and Guildenstern and boarding a pirate ship. But by the play's end (and the end of his life, as it turns out) Hamlet understands that there is "providence in the fall of a Sparrow," and neither thinking nor action are always reliable, but—"The *readiness* is all."

The lightning bolts we need will appear. Returning to the story of my gerbil-like ADD mind at the beginning of this chapter, I've learned I discover more and more often that if I simply stand still a moment and stop dwelling on what's lost, an image of where (and what) my desired object is pops into my mind. Perhaps I'm creating a virtue of empty-headedness, but I'm pretty relaxed most of the time, and things just seem to work better when I relinquish being in control. When I was younger, I was neither happy nor relaxed. I used to be obsessed about being happy, and of course spent most of my time cataloguing the ways and whys I was unhappy. One day a "lightning flash" illuminated the issue for me, and I decided I would give up worrying about how I *wanted* to feel and concentrate on how I was actually feeling. After that, I discovered I was usually happy nearly all the time.

O

During a dharma talk once, I was asked, "Could you talk more about Not Knowing or Beginner's Mind, especially during these times when not knowing in the conventional sense is dangerous?"

The phrase comes from Suzuki-roshi's book *Zen Mind, Beginner's Mind* and the actual statement "In the beginner's mind there are many possibilities, but in the expert's there are few."

The expert has learned to conserve his or her energy, to conserve her gestures, to express what they are trying to do efficiently. That always involves some routinizing of practice and may result in not seeing each encounter with your work as a fresh and new opportunity. A consequence of this conservation is a diminished palette of choices.

A beginner has no idea. When you watch kids playing with blocks, they pound them, they make noise with them, they pile them up, they knock them over and put them on their heads. When they color in coloring books, they color on both sides of the lines, and everything is an expression of creative play.

Beginner's Mind is our wild mind. Gary Snyder helped me see that *wild* means self-organized, not crazy. Wild animals and plants are not organized for human purposes but their own. The Port Orford cedar grows for itself, the coyote, the falcon, the brook trout exist and follow their own coded intents and purposes, not ours. It's a function of human self-importance and ignorance that we consider their concerns less significant than our own.

If you enter a room in a state of Not Knowing, without preconceived ideas about the people you're about to meet, you'll learn more than you could have predicted and will miss less by removing the discriminating filter of your self-interest.

Whether or not you are white, it's better not to have too many ideas when you're stopped by a policeman. I drive rapidly most of the time, and when they catch me, I pull over, turn off the car, and roll down both front windows. When an officer comes to the window, I put my hands on the steering wheel, and, if it's dark, I turn the interior lights on, because I can feel their alertness when they approach

When I'm asked for my license, I tell them, "I have to reach in my back pocket." And I don't move until I hear his "Okay." I may have to add, "I have to go into my glove compartment for my registration." I can't tell you the number of times that an officer has thanked me and said, "You have really good manners. Thanks. Just slow down, will you?" They're relieved at having survived an encounter that could have gone any number of ways and relieved not to hear excuses and arguments.

However, neither is there is any getting around the fact that they see me as a white man and extend the privileges of that race to me. I don't like that that is the case, but I'm not going to argue it out in that arena. White policemen are not as on guard with me as they are with black men and women, but they're still on edge, and my understanding of that gives me an advantage in ensuring how things will go. Black policemen tend to read me intently, perhaps to see how I'll respond to their authority. If I believe that I am dealing with a fascist pig who is the fist of the state (which is one possibility), I'm going to be frightened and/or angry, and my feelings will leak out through my eyes, speech, and behavior. It's to my personal advantage to be calm and relaxed. It's not to my advantage to try to outwit the officer or lecture them on social justice.

Knowledge also makes me consider how much more difficult, frightening, and complex it is to be pulled over if you are an African American, Latin, or non-white man or woman. By now the videos of well-behaved, compliant African Americans pulled from their cars, tased, and in some cases killed by police are ubiquitous. We've seen them shot in the back running away, and we've seen them executed on the ground by guns or choked to death. There is a long, well-known history of black relationships with the police that devolve from slavery and Reconstruction days when the police were overt agents of white repression. This lore has been passed through the conversations of generations of African Americans who understand with unswervable clarity that one function of the police has always been to keep them in "their place"—namely, the lowest caste—in society.

I have African American friends and query them about this and follow the online discussions where some African American parents have argued for the necessity of allowing their children to defend their personhood and dignity in the face of police affronts. Unless we're extremely close, I never intercede in these debates, because the threat levels we face as black and white citizens are so differently freighted with deadly danger that it's often disrespectful to assess a black experience with the police from my point of view.

If I were asked, however, I'd argue that I would rather have my child *survive* an encounter with a potentially dangerous law officer, even shamed, to live and struggle for justice another day, to live to care for their children and family. I see little dishonor in acknowledging the power imbalance of police and young black men and women. That is not an equation, because there is no such thing as a fair fight. Even as white citizens, when we deal with the police we are dealing with a person who has been given a license by the state to kill. Furthermore, he or she has been culturally trained to expect deference and subservience and may have even joined the police seeking such advantages. We simply don't know, but I would never want to lose a child under any circumstances and would rather he struggle to live with the trauma of humiliation than not at all.

Were it a fair fight between unarmed individuals, I would say, by all means, stand up for yourself and your values, but there is another level that must be addressed here, which is the centuries of organized violence and suppression of black folks, *which been tacitly supported by the white majority*. The 2002 census determined that 12.1 percent of the population is African-American. If they are ever to be included politically under the umbrella of rights guaranteed by the Constitution, black folks must be supported by 38.9 percent of white people to have any majority, guaranteeing them access to democratic institutions and relief. This means, literally, that their problems are our problems too. Caucasian Americans who will not come forward to demand the Constitutional rights of citizenship for *all* Americans are coasting on their white privilege, which is demonstrated by the fact that they can. There is no neighborhood or store they can't enter at will. They are not always suspected of shop-lifting or regarded as potential threats. I challenge people who dispute this to name *one* white American shot by police while fleeing. I can't, but I could probably name nearly twenty African Americans who've suffered that fate or were simply murdered by police for looking out a window.

I would not want to use my child as a chip in the gamble that perhaps their death will finally change public opinion and the law. I have seen too many ground up in the maw of racism or ignored by the white majority who "refuse to pick up the speck of dust."

Beginner's Mind or Not Knowing is not being naive. It's entering each moment with an open and receptive mind, without predicting conclusions we really don't know. Behind those ideas of white cop/black cop is a human, perhaps struggling with divorce, a sick child, an unhappy encounter at work, or a child who's an addict. Perhaps he or she was once frightened by a black child at his school. We never know. I always release a full exhale to clear my thoughts and activate my Not Knowing sense before I begin to speak in such situations.

Beginner's Mind is always open. It's difficult to get into too much trouble when we are paying attention to what's happening in the moment. If we trust Big Mind, if we trust relaxing, we may discover that our *intuitions* are far more sensitive than our intellect.

According to current research, intuition is a much older mechanism than intelligence. It activates larger areas of the brain on an MRI scan than logical deductions do. A psychiatrist once explained to me that healthy decision-making involves 80 percent memory, 18 percent emotion, and 2 percent intuition. Given the power of intuition, we only need to use a little, but it's important to keep the channel of communication with it open. Millions of years ago, the little monkey, eating a nut and startled by rustling in the brush, dropped her prize and scampered up a tree. When another monkey, and not a lion, emerged from the foliage and ate the nut, datum was added to her understanding and her perceptions, including her intuition, became sharper. Refined over millions of years in this manner, intuition often exceeds the reach of logical problem solving.

In the Big Mind field and the interconnections of all things, intuition is the only capacity capable of guiding us through the inconceivable Gordian knot of possibilities. I've spoken before about the dangers of attempting to observe ourselves from the outside, as if we could regard ourselves from an imagined viewpoint, as a fact. When we do this, we're attempting to mimic the "objectivity" of science, where a fact in Philadelphia is the same fact in Akron. But that's not how humans live and experience our lives.

We live in the welter of our feelings and thoughts and impulses and sensations, and they have guided us so reliably over the millions of years of hominid evolution that our planet is overcrowded with representatives of our overly successful species. The attempt to be objective appears reasonable enough. If we sense that our personality has biases (it does), wanting to perceive without them to obtain accuracy of information and clarity appears laudable. However, seeing ourselves objectively is an act of the *imagination* not science, because we are still regarding ourselves through the distorted lens of the personality. Our intuitions fire enormous areas of our brains because they combine memory, logic and emotion. We are on much surer footing consulting our intuitions and feelings, and the hunch in our gut than trying to parse every problem logically. Trusting our gut is a more reliable way of moving forward, in a more integrated and collected manner.

Our gut (or wherever your intuition speaks to you) will usually offer us clear directives. "Oh, this guy is fibbing. Okay." Fibbing is not a mortal sin, but now you are alerted. That's the little lightning bolt in the darkness.

17

On Anxiety

·····

July 1, 2020

A NUMBER OF PEOPLE HAVE WRITTEN asking me to discuss anxiety. Given the stressors of the pandemic, it seems appropriate to discuss and include more about dukkha, what it means and how it translates to us right now.

Remember the First Noble Truth in the Buddha's first talk to disciples:

> The noble truth of dukkha, affliction, is this: birth, old age, sickness, death, grief, lamentation, pain, depression and agitation are dukkha. Dukkha is being associated with what you do not like, being separated from what you do like, and not being able to get what you want.*

Dukkha is the mental/physical element of affliction. It's not just that you're sick, or you have a pain, or you've been hurt in a car crash, there's also the accompanying "agitation" of worry and fear of being unable to help oneself, children, or people for whom we're responsible.

During the Covid-19 pandemic's moment of bodies being stacked

---

*David Brazier, *The Feeling Buddha* (New York: St. Martin's Griffin, 1997), appendix 1, p. 185.

in freezer trucks and hundreds of thousands of people ill and dying, dukkha was moved into prominence in our culture. When I watch the TV news reports, the underlying hysteria of the anchors feels barely sublimated and about to break free. Some people respond to fear with rage, others with confusion, and it is hard to blame them as so many norms, rules, and conventions collapse around us; so many social institutions were unprepared and and failed to fulfill their responsibilities. So many things we always considered as firm, fixed, and impregnable are not that it is difficult to maintain one's balance.

It might be useful to remember that life during the time of the Buddha was the same, only worse. Power had few limits. The poor lived lives of unimaginable suffering and death. There was no Bill of Rights guaranteeing civil liberties and equality under the law. No institutions were independent of the monarch. There was no Social Security, no Medicare, no emergency rooms or drugs stores stocked with remedies. While things have certainly improved materially, none of these problems have been completely vanquished by our technology, wealth, and creature comforts, and our mental reactions have changed very little since the time when the Buddha preached 3,000 years ago.

This was the reality he addressed with the Four Noble Truths.

Anxiety takes many forms, sometimes it is masked by an apparent certainty or fought off with anger. It is often related to an interruption in breathing, in the way that hearing an unexpected noise in the middle of the night might make us hold our breath to listen more closely. At other times, it can be so overwhelming it must be pushed below consciousness and one might question whether the degree to which we lavish attention and wealth on sports events, consumer toys, comedy clubs, and our computers and phones is not related to such suppression.

I was speaking to a friend of mine the other day, inquiring how he was doing. He replied, "I'm fine. I'm not worried about this virus at all. It's a hoax." I was shocked because he's a smart fellow, employed in technology and security, and yet, ignoring every credible, monitored data source, he indignantly supported his belief by relaying fringe information and conspiracy theories to me. He turned on his heel to leave, practically spitting, "I thought you was woke."

I was as surprised by his purloining of a Black Lives Matter slogan to describe his plunge into the information netherworld as I was by his wholesale rejection of science and his substitution of a grand paranoid worldview that imagined virtually the entire economic and political world consciously collaborating in a fiction dedicated to drive President Trump from office.

Despite his censure of me for accepting "bullshit," he was adamantly not skeptical at all about his own thoughts and points of view. At one point I asked him for the evidence behind his assertions, and he proceeded with a long and complex rant based on a video he'd seen by "Front-line doctors" refuting the CDC (Centers for Disease Control) and government spokespeople Drs. Brix and Fauci. Later that night, I watched the video he'd mentioned and was stunned by its hokeyness and amateur production values and could not believe that people found it convincing.

One of the doctors, a black African woman, insisted that vaginal infections were a result of "sleeping with demons" (a literal quote)! I felt as if I'd slipped into an alternate reality. "We can open up the society," the video doctors insisted, ignoring all the empirically verifiable data put forward by Drs. Fauci and Brix about masks and the protocol to maintain 6 feet between people to lower the risk of spreading the virus.

I appreciate skepticism, so I researched the video and discovered near unanimity among accredited health experts and physicians, all of whom criticized it for extrapolating from an extremely small subset of the population on the national scale. The individuals in this video were so inept they beggared belief. I wouldn't have let them examine my dogs. My friend had marshaled a vast and seamless web of data from sources that have no published standards, whose authors are often not publicly known, reviewed, or trusted and thus never available for refutation. For whatever problems they might have by being under the sway of advertisers, mainstream news media (which my friend dismissed as bought and sold) *compete* with one another and critique one another for reported inaccuracies. Furthermore, nearly all adhere to the same standards of journalism, which is rarely the case with blogs and internet news sources, which have elevated opinions to the status of facts.

The backdrop to our conversation was a rapidly rising death rate, pleas from emergency rooms to be careful, and bodies being stored in refrigerated trailers because the morgues were full. It felt as if I were standing in a burning building chatting with a man insisting that the danger of fire was overrated and inviting me in for a beer.

My friend's passion, expressed without a scintilla of doubt, led me to believe that he was truly suffering. He was angry and agitated. He felt beleaguered, as if he and his friends were the only people who had seen through the myths blinding the rest of us. He was warning me of the grand hoax being perpetrated on the planet by an unidentified cabal—which involved the Italian government, the Jews, and the Deep State. His list of malefactors was so extensive I would not have been surprised had he included Santa Claus. He felt insulted and condescended to by "the experts" laboring to protect his life. I wondered what it must be like for him to feel that the entire superstructure of society had conspired against him. At that level of anxiety there is no refuge from it. What is more troubling is that apparently tens of millions of people agree with him.

This is not the place for an in-depth discussion of why so many feel that there is a reality going on that is hidden from them. (There is.) Buddha observed that humans enter this world with the evolutionary heritage of greed, hatred, and delusion. If we don't know the reason we are suffering, we create narratives to explain it to ourselves. In the absence of available facts, these narratives may be delusionary. I'll discuss this at a later point in the book, but for now let me just offer that what is hidden from the majority of citizens is the pernicious role that money and its ability to buy political power plays in our political system. The evidence is available on a daily basis that the wealthy and powerful elude the limitations most others face. As the average citizen has found themselves being paid in less valuable money (inflation); as costs skyrocket and they fall farther behind, the desire for power and understanding (in the absence of information) creates these narratives. More to come on this.

One consequence of not understanding our connections to every-thing is that we are left with a tiny isolated self being forced to contend with the immensity of the Universe. This is a nearly universal response. On the political spectrum, this is how poor people often feel—weak and impotent facing the immensity of the power of capital. Such feel-ings generate anxiety because next to the immensity of what surrounds us, we don't amount to much when we remain isolated . . . and yet, we are the center of our world. The conflict between the ego's self-impor-tance and the Universe's lack of favorites is always a losing battle for narcissism.

Anxiety operates from within our self-centered, self-concerned point of view. I don't want to judge anxiety as a negative (though I've never had much fun when I was anxious) because there are many posi-tive protections and defenses anxiety may afford us. Richard Baker-roshi once said, *"Feeling anything is not crazy. Feeling something and not wanting to feel it, is closer to crazy."*

Once we understand that there is no permanent self inside us, being warped, hurt, or damaged by our past or current beliefs and behavior, we can regard our thoughts and inner visions in somewhat the same manner we regard a movie. We can watch Freddy Krueger and the Chainsaw Massacres because we know it's just a projection on a screen. We know the actors remove their makeup afterward and go out and have a drink. Freddy might be dating the woman he just dismembered on camera. Consider for a moment that horror films like this may be a public way of managing anxiety, by giving it a locus and frame as entertainment. We can enjoy the story, without ever considering that it is only the blank screen itself, and its lack of qualities, that makes it the perfect recipient of projections. We don't often consider that our thoughts are projections as well, by-products of awareness and mental energy on the screen of the mind, which, in the final analysis, is also awareness.

Meditation offers us an imaginary perch in that aware space. The *form* of Zen meditation—posture, attention to breath, mudra—sequesters enough of our attention that the mind can't seize and run away with all of it into compelling and hypnotic scenarios. From that secure perch, with a part of our attention insulated from the objects that energize our emotions and mental processes, we can practice observing and accepting the mind and our responses.

Even when we meditate for as little as ten minutes, if we pay attention, we'll perceive little caesuras—little free-zones—in our internal narratives that become more extended the more consistently we do it. We will begin to experience what a quiet, calm mind actually feels like and how accurately and with how little distortion it registers the world. This is not to say thoughts stop—please don't go there—but that they arise and fade without interference, and the mind is neither overly interested nor repelled by them. It requires time and attention to end our addiction to our habitual narratives: "My daddy did this, my mommy did that." Indulging in such reminiscences will insure that we are missing the one and only present moment where our lives are actually lived. Returning over and over to our compelling personal narratives keeps us chained to our personality and its personal history. After clearly witnessing such attachments a moment often may arise when we can't bear to repeat the same whine once more and drop it. To be sure, there are traumas of such severity that personal discipline cannot banish them. They are lodged in the body itself. In cases such as that, therapy is called for and should not be avoided. Meditation is not a panacea.

The thing about suffering (dukkha) and its response (samudaya—what arises) is that it is always related to some conscious or implied grasping or repulsion. Either we don't like what arises and want to push it away (grasping after some alternative state), or we do like it and want to prevent it from changing into something we don't. Perhaps we have an emotional response to something that seems overwhelming—a condition over which we have only minimal control. Whatever arises has snared our personal comparative value system. We either like it, dislike it, or are neutral about it—each of which is a spectrum of judgments we identify as part of "us."

There are methods that I've found helpful for interrogating states like that. First, see if you can identify which thoughts, events, or sensations you're grappling with. Examine them in detail, catalogue the feelings you have about the details. Question yourself: What *don't* I want to change? What *do* I want to change? One of the continually reinforced inducements a fixed self beguiles us with is its perennial hints that it is somehow ultimately malleable and under our control. I was taken by David Brazier's response to this subject.

> When a person who is following this path conscientiously feels anger or disappointment or greed or any such impulse rising up, they do not immediately start to look for someone or something outside themselves to blame . . . they welcome it. For spiritual training this is very profitable, provided that we can keep our nerve, . . . the habit of angry thought, when seen clearly, becomes a source of fire for our furnace.

Suzuki-roshi repeatedly urged his students to "Just say 'yes'"—to accept what's present before us whether we like or disagree with it. The Universe is breathing us and energizing our minds. Much of what passes through our awareness is meaningless except to the degree that it affects our appreciation of this moment. Whatever the situation is, its existence is the product of many previous conditions and states. Observing them as they come and go is different from controlling them. If we don't care what arises, "the mind is no hindrance" (The Heart Sutra).

Let me state unequivocally: saying "yes" does not imply accepting or tolerating actions that violate your moral principles or promote the injustice and oppression of others, to seek shelter in a bland neutrality. Studying our reactions and feelings without ever committing to act on our beliefs is an act of intellectual and moral cowardice. As my friend the writer David Harris observed, "*Unexpressed intentions don't count.*"

Saying "yes" *does* imply that while we try to protect the weak, defuse anger and violence, exercise our free speech, and model alternatives to greed, hate, and delusion we do not sacrifice our state of mind or the Buddha's precepts. One of the reasons we carefully consider our inner directives before acting is because we don't believe everything we think. Too-rapid responses knock us off-plumb emotionally, making it harder to remain helpful to ourselves and others.

Ideas based on the certainty of separate existences and an independent self are an invisible prison, empowering us in many ways and obviously important to our evolutionary history. They narrow our focus to what my beloved college English teacher, Sheldon Zitner, referred to as "well-rounded and half an inch in diameter." It's not as if *self* is false and *everything else* is the truth. In a Universe in which everything is boundaried by and composed of everything else, the formalities of Zen are excellent practice for expressing our essential freedom in the midst of limitation, which includes anxiety.

Suzuki-roshi used to say, "*Everything is perfect until you compare.*"

At this time of national anxiety, America and its cherished and vaunted institutions are losing centrality and trust with the American people. But compared to what? Certainly compared to our past perception of them. However, contrary to popular belief, hindsight is not always 20/20. Our fond memories of our favorite (usually idealized) past may exclude many people who were not allowed to participate in the good times our memories represent. Our memories were certainly based on less understanding than we have today, but they may also be based on prior belief in fictions that comforted us. It should not surprise us that those souls that were not comforted may have run out of patience waiting for us to wake up.

Amazing how "waking"—a measure of high awareness—has been transmuted from the present to the past tense, consigning it to the status of a relic. The term "woke" has apparently driven a number of political figures barking mad and actively campaigning to eradicate it. I suppose it is easier to campaign against a meaningless word than to specify that you are trying to obliterate racial justice, gender equity, free and fair voting, and human rights.

Many people forge strong identifications with their nation (or sports teams, political parties, and social networks). I suspect they consider it an empowering expansion of themselves to a larger, more powerful body. The fact that these teams and parties are usually competitive should give us some clues about the degree to which our ideas of competition ("May the best man win"; "survival of the fittest") factor into our lives. It's not that competition per se is harmful. The idea of testing one's limits against another human, whether a physical or mental challenge, is good. But when competition becomes a metaphor for the entire culture, as ours does, virtually every news story is formatted to be one side versus another (as if there were only two). Our political coverage is always about the strategies the campaigns are utilizing to vanquish one another. Virtually no time is available to study the consequences of any policies in depth.

Imagine how a cooperative model might alter these cultural instititutions.

O

When my teacher first asked me to consider being a priest, I demurred, saying, "No, I'm not ready yet." His response was instructive. He said, "There'll always be others ahead of you, you can learn from, and others behind you, you can help," and that turned out to be true.

At this time of heightened attention to people of different colors and cultures, many of whom are achieving new prominence and success, it's not difficult to understand how many Americans could feel that they had been in line for decades, waiting to receive the bounty

America promised them, only to be replaced by newcomers, often of different races and ethnicities. It's a narrative primed for resentment, and that resentment has common roots in systemic inequities that the victims may not fully understand, despite suffering their consequences. To those feeling perennially left behind, they don't want to hear that historically we have taken unfair advantage of others who, up until now, have not been able to assert themselves and claim their promised rights. If we feel that we, too, have been taken advantage of and are in some degree powerless, then it's understandable why our perspective would be anxious, angry, and threatened, but the problem will not be relieved until it's correctly analyzed. There is much making up to do before America can assert it has become the country it has always claimed itself to be.

Despite our enormous opportunities, America has a long, documented history of taking advantage of the powerless, utilizing its economic power to weaken labor and warp the law to the advantage of the wealthy. Anyone who can read a book can uncover the details of these assertions. Had our underserved (a euphemism for "ignored") populations—especially poor or rural non-college-educated white people—been effectively served by the political system, that groundswell of xenophobia, racism, and the feelings of being replaced by foreigners would never have gained so prominent a foothold. I would posit that people are not defecating in the Capitol because they love ex-President Trump but because they feel betrayed by the system itself.

If I am not getting what I need to survive and others are, it's too easy to believe that there's not enough to go around and those others have been favored over me. The truth is that there *is* enough to go around. There's always enough for sophisticated weapons, huge infrastructure projects, trillions dedicated only to making more money, and giving special advantages to the wealthy, while mothers cannot find affordable day care so they can work. People cannot find affordable medicines. Schools are overcrowded and unrepaired, and lead water pipes are literally crippling future generations. These are called "political problems," but they are really value problems. Watch how a person spends their money and you'll learn their values, despite what they proclaim. The same holds true for our nation.

These values are not carved in stone as the way things must be. They are mechanized by playing needy populations against one another. Should those populations join forces, which implies seeing others as allies and not competitors, they might carry the day, but there are entire industries dedicated to seeing that they never do. Seeing others as competition is another way of describing the spiritual problem this book is addressing.

We project the thoughts, attitudes, and impulses we can't accept about ourselves onto others, to remain blameless in our own eyes, always able to reassure ourselves that we are the good guys. By postponing the processes of reconciliation once-shredded Nations like South Africa, Ireland, Bosnia and Herzegovena have done, we continually postpone cooperative, win-win outcomes.

When we are not anxious or frightened, we can accept our shadow sides more readily, which allows us to take better care of ourselves and others. A divided nation is the product of a self divided into multiple parts. It is, at root, a spiritual problem disguised as politics. We can address the problem from either direction. If my employment is insecure or my salary insufficient, I may become obsessed about too many "others" in the country, even if they are doing work I would never want to do. If I am a member of the majority race and am fixated on what others are receiving, I may not recognize the invisible benefits and privileges I'm receiving, which are often denied non-white or less financially well-off citizens. The operative word here is *citizen*. In a liberal* democracy all citizens are equal under the law (theoretically). If the law is applied

---

*The word *liberal* here does not mean the opposite of conservative as it's used in everyday speech. Rather, "liberal institutions effectively protect the rule of law and guarantee the individual rights—free, fair and competitive elections, Universal suffrage, Protection of Civil liberties—freedom of speech, the press, and associations." Yascha Mounk, *The People vs. Democracy: Why Our Freedom Is in Danger and How to Save It* (Cambridge, Mass.: Harvard University Press, 2018).

differently to different classes, races, or economic strata, such a system is known as an *illiberal* democracy. Though it may retain some vestiges of voting, the system will conscript the law, press, and government agencies under an autocrat's control.

Let's return to the subject of anxiety.

One way to approach anxiety is to become intimate with it. For most people, as I said earlier, anxiety is linked to the shortness or interruption of the breath. If, on the other hand, we're paying attention to our breathing and allowing it to cycle uninterrupted, it serves as a specific antidote for anxiety.

If we allow our anxiety to arise, it will begin to morph into images and narratives that may reveal information we had not yet discovered about it. There's nothing wrong with being anxious, but the *flight* from anxiety, especially if it is thoughtless, can get us into trouble. Consider that your anxiety is a part of you trying to communicate. It has always seemed to me that what we call the unconscious is the body itself. It's where we store things too important to forget, in our muscles and ligaments. Consult your body to discover where your anxiety resides. As you examine it, see if you can find language to describe it, or ask it to reveal images of what it fears to you.

I've had the experience during long periods of sitting zazen of having a muscle or ligament suddenly soften, flooding me with strong emotions. The more you allow your anxiety to communicate, the more you can be compassionate with yourself for being afflicted by it, and the more nuanced your understanding of it will be. Recall Suzuki-roshi's caution on the subject: *It's okay to allow your thoughts in. You don't have to invite them to tea.*

We can't hold on to a good mood and if we struggle against a bad mood we strengthen it in the same way we strengthen a muscle at the gym, by creating resistance. Resisting anxiety means it owns you.

The mind will change on its own. By focusing attention on your breath or posture you can summon your zazen mind. By directing all of your attention completely to one, slow exhale, you will clear and refresh your mind. It's a secret practice that no one will necessarily be aware you're doing. I perform this simple practice before I answer the phone. I don't know who is calling or what events the call might precipitate, and neutrality offers me the most freedom of movement—like driving in the center of an empty road so that if you get a blow-out you have protected room to maneuver in. I practice such exhales before meeting anyone, to enter the moment with a clear mind, not imagining the circumstances but being open to what actually exists in the new moment.

Another practice that is helpful for anxiety is maintaining a Not Knowing attitude. We don't always know the degree to which our anxiety is justified, so why not interrogate it? Why assume you know everything about it? Byron Katie is not exactly a Zen teacher, but then again she's not exactly *not* a Zen teacher. She has developed a four-question interrogation of circumstance and feelings that is quite practical and often useful. She asks:

Question 1: *Is it true?*
Question 2: *Can you absolutely know it's true?*
Question 3: *How do you react—what happens—when you believe that thought?*
Question 4: *Who would you be without the thought?*

She counsels people to turn a troubling thought around, which might mean changing "She doesn't love me" to "I don't love her," or changing "He was so mean to me" to "I was so mean to him" to see what you can learn. Her point is to inhabit these thoughts and see what they do to you. Do they open up space in your thinking and create the possibility of new ways of looking at the subject? It's a kind of restatement of the axiom "Don't believe everything you think." To the extent to which we believe we know things, we believe we may be in some sort of control. But many things we believe are actually delusions. I was thinking about this in the context of the Vietnam War because I heard today on the news that the number of people who have died from Covid-19 in the past three months is now larger than the number of American people who died over the ten or twelve years of the Vietnam War.

In October of 2020, every day 3,750 people were *dying* of Covid. That's the equivalent of a 9/11 catastrophe every day. How could that be a hoax and how could such a hoax be carried out on so grand a global scale? Anyone could call funeral homes, morgues, hospitals and find out the truth for themselves, and yet highly educated adults were insisting that Covid is a hoax, which to me indicates the depth of their fear and/or anger clouding their clarity. It feels more powerful to be angry than frightened. It offers us a feeling of agency and control, which offers the fearful some comfort. However, in the face of catastrophic death counts and the near collapse of our national health system and economy, this self-comforting shift leaves everyone vulnerable. I think there are two things worth noting about this.

The first is that the anger and disaffection is real and virulent enough to elect a potential dictator to the presidency. While there has been extensive investigation into *how* it happened, there was very little introspection as to *why* it happened, because neither party wants to investigate the root cause of immense dissatisfaction in blue collar communities.

The second noteworthy event has to do with what I learned about the Vietnam War narrating the sixteen-hour documentary on the war for Ken Burns and Lynn Novick. Our forces killed three million people in Cambodia and Vietnam. We lost fifty thousand Americans and wounded and traumatized hundreds of thousands more, and then one day it was over. Five U.S. presidents knew the war was unwinnable, yet never told the American people because they could not figure out how to get out of Vietnam and save face. General after general and policy wonk after policy wonk insisted we were "turning the corner" and about to win. Of such flimsy stuff are our certainties made, "and yet" (see chapter 23 for a discussion of Issa's "and yet") the consequences, the trauma, and the suffering remain as a stain on memory and deep suspicion lodged in the hearts of many Americans.

There are many who still do not believe the Warren report on the assassination of President Kennedy. It is not wing-nut conspiracy theorists asserting this, but it was Congress's House Subcommittee on Assassinations which uncovered later evidence of multiple rifle shot at Dealey Plaza, which called the president's murder "a conspiracy." Add to this, distrust concerning the twenty-year war in Afghanistan, Iraq, a host of Savings and Loan failures, and the near collapse of the entire economy in 2008, and one can understand the deep, abiding suspicion of the American people. We may laugh at their uneducated conspiratorial rationales, but we are laughing while they are routinely buying guns and assassinating our fellow citizens and children. Younger people may have forgotten or never known about the war, but many Americans have not forgotten that their government routinely and sequentially lied to them for two decades. Those were not the only lies, either. President Reagan broke multiple laws to run his war against "communists" in Latin America. Democrats and Republicans sat on their hands while wages were frozen from 1973 until a year or so ago, costing every salaried American 2–3 percent a year as normal inflation ate away their net worth. Each and every one of these events caused anxiety and fear as once-middle class families edged closer to or fell into poverty. Social Security has been borrowed against by both parties and not repaid, but all the public is ever told is about the frailty of the system.

One reason Buddhists practice being mindful is so that we can sort and select among what arises over the spinal telephone. What are we thinking in this moment? What are we feeling? Are we being rational, obsessive, indulgent? Kind? Are we in the grip of strong emotions? No matter what, it is *our* job to contain them to prevent them from doing harm to others and the world. That's the point.

Thinking is a mental act, and mental acts prefigure physical acts. I've previously shared the example of how irritation at another driver can lead to giving someone the finger if they cut you off in traffic. And today we have no assurance of what anxious and suspicious people may be carrying in their glove compartments, which could turn an irritated gesture into a deadly incident.

I've struggled my entire life with anger and resentment at bullies. I'll be eighty-two when this book is published now, and after fifty years of disciplined meditation and study, if I'm not paying attention I can still snap off a harsh word as reflexively as one might slap a mosquito. (Something else I try not to do.) The level of observation and calmness required to stay on top of such things is ceaseless, and when our attention is distracted by anxiety and/or fear, we're bound to stumble. Some days it feels as if the entire nation is stumbling.

Zen is no practice for weaklings. I sometimes feel that people have to be deeply troubled or out of options to submit to its disciplines, and yet, without trying, we can still find ourselves contributors to a savage, pitiless world. We are all "Bozos on the bus," as my friend Dick Grace says—by which he means that each human being is unique, but none are special. The surest prescription I know for alleviating anxiety is to help others. I can guarantee that if you shift focus from your own dilemma to consider someone who's suffering and how you might help them, your anxiety will disappear while you are engaged with them.

It may not mean that your problems have disappeared, but they have been altered from a fixation you can neither ignore nor eradicate to one among many claims on your attention, which can be owned and redirected. They will have lost something of their urgency when they are demoted beneath kindness to others, and once you realize that you can contain whatever arises, the mind ceases to be a problem.

It requires some practice to get the hang of this because our minds are endlessly interesting. *My* dramas, *my* story, *my* struggles, the ways *I've* been abused—all personal narratives can remain perennially absorbing, triggering and linking other trains of thought and emotional states into a geodesic-like narrative of great durability. Following these narratives can also lead down an endless rabbit hole that rarely delivers substantial change.

I am not suggesting that personal therapy does not have intrinsic value. I benefitted substantially from it, but for many, the endless preoccupation with personal narrative can become a substitute for doing the work of changing patterns and habits of thought and behavior. If we're not careful, we can find ourselves continually rewriting a mental autobiography titled *Self-Involvement as a Way of Life.*

The most effective method of dealing with anxieties is to face them without shame. Remember the First Noble Truth—suffering exists—reminds us that *Truth* (meaning "real, actual") and *Noble* (meaning "worthy of respect, dignified, courageous") were expressed in this manner because Buddha is reminding us that suffering/affliction happens to everyone. Your problems are not indicators of spiritual insufficiency. The energy of your affliction and arising is also the energy of your positive change. As the old Zen adage reminds us, "The ground you fall on is the ground that helps you rise."

The posture of zazen itself induces strength and confidence. Uprightness, leaning neither into nor away from what assails us, and trusting that our body/mind is a suitable vehicle to experience and contain whatever arises is a profound lesson.

I'm not suggesting self-pacification techniques or tricking ourselves to feel nothing. I'm suggesting toughening up a bit, finding the true grit to experience and interrogate the anxiety, face the fear. You'll eventually be able to say with some deserved satisfaction, "Okay, I can do this." Eventually, "doing it" to help others helps us and demonstrates to all that it is possible. It's the constancy that makes a difference. Zen students do not limit themselves to the possible. Their determination to fill impossible vows is what motivates them and actually secures greater changes than one might have thought possible. The moment-by-moment dedication to model an enlightened life is what Zen master Shohaku Okumura refers to as "living by vow." It's beyond our comprehension, but we do it anyway, requiring only faith in Buddha-nature—our own nature, which is "not one, not two" with the formless, boundaryless energy of the Universe.

18

On Busyness

·····

February 23, 2021

To allow oneself to be carried away by a multitude of conflicting concerns, to surrender to too many demands, to commit to too many projects, to want to help everyone in everything, is itself to succumb to the violence of our times. Frenzy destroys our inner capacity for peace. It destroys the fruitfulness of our work because it kills the root of inner wisdom which makes work fruitful.

THOMAS MERTON

ALL OF THOMAS MERTON'S CAUTIONS could pertain directly to me. I tend to be the type of person he describes, easily carried away by the desire to be helpful and therefore often overwhelmed by a multitude of conflicting concerns.

In the 1940s, I had family members who were Communists for some period of time. They were basically educators and garden-variety union organizers. In the 1930s and 1940s, Communism and Socialism were still recognized as constitutionally protected political *philosophies*. At the end of World War II our political elites recognized that they would be in postwar competition, materially and philosophically, with Russia. For this reason some prosecutors at the Nuremberg trials were instructed by President Truman to be "easy" on certain German scientists and industrialists we might need for the coming competition.* These elites (cultural and political) pursued strategies to ensure that our citizens would not become vulnerable to Communist and Socialist ideas. Apparently, our elites feared exposing the general public to Marx and Lenin's analysis of capitalism. Communists may not have many examples of running a country successfully, but Karl Marx had analyzed capitalism quite clearly and coherently, and even an uneducated American could understand that if his labor generated $5 an hour for his employer and he was only paid $3, then the $2.00 per hour difference, known as *surplus value,* accrued to the employer's benefit.

The policy wonks' antidote to such a state of affairs was to launch a crude plan to link those philosophies with evil and to deprive anyone who subscribed to Socialist or Communist ideas of even the smallest audience. Senator Joseph McCarthy (an uncanny doppelganger for today's Senator Ted Cruz) insisted that all "fellow travelers" (Left-wing sympathizers) were spies or stooges for Russia's dictator, Joseph Stalin. He ran congressional hearings that forced people, under oath, to declare if they had ever subscribed to such ideas or belonged to any organizations or groups that did. If so, those people would be forced to name fellow members or risk losing their jobs. Industry climbed on board and the mere accusation of being "pink, Leftist, or Red" could end one's employment. The atmosphere was so overwrought and hysterical that the highly respected playwright Arthur Miller wrote a play called *The Crucible* about the Salem Witchcraft trials as a way of discussing the mass hysteria and betrayals wracking the country. As a young boy of ten and eleven, I saw adults in my living room weeping and broken as their livelihoods disappeared.

Their ideals were betrayed by the dictator Stalin, and many had left the Communist Party years earlier, but they were never safe from

---

*The person who told me this was a family friend, an attorney named Abe Pomerantz, a prosecutor of German industrialists at the Nuremberg trials.

Senator McCarthy's persecutions. The program was so successful that many today (not yet born in the 1950s) still spin the word *Socialist* as an accusation of evil, with little idea that our military, Social Security, Medicare, veterans' hospitals, police are all public, government-run institutions, not privately owned, and that one of the functions of liberal government is to protect the weak from the predations of the powerful.

Anyone who marched in the streets against the Vietnam War or our "preemptive" war in Iraq could have been tarred by that same brush had they marched in the 1950s. Many idealistic people, caught up in the fervor of what they perceived as a great cause of economic justice and high ideals, also neglected their children and families, extending the sacrifices on all sides.

I certainly did. In the turmoil of the 1960s, in the fever to end the Vietnam War and invent cultural alternatives that would be more sustainable, compassionate, and humane for *everyone's* children, I left most of the raising and nurturing of mine to their mothers or the clusters of dedicated women whom I lived with communally. Those women were the actual source of enduring wisdom: caring for the children, ensuring everybody was fed and in good order, and their quiet and unassuming efforts were usually overlooked, while the world and its media concentrated their attentions on charismatic men.

When I reread Thomas Merton's quote, these memories return to me and, in today's moment in particular, return with vigor. Every day that I open my seventy or eighty emails, the overwhelming majority are desperate pleas for money to fund some critical issue—saving the wolves, the whales, the rivers, Indigenous people, the Barrier Reef, even our government itself. It is ALL worthy of my time, attention, and money, and yet, without concentrating my attention and my resources, it does very little good.

By restraining my own greed and acquisitiveness through daily practice, and modeling the life of a Buddha as best I can, I am following in the footsteps of my political and Buddhist elders, so that others may see and model their efforts after mine, as I model theirs. That is the way that Buddhism is passed through time to "save all Beings."

And yet, despite the dedicated efforts of millions, from every faith and belief, our country and its political system based on collecting and disbursing money continues pumping 35 billion tons of carbon into the air every year, continues selling 400-horsepower cars as "escapes" and symbols of "freedom" as if they had nothing to do with the crazed and terrifying fires and floods scouring the planet. Humans have raised the temperature of the planet 1.85 degrees Centigrade, and another 1.7 degree Centigrade (about .5 F) increase is expected over the next few decades even if all emissions from human activities suddenly stopped.* The hurricanes, fires, and repeated once-in-a-century floods all derive from that 1.8 Centigrade rise. We are moving toward 2 degrees, and the science tells us that by mid-century 2100 CE it will be 3 degrees.

We are making the planet unlivable in the present and condemning our children to a drastically reduced and impoverished future, both biologic and economic. How can it not be the province of spiritual people to address such dilemmas? It can only be if one separates ideas of *matter* and *spirit* in a hierarchical way. That's a direct consequence of conceiving of the world in contradictory terms—self and other.

It's difficult not to be so snared by such facts we might conclude that most of what we consider important in our daily life is indulgence. But the quote by Christian monk Thomas Merton at the chapter head cautions us to be careful, because such thinking can unbalance us.

When we travel by plane we are cautioned that in an emergency, we must put on our own oxygen masks before helping others. The warning is given because airlines have learned that people can become so fixated on insuring their children are masked, that they pass out from lack of oxygen, leaving the children helpless.

Something similar is required with overwhelmingly large and pressing dilemmas. The scale of them can delude us into believing that our

---

*According to the National Climate Assessment Report available on the website of the U.S. Global Change Research Program, GlobalChange.gov.

own lives and concerns are meaningless. If we abandon our children, or our health, or our states of mind in the pursuit of such causes we will be perpetually re-creating the dilemmas.

Sitting zazen requires only enough floor space to sit down. In "vertical" we are working on the core human engine of the worlds' difficulties: greed, hatred, and delusion. We are learning how to keep a clear head and react with calmness, and in times of crisis such people are immensely valuable. Furthermore, people who are usually calm and internally satisfied require less from the world than those who aren't. Brand names, displays of wealth, status competitions are meaningless to calm and generally satisfied people. So for those who would proscribe cutting down on consumption as a worthy goal to secure a brighter future for all, the simple act of sitting still is doing more, with less unintended consequences, than anything I can think of.

The appropriate words rising to mind are *poise* and *balance*. If we take care of the little things thoroughly we are also preparing the future (the next moment) for the larger issues. We can dedicate ourselves to both—and must do so conscious of both *constancy* and the impossibility of attaining purity in our labors.

The ancient Zen riddle (koan) of Fuketsu's speck of dust, which we discussed in chapter 16, speaks to this issue. "If you pick up one speck of dust, the nation will increase. If you do not pick up one speck of dust, nothing will happen."

If you are interested in spirituality or reading this, you are probably not like that and would like to do something to aid people and animals and relieve their suffering. So, you will pick up the speck of dust.

The critically important thing to remember from the previous discussion of Fuketsu is once you pick up the speck of dust, you activate the entire world. You bring everything into being. Here's what Suzuki-roshi had to say about this:

It's not that we just do a good thing. We bring up enlightenment and we bring up delusion. We bring up good and bad. We bring up birth and death—it's all there. It's important that we understand that.

This is the *Genjōkōan* (to manifest or completely share), the complexity of our actual everyday living.

Our job as Buddhists is to help others find their own authentic way, to contact their own fundamental intention, and to keep a wary eye on themselves so they don't harm others, or at least minimize their harm to others. Whenever we attempt to serve our personal point of view of and our personality, the odds are it's not going to go well.

Suzuki-roshi warns us:

> We should not be proud of our faculties, our personality, or our bright, smart mind. When you have a good practice, that is also an enemy of Buddhism. They don't pursue the Buddha Way for the sake of change or for your own personal interest. In the same way, we seek some advantage in our own everyday life. Whether people like what you do or not, it doesn't matter. If it is necessary, you do it.

When we do it, we also know that on some level it is a delusion. We know we are doing good, and we are also doing bad at the same time. It's unavoidable. This is the "full manifestation" the Genjōkōan refers to.

So, what *do* we do? How do we behave in the face of this? One way we can be guided by these facts is to behave tentatively as if conditions might change at any moment. It's important to remember that "good people" are creating bad karma unavoidably, made worse by the fact that we never consider it when we refer to ourselves as the good guys. We have to know fully that every action we take is simultaneously positive and negative, or we can never mitigate the consequences.

We shouldn't be overly bothered by concepts of good and bad, which are relative to one another. We should be concerned that our practice is sincere and supported by Big Mind. When I'm in my thinking mind, I struggle with contradictions like looking after myself and what's helpful

to others? I'm not sure how helpful I am whenever I sign online peti-
tions, for instance. It makes me *feel* as if I'm doing *something* constructive, but I don't know if anyone reads them or cares about them, and
they may be distracting me from more important work. I may just be
delivering my email to marketers, and it certainly interrupts the flow of
what I was doing before the request caught my eye. Signing my name
or giving a little money feels more like virtue-signaling than real work.

One of the things meditation accomplishes is unification of body
and mind. Collectively it unifies individuals with the largest common
denominator—Formlessness or Buddha Mind. When we are sitting,
everything is included in mind-body. The mind-body is not a dualism
made of two parts. When we extend the mind to cover the entire body
it is one thing. Because we are attached to the entire Universe, we can
also assert that when we "sit," the world sits with us.

From that unified perspective we achieve a deepened sense of calmness in which we are not afraid to observe the world as it is. As it *actually* is, as opposed to what the filter of our ideas and concepts and
desires presents to us. Collectively, it allows us to see and feel each other
clearly, making cooperation more viable and easier.

Earlier, I made a point about making sandwiches for the hungry,
because the behavior could be modeled. This also holds true for calmness and kindness, for maintaining your stability and your emotional
poise in the face of rancor and facile arguments. Others can perceive
calmness and concentration, and it calms them as well.

So, in the same spirit of helping yourself first with an oxygen mask,
we need to consider self-care. We're awake twelve to eighteen hours a
day. There's a certain amount that is required of us every day if we are
going to treat our lives respectfully with the attentiveness they deserve.
Maybe it's doing the laundry, caring for children, or being available to
them. These pressures never disappear and are never done. As soon as
you get the laundry washed, dried, folded, and put away, you're already
filling the laundry hamper for the following week.

The question then becomes not *What are we going to do* as much as *How* are we going to do what we must? In the spirit of calmness, with full attention and humor at our own failures, or being blown like a leaf in the wind, constantly interrupted by random thoughts and impulses?

If I were a Yanomami Indian living in the Amazon, when gold-miners and timber cutters invaded my land, threatening my home, I would have to put my ordinary life on hold. I would have to go on war footing to protect my land and my way of life. That's precisely what Indigenous people are doing in the Amazon and at Standing Rock Sioux Reservation in North Dakota, where Native people are resisting the imposition of an oil pipeline crossing their land.

Chevron lost a $9.5 billion lawsuit for poisoning an area the size of Rhode Island in the Ecuadorian Amazon (and simply refused to pay the fine). Numerous American corporations are invading Indigenous tribal areas to extract their exotic timbers and precious metal like gold, silver, palladium, rhodium, platinum, and tellurium "required" by our cell phones and computers for exports for their profits and our comforts. These efforts are degrading the environment, threatening the lives and cultures of Indigenous peoples, but it is difficult for us to connect our beloved cell phones and computers with this destruction. There is nothing about Buddhist practice that demands that we be nice about this.

If you feel deeply that you want to do something, before you do anything, think deeply about what you can do and the best way to maximize your efforts. I have a list of things that I can do. But that list is overwhelmed by the scale of the list of things that I can't do. I can't read every political email begging $8 for Joe Biden. I can't read every letter saying, "Oh my god. Amy is almost beating Mitch! If you just send us $100, we can do it." I have received ten fundraising requests from a candidate to whom I once sent money.

What I'm trying to get at is that neither myself, nor the Indigenous Yanomamis, nor Native Americans nor African Americans can live on a permanent war footing without destroying our lives to some degree by surrendering to bitterness, frustration, rage, or despair. Even people who are on a war footing—Ukrainians at this moment—still discover and foster pauses where they can sing, rest, walk outside, and play with their children. These are not idle concerns. They are vital to our health, and if we want our solutions to be healthy we have to be healthy to conceive them.

The pace and scale at which we live will be the rate at which we may save the world. That pace should be measured by determining a pace and constancy that we can keep going *indefinitely*. It's important to search our psyches and inventory our needs and priorities to discover our limits. Those limits can be expanded by bathing in meditation and by exploring your *fundamental intention and then practicing it with constancy*. What do I most care about constantly, just like breathing?

When you align yourself with your fundamental intention you have embarked on "a path with a heart," and your life will probably go well.

In my experience, Buddhism expresses the largest intention that includes all options I've ever encountered. That's because absolutely nothing—human or nonhuman—is excluded from Buddha-nature. Finding the path with a heart and adhering to it as consciously as we can, consciously dedicating those free moments left after caring for children, family, community—all the myriad responsibilities that we have—will strengthen the boundaries of a dignified, orderly, productive life, the Grand Story that Buddha has introduced us to. If we're not going to burn out and quit, we'll have to set a pace and parameters that we can observe for the rest of our lives.

One of the deepest lessons of my life began at ten years old, the first summer my dad put me to work under our ranch foreman, Jim Clancy. Every day I worked for eight hours with Jim and our hands, Walt Poliskewicz and Bill Jelinek. My friends were off swimming and playing and my sister was at camp, and I was jealous of them but determined to keep up and win the respect of these men whose lives were forged in the crucible of work. There was no going to school in the autumn for them, or catching a lucky break with a cushy job. Life tomorrow would be similar to life today, and that was a life of hard, unremitting work, leavened only by humor and pride in the job you were doing.

What I learned from those men was *pace, standards, and constancy.* They did everything at the same speed and to the same degree of thoroughness. They worked, took a break, had a beer, made repairs, rolled a smoke, played on the local softball team—all at the same relaxed, concentrated pace. This was their life, and they could not afford to burn out. Their lives (like ours) were boundaried by uncertainties. Would it rain when they needed it? Could we get the stones cleared and the fields harrowed and planted early enough to get three cuttings of hay? Would any animals become ill? Would they become injured from their work?

As a culture, we appear to be in ceaseless, restless motion, impelled by our anxiety to "get enough" done. During the Vietnam War, my friends and I were so wounded by the moral transgressions perpetrated in our name—seared by pictures of children on fire, prisoners executed in the street or reports of prisoners being thrown from helicopters. It was unbearable, and I often felt that if I was not impeding the war, I was supporting it or coasting on the privileges our system had afforded me.

I never disparage such moral outrage or the quest to find a moral response to injustice and oppression of others. But I can see how, absent restraint, such feelings can push people of good conscience off center. The suffering drove friends of mine to set bombs in government buildings, go to prison, and pursue virtually any strategy or act to stop the juggernaut of the country's moral disaster. I disagreed with friends who set bombs or plotted armed revolution, but our disagreements were over strategy, not dedication to the goal.

And here's the rub.

In the early 1980s, James Carse was invited to participate with a group of mathematicians to investigate game theory—the mathematics and probabilities of winning conflicts or minimizing losses when you cannot win. Carse was not a mathematician, so he developed other ways of expressing himself. Here is the entire first chapter he published in a book titled *Finite and Infinite Games:*

> There are at least two kinds of games. One could be called finite, the other infinite. A finite game is played for the purpose of winning, an infinite game for the purpose of continuing the play.

There are serious implications for everyday life in this simple chapter. For instance, sporting events are finite games, played to be won. However, without rules and norms they cannot exist. So, if a basketball player should suddenly seize the ball in both hands and race down court, people would be outraged, because they understand that the difficulty of avoiding intercept while dribbling is one of the ways we judge the skill of participants, The difficulty handicaps everyone equally and makes it a game.

However, the United States of America is an infinite game. We play to keep the game going. Prior to President Trump, we never suggested ending the game when a president's term was over. However, the same necessity for rules about norms and laws apply. If players go to any length to win, and seek advantage by violating the rules and norms, they are ending or at least threatening the game of America. That is the part of the equation I didn't understand as a young man.

When an athlete loses, they hold their head up and retreat to study and train harder. They do not (or only rarely) scheme to bribe the referee, challenge the rules, or shout that they were cheated. We instinctively understand that, so in 2015 when Quarterback Tom Brady was suspended without pay for four games from the National Football league, we understood why. "Substantial and credible evidence" proved that Brady knew that his team employees were deflating footballs to give him a better grip. He failed to cooperate with investigators, and he received punishment because both the fans and the NFL knew that cheating would risk the life of the game itself.

In politics, conventional wisdom dictates that those who do not pursue *every means* to win are not trying hard enough and are somehow violating their responsibility to their constituents. They are overlooking that their argument never considers that they might be violating their responsibility to the game of America itself. Sometimes we win, sometimes we lose, but if our goal is to keep the infinite game—humanity, the planet, our nation—alive, it can only be done within the limits and strictures of rules and norms.

It is only today, after nearly fifty years of submitting to the rigors and forms of Zen practice, that those lessons have permeated my muscles and marrow; where my ideas about myself have softened to the degree that whispers of intuition can intercede and restrain my often overbold impulses and return me to plumb. Failing some similar understanding, our public life begins to resemble gerbils running on an exercise wheel, mistaking our effort as progress and deluding ourselves that we are getting somewhere. When I read Thomas Merton's quote today, I can see that he's reminding me of the wisdom and sanity in understanding that there's only so much we can do.

In closing, I want to share one last quote to consider. It was written in the mid-eighth century CE by Shantideva, an Indian Buddhist monk, philosopher, and poet whose reflections on the overall structure of Buddhist moral commitments reach a breadth and theoretical power that is hard to find elsewhere in Indian thought. He was a major influence on Tibetan Buddhism, and one of his two major works, the Bodhicaryāvatāra, is described by the Dalai Lama as his favorite religious work. Shantideva says:

When one sees one's own mind to be attached or repulsed, then one should neither act nor speak, but remain still like a piece of wood.

When my mind is haughty, sarcastic, full of conceit and arrogance, ridiculing, evasive, and deceitful, when it is inclined to boast, or when it is contemptuous of others, abusive, and irritable, then I should remain still like a piece of wood.

When my mind seeks material gain, honor, and fame, or when

it seeks attendants and service, then I will remain still like a piece of wood.

When my mind is averse to the interests of others and seeks my own self-interest, or when it wishes to speak out of a desire for an audience, then I will remain still like a piece of wood.

When it is impatient, indolent, timid, impudent, garrulous, or biased in my own favor, then I will remain still like a piece of wood.

Remaining still like a piece of wood is an apt description of zazen meditation. What I appreciate about this quote is that it catalogues so precisely much of the content that crosses our human minds. It doesn't pretend to be less than fully human and does not require that of us. What it does do is urge us to contain our negative thoughts and urges.

Remember, containment (nirodha) was the Third Noble Truth of the Buddha's very first teaching. We've all experienced these thoughts and feelings; we all know what those words mean. We've all caught ourselves swirling in mental realms that are not necessarily wholesome and positive.

Shantideva reminds us that we can check everything, keep it all behind our teeth and within the stillness of body. We don't have to overreact because someone frightened us when they cut us off. It probably wasn't a personal insult, but we'd rather feel powerful (aggressive) than frightened. To stay stock-still is a kind of discipline that comes from being *concentrated*—which is to say, too balanced to be thrown off your game. Suzuki-roshi referred to such a state as "being the boss of everything." When you are the boss of your internal states, when you can hold whatever arises with equanimity, being neither repelled nor attracted by it, you *are* the boss of everything.

Buddhist practice is based on the disciplines of patience and constancy. To live and practice in the world (as opposed to in a monastery) one must be *very* patient. Ordinary humans are impulsive, angry, vengeful, deluded, and change slowly. When you see through those feelings and impulses and understand that *within* this world and those imperfections enlightenment exists; when we realize that human thoughts, feelings, impulses, sensations, and consciousness are as transparent and empty as soap bubbles, we still must develop patience to deal with the many who may not yet have considered or experienced this. We are all stuck within this delusional world. There is no other place to be. Buddhists included, so we should be cautious about insisting that our way is the best way. If we are going to be helpful to others, we have to help people see for themselves, and most of what they will see is the way we behave and comport ourselves. We can't hurry them along by insistence . . . or ourselves. We can remain still.

19

Wild Body, Wild Mind

· · · · ·

September 16, 2020

FULL DISCLOSURE: THOUGH I NEVER HAD a formal teacher-student relationship with Gary Snyder, I consider him my first teacher and exemplar of Buddhism. He cosigned my first rakusu alongside my formal teacher and I've read and considered his work seriously over many years. I've read Gary's *Practice of the Wild* many times, and each time I learned something new. I want to discuss an essay from that book, "The Etiquette of Freedom," because lately I've observed how our culture has altered the word *freedom* into some unstated but agreed upon national myth about the word, being claimed to justify personal behaviors as diverse as owning a silencer or refusing to mask during the Covid pandemic. Buddhists use the word *freedom* when describing attributes of enlightenment, but the colloquial meaning of the word has been strained by overuse, so some discussion might be appropriate.

Colloquially, the word *freedom* has been massaged to indicate a constitutionally guaranteed right to do apparently whatever we want, whenever you feel so moved. If a city tries to regulate the sale of armor-piercing bullets or prohibit gun sales to persons on the government's no-

fly list, they will be attacked for infringing on our constitutional rights
and god-given freedoms, and the assault is paid for by the American
armaments industry. That connotation of freedom was never the understanding nor the promotion of the Founding Fathers, who at the time
of the crafting of the Constitution did not include women, negroes, or
non-property-owning whites to share the franchise for voting. Snyder
refers to such distortions of language and policy as "consumer baubles."
His description of the Universe we actually inhabit has a specific deno-
tation of freedom.

> Our bodies are wild. The involuntary quick turn of the head at a
> shout, the vertigo at looking off a precipice, the heart-in-the-throat
> in a moment of danger, the catch of the breath, the quiet moments
> relaxing, staring, reflecting all universal responses of this mammal
> body . . . [which] does not require the intercession of some conscious
> intellect to make it breathe, to keep the heart beating. It is to a great
> extent self-regulating, it is a life of its own. Sensation and perception
> do not exactly come from the outside, and the unremitting thought
> and image-flow are not exactly inside. The world is our consciousness,
> and it surrounds us. There are more things in mind, in the imagi-
> nation, than "you" can keep track of—thoughts, memories, images,
> angers, delights, rise unbidden. The depths of the mind, the uncon-
> scious, are our inner wilderness areas and that is where a bobcat is
> right now. I do not mean personal bobcats in personal psyches, but
> the bobcat that roams from dream to dream. The conscious agenda-
> planning ego occupies a very tiny territory, a little cubicle somewhere
> near the gate, keeping track of some of what goes in and out (and
> sometimes making expansionistic plots), and the rest takes care of
> itself. The body is, so to speak, in the mind. They are both wild.

Because the concept of freedom is so central to our political history and culture, and because wildness is often invoked simultaneously
as both the ultimate freedom and the site of savage danger. Because

contemporary definitions have become unmoored from any observable reality, in the spirit of clarification, I'm going to quote Snyder's observations more extensively, because they serve as clarifying intelligence illuminating the darkness of polluted political discourse.

> Like imagination and the body, language arises unbidden. It is of a complexity that eludes our rational intellectual capacities. All attempts at scientific description, of natural languages, have fallen short of completeness. . . . Without conscious device, we constantly reach into the vast word-hoards in the depths of the wild unconscious. We cannot as individuals or even as a species take [credit] for this power. It came from someplace else. From the way clouds divide and mingle, and the arms of energy that coil first back and then forward.

This quote could be a vernacular reference to Buddhist Emptiness and the observation that we are intimately connected with all of it and exist as manifestations of its vast, formless energy. This may strike non-Buddhists as an unsettling surprise.

Humans take pride in our species' unique accomplishments, our domestic sophistication, and our distinctions from (and only rarely similarities to) animals. But we *are* animals. We are indisputably animals with our own specific capacities, quirks, talents, and limits. Most animals are faster than we are. Some can fly. Many can outrun us. Many can eat us, and yet to most humans, *animal* represents a lower order of existence, justified by spurious comparisons between skyscrapers and termite mounds. Snyder specifies the denotations of *wild* more precisely:

> **Of animals**—not tame, undomesticated, unruly
> **Of plants**—not cultivated
> **Of land**—uninhabited, uncultivated
> **Of food crops**—produced or yielded without cultivation
> **Of societies**—uncivilized, rude, resisting constituted government

Of individuals—unrestrained, insubordinate, licentious, disso-
lute, loose

Of behavior—fiercely resisting any oppression, confinement, or
exploitation. Far-out, outrageous, "bad," admirable

What I appreciate particularly about this essay is the way that the
non-anthropocentric view simply ignores the premises of human exceptionalism. It does this by flipping the perspective to observe everything
from Nature's point of view:

Of animals—free agents, each with its own endowments, living
within natural systems

Of plants—self-propagating, self-maintaining, flourishing in
accord with innate qualities

Of land—a place where the original and potential vegetation and
fauna are intact and in full interaction and the landforms are
entirely the result of nonhuman forces, the natural excess and
exuberance of wild plants in their growth and in the production of quantities of fruit or seeds

Of societies—societies whose order has grown from within and
is maintained by the force of consensus and custom rather
than explicit legislation; societies whose economic system is in
a close and sustainable relation to the local ecosystem

Of individuals—following local custom, style, and etiquette
without concern for the standards of the metropolis or nearest
trading post; unintimidated, self-reliant, independent; "proud
and free"

Of behavior—artless, free, spontaneous unconditioned; expres-
sive, physical, openly sexual, ecstatic

It is worth recognizing that Snyder is, in each of these examples,
refining the definition of *wild* to mean "self-regulating." Redwood
trees grow for redwood trees; mullein for mullein; skinks pursue their

biological chores for skinks; deer, mice, voles, and pumas are equally dedicated to their own purposes. Each has its own gifts and limits, but all share the same energetic operating system we call life, which, if anything, includes awareness among its categorical definitions. It is multidimensional and nonhierarchical, except in our own minds, which insist on regarding humans as the apex species, the tip of the spear of evolution, demoting all other forms of life to secondary and tertiary status without becoming aware that it is the ruler and terms of measurement creating the hierarchies.

In precisely the same way, humans normally privilege the idea of a self as the king of the mind-body dichotomy. This may go some way toward explaining the general rudeness and ignorance of Western humans when dealing with nature.

I had a friend a long time ago named Tim Treadwell who became fascinated with grizzlies, the hump-shouldered, 400- to 650-pound behemoths of the bear world. A black bear, by comparison, may weigh 200 to 300 pounds, with claws about an inch and a half long, compared to the six-inch claws of a grizzly.

Tim began traveling regularly to a remote Alaska island where the bears congregate in numbers during the salmon runs, generally observing peaceful relationships as they hunt the upstream swimmers to store up winter fat. For thirteen summers Tim communed with the grizzlies there, writing to me about the mystical connections growing between them, and once including snapshots of a grizzly bear laying his suitcase-sized head across Tim's legs and napping.

It scared me to see his belief in magical thinking about a cross-species "understanding" between them that would make the bears "love" him. I told him so unequivocally, writing with some urgency: "Tim, this is not a good idea. These are independent creatures, not your buddies. Your affections are not theirs. They have their own ways and you need to respect those differences."

We all have the freedom to be deluded. On October 5, 2003, Tim and his girlfriend, Amie Huguenard, were both killed and devoured by a single large rogue bear. The microphone in their video-camera was on during the bear's attack, and the soundtrack of their grisly deaths recorded Tim's last words, which were to Amie—"Get out of here. I'm getting killed."

Werner Herzog, the celebrated German film director, made a documentary about Tim titled *Grizzly Man*, and in that film, Herzog listens to the couples' last moments through headphones and cautions Tim's longtime friend and former girlfriend Jewel Palovak, "You must never listen to this." The rogue bear was eventually killed, and in the film, the two intact spines of both Tim and Amie are recovered from the bear's belly. I repeat this story to introduce the idea of respect as one of the critical limits to freedom and wildness.

Both self-respect—treating yourself with the care and consideration that a devotion to the natural world might inspire—*and* treating everything *else,* such as butterflies, habitat, dolphins, frogs, and salamanders, with commensurate respect, follow directly upon the perception (or at least intuition) of a universal, formless, boundaryless energy web Buddhists refer to as Buddha-nature and considered a common denominator of Creation. If individual plants and species could be considered sacred, how much more so should we consider the source? The observation that our lives interpenetrate the lives of other species, wild creatures (including plants, animals, and geography), might normally induce respectful behavior without much effort if we were not blinded by our personalities and "civilized" responsibility to exploit and "improve" everything according to personal, human standards.

On the news the morning I was writing this, during a discussion of this season's raging wildfires. My old boss, Governor Jerry Brown, responded to an interviewer's question about his opinion of the fires with remarkable clarity. The governor pointed out how the scale and ferocity are unlike anything he ever witnessed in his long lifetime. He continued by analyzing the political failings that to date have done nothing to check our destructive human behaviors so antithetical to natural systems, saying, "I've been a politician for fifty years. I've seen the good, the bad, and the ugly. I've never seen anything like this. I've never seen such a dereliction of duty."

The consequence of such "dereliction," he continued, compounded by the accumulated carbon release of a culture animated by the burning of fossil fuels, will require us to spend billions and billions of dollars managing our forests; hiring more firefighters; building more helicopters, tanker planes, fire trucks; and prohibiting people from building wherever they want. If we shirk or fail in this endeavor, we will bankrupt ourselves by continual rebuilding, which will be decimated by the next fire.

That chain of events, a direct consequence of extreme drought and "global warming" (the corporate-approved term for climate change), has raised the planet's temperature and reduced snowfall, so that what does reach the earth is dissolved too precipitously by warm rain before it can leach into and replenish the aquifers.

The trees and underbrush are tinder dry. Heat lightning in August 2019 was unprecedented, and heat strikes caused 650 fires. This is the world our extractive economy and indulgences have created. We have not, as a culture, accepted responsibility for these failures.

When Snyder mentions freedom from responsibility to civilized societal norms he is *not* advocating for dismissing responsibilities to *compassionate* norms and compassionate regard for other forms of life. Humans caused these problems, in part by imposing small-mind, self-centered notions on wildness and doing so with no sense of reciprocity or mutual responsibility. Do we really believe that nature exists as an inert potential, remaining dormant until "improved" by humans? Another name for such rationalizations is greed.

The poet Robert Bly once observed that one of the first "civilizing"* events on the Kansas and Oklahoma frontiers occurred when women

*I have always understood Bly's use of the word *civilizing* as ironic, because I don't believe he had any intention of denigrating the evolved, Indigenous Plains cultures—centuries-old farming-hunter communities and the later horse cultures that began in the seventeenth century—as uncivilized.

received mail-order Sears catalogues, introducing them to a plethora of "time-saving, labor-saving" machines and attractive goods from the distant cities. The men saw useful tools and wanted them as well. As a consequence of these desires, they were forced to transform the thick, fertile soil of the ancient, undisturbed tall-grass prairies into money—a nearly impossible task given the tools they had at hand. Some of the natural grasses had roots that grew 12 feet into the earth.

In 1837, a young blacksmith named John Deere cast a very smooth, self-cleaning, moldboard plow blade that cut through these roots and turned over extremely deep furrows. The process of turning America's once bountiful prairies and savannahs, one of the richest ecosystems on Earth, into the Dust Bowl of the 1930s had begun.

The early settlers of the frontier (the edge of civilization opening onto the vast panoramas of the West) resolved their "Indian problem" by exterminating their primary food source—500 million buffalo, a creature perfectly tuned by evolution to this environment, a nimble grazer who eats while moving, whose consumption of grass does not rip it up by the roots. The buffalo were replaced with an equal number of cattle from riverine Asia that traditionally passed their days knee-deep in water while uprooting their food. Their newly formulated pastures were thenceforth defended by the United States military.

I want to share another cultural memory of the frontier from Gary's piece, to remind us of another boundary that we failed to acknowledge but that we may still possess enough honor to recognize.

It is often said that the frontier gave a special turn to American history. A frontier is a burning edge, a frazzle, a strange market zone between two utterly different worlds. It's a strip where there are pelts and tongues and tits for the taking. There is an almost invisible line that a person from the invading culture could cross out of history and into the perpetual present. A way of life attuned to the slower and steadier processes of nature.

The possibility of passage into that myth-time world had been all but forgotten in Europe. Its rediscovery, reminding many of the unsettling vision of a natural self, has haunted the Euro-American people as they continually cleared and "roaded" the many corners of the North American continent as if it were God's own mission to scrub the place clean of it wildness.

Wilderness today, for much of North America, are places set aside from commercial development on public lands, managed by the Forest Service and Bureau of Land Management. These are the shrines saved from lands that were once known and sustainably exploited by the original people—the last little bits left, as they once were. Today, such places represent only 2% of the land of the United States, the last little places where intrinsic nature still "wails," playing its own jazz, with what remains of its original orchestra.

When settlers came here, a choice existed they could have made, if their imaginative bandwidth had not been stuffed with their own cultural narratives and history of Europe. They might have taken the equivalent of a deep breath, looked around and understood, "Oh, *this* is the appropriate way to live in this place."

Western European culture executed a devious pivot (with powerful unanticipated consequences) around the beginnings of the European enlightenment. For all the benefits logic and scientific analysis afforded human culture, the lineage of Descartes and Newton—urban geniuses with little patience for the apparent chaos and disorder of Nature—conceived the Universe as a mechanism, and perhaps with no intent, by attacking the mysteries of Earth, banished spirit to the sky, the province of their Christian sky god. This left the rest of matter on Earth to be considered as "resources" to be recombined, swapped, and altered like auto-wreckers exchanging parts. Perhaps one reason the new immigrants were not awed and intimidated into respect by the majesty of a 750-year-old redwood tree or the millions of acres of grassland, to the point that they refused to cut them down or plow them under, might be because by the time they arrived they no longer regarded anything on

Earth as a spiritual entity. Therefore, no cautions, protocols, ceremony, or even remorse was required when virtually every form of life on the new continent was transformed into articles of use to humans. They were taken with no fear of offending a Creator who had given them "dominion" over the planet. With the extinction of Indigenous people, the banished spirits had no spokespeople, and for those who remained, their perception of animals, plants, and trees were consigned to the realms of superstition or resources.

We are all mired in the karma of our forebears' historical biases and choices. We cannot blame only the Abrahamic religions—Judaism, Christianity, and Islam. Judaism was the product of a nomadic herder culture, and it was their creation myth (Genesis)* that codified human *dominion* over the Earth. It's not well understood that the concept of dominion derives from a translation of the ancient Hebrew word *yiredu,* from the root word *radah,* meaning "to subdue." Absent any concept of responsibility or reciprocity (the sole protection against historical indulgences of freedom), subjugation blossomed as an irresponsible, extraction economy, ravaging the natural world.

Perhaps because the commission members assembling and revising the King James Version of the Bible were serving a king, they felt that such a translation of *dominion* might be appropriate, but learned, contemporary rabbis say that this translation is incorrect—the root word of *dominion* is not *viredu* at all, but *yarad,* which means to "come down, to lower oneself." The mistake is worth noting because it demonstrates the way small things may have outsized consequences. It is explained this way:

Seven hundred years after the birth of Christ, the Masoretes (Jewish scribes in Palestine, seeking to standardize pronunciation and grammar in Hebrew) put a *chireq* (one dot) under the Resh in yarad,

---

*Every culture has its own creation myth. Genesis is on a par with but not superior to the Kalevala, the Epic of Gilgamesh, the Babylonian Enuma Elish, the Akkadian Atrahasis Epic, the Blackfoot Colored Language Water, or the Aboriginal Rainbow Serpent. It's a story—a comfort to "explain" the way things are. It is not law.

[the twentieth letter of the Hebrew alphabet, sound R, meaning "poor," "wicked," "head"], making this the root word *radah,* which means "to subdue." Had they put a *tsere* (two dots) under the Resh they would have had the root word *yarad,* which means "to come down or lower oneself." The original inspired Word of God had no dots and I believe this old rabbi was correct in using the root word *yarad* (to lower oneself) rather than *radah* (to rule over). In the original Hebrew the word starts with a Yod [the tenth letter of the alphabet, meaning the "power of God," often simply a dot], which is a picture of a heavenly messenger, or *yarad,* which means to lower oneself, and not a Resh, which means to rule over.*

I choose to believe this because the love and respect of Nature seemed to be a universal quality among humans before the Enlightenment.

It would be ironic if something as inconsequential as a misplaced dot justified millennia of unabated extraction and exploitation of nature by our forebears. If true, the consequences are beyond ironic—they are tragic.

Failing to consider interdependent (spiritual) dimensions, the embrace of convenience has gradually lulled Abrahamic cultures into believing that dominion implies the "freedom" (there's that word again) to do whatever we want with natural "resources." The consequences of that uninterrogated belief (which also implies human independence from all restraints and obligations, which is another way of describing human superiority) have scorched, parched, and dismantled our incredibly rich and interconnected world, passing that bias down as an intergenerational toxic legacy. Once humans perceive themselves as separate from nature, dominion becomes the rationale for exploitation and convenience the rationale for excess. Actions have consequences, and the karmic traces of those decisions can be seen in the culture they nurtured.

---

*According to "Hebrew Word Study: Dominion," ChaimBenTorah website, June 4, 2015.

In 1904, Henry James returned to America after an absence of more than twenty years. In his book *The American Scene,* a diary of his travels and observations upon return, he describes the changes he observed since his departure. In this quote he observes the relationship to Native Americans.

> Beauty and charm would be for me in the solitude you have ravaged, and I should owe you my grudge for every disfigurement and every violence, for every wound with which you have caused the face of the land to bleed. . . . You touch the great lonely land—as one feels it still to be—only to plant upon it some ugliness about which, never dreaming of the grace of apology or contrition, you then proceed to brag with a cynicism all your own. You convert the large and noble sanities that I see around you, you convert them one after the other to crudities, to invalidities, hideous and unashamed; and you so leave them to add to the number of the myriad aspects you simply spoil, of the myriad unanswerable questions that you scatter about as some monstrous unnatural mother might leave a family of unfathered infants on doorsteps or in waiting rooms.*

James's choler caused his nervous American publisher to excise this paragraph from the American version, but it was retained in the English edition.

Previous to the European invasions, Indigenous minds were everywhere exploring, cataloguing, cross-breeding plants and other species and learning to coexist with them. This would have been visible to anyone who took the time to consider what they saw. Modern scientists have calculated that in forests where Indigenous people lived, nut-bearing trees were 40 percent more prevalent due to the care and breeding by Native American farmers. I am assuming that this human-managed

---

*From Peter Brooks, "Visions of Waste," review of *The American Scene,* by Henry James, ed. Peter Collier, *New York Review of Books,* March 24, 2022.

bounty contributed to the observation of natural wealth motivated the European settlers toward ethnic cleansing and genocide.

The logic blooming in the European Enlightenment had, among other things, selected a mechanistic model as a metaphor to explain the Universe. Just as in Genesis, the serpent who bewitched Eve is the creature closest to the earth; the devil's hooves, tail, fangs, and hairy haunches represent nature as evil. That which was closer to spirit (God's sky home) was privileged over the matter of Earth. The life of the mind was celebrated over the life of the body, and the domestic over the wild. Even the orderly pre-Enlightenment feudal farms and households of Europe remained in intimate dialogue with wildness, leaving hedgerows and drainages as borderland spaces hospitable to other species; in America these were ravaged by the economic power unleashed by machines and mechanistic modeling beginning to generate unimaginable secular wealth.

Consider how a line of nineteenth-century U.S. calvary horsemen closing for battle with Sioux or Comanche warriors appeared to these guerrilla fighters. Spread out in a line, identically uniformed, wielding identical rifles and sabers as they approached. They were actually imitating a mowing machine. It was the superiority of American technology (repeating rifles) and their compartmentalization—there were no women and children traveling with them to be cared for—not military strategy, courage, the Abrahamic God, or the benefits of the civilized mind that vanquished the Native's anarchic battle practices which featured public displays of bravery.

Today, absent any Native threat, twentieth- and twenty-first-century descendants of Western European settlers wax nostalgically about Native Americans. They adopt Native jewelry and aesthetics to signal love of the Earth and the ancient values in the iron and steel cities built over the ancient villages and fields. Wealthy white women in Santa Fe sport intricate, old squash-blossom silver necklaces Native artisans had to pawn to buy silver and dyes for the intricate blankets, which today can sell for hundreds of thousands of dollars—wealth now funneled into art galleries, museums, and the homes of wealthy collectors. There is an ambiguity to the display, a simultaneous appreciation of a complex aesthetic and the flaunting of battle trophies by the victors. Despite the advertised ecologically harmonious lifestyles of the Range Rover set and Chevron's "green" advertisements, neither the environment nor the Natives have fared well under dominion of the people of the plow and refined oil.

The conflict between the two cultures was a collision of belief systems and minds—wild and domesticated. For the Natives, wildness was the Great Spiritual model. Their continent was filled with autonomous beings—plants, animals, birds, insects, and humans—who had to be negotiated with and whose deaths were placated with ceremonies and meticulous use. Like Buddhist Emptiness, the Great Spirit was the formless energy expressed as the various "peoples" of the animal, plant, and human communities. Birch trees were propitiated before being skinned of bark for canoes.

For the Europeans, the physical world had, centuries before, been reduced to matter, and, in that environment, newly severed from spiritual constraints, America was a tabula rasa of opportunities, unencumbered by the history, husbandry, spirituality, conservation norms, and customs of Europe. What was left on Earth and after spirit had been banished to Heaven was reduced to resources for the benefit and exploitation of man.

A lifetime of observation leads me to believe that despite our preoccupations with riches and distracting entertainments, the hunger for the human birthright of undivided wild minds still resonates at deep personal and cultural levels. Our earliest experience as infants is such an undivided state, and who is to say to what degree dim memories of such "wholeness" may be animating the rise of interest in Buddhism or whether the despoilation of our only home has awakened the need for more sustainable values among many people.

The Pew Research Center estimates the current number of American Buddhists at about 4.5 million, predicted to rise to 6.5 by 2050. There are more than 15,000 organizations registered as either environmental or animal-care organizations in the United States, and in his book *Blessed Unrest,* author Paul Hawken, after global research and study of the hundreds of thousands of small environmental clusters fighting to save a local creek, watershed, forest, or species, declared environmentalism as "the world's largest movement."

A shaman may appear to be curing only an individual, but he or she is actually adjusting the dynamics between human and natural communities, practicing a diplomacy of health. While New Age magazines are filled with advertisements of self-appointed shamans, the Indigenous cultures that specialized in such human/natural mediations remain impoverished and ignored. Perhaps it never occurs to Europeans to pray, apologize, or entreat Nature itself after having been inculcated with the notion that matter and spirit are mutually exclusive for so many centuries; as in most relationships, poor communication fosters misunderstanding..

Bars are filled with people who can't stand to be alone. Drug addiction, alcohol addiction, gambling addiction, sexual addiction, addiction to power and status, shopping addictions—all are attempts to stop or mask the flow of thoughts and associated feelings that people, for one reason or another, cannot abide and have never learned to master.

While the *content* of each person's feelings may be radically different, everybody understands anxiety, joy, pride, fear. No two personal histories are exactly alike, but movies, theaters, gossip, and empathy offer proof of the commonality of human feelings.

Zen practice actually fills and serves the overlooked niche that we're all in this together—walking around in the starlight, stepping over the graves of our forebears, sleeping, eating, pooping, fornicating, raising our young as every species has done for millennia. If we dwelled more on our commonalities with other species, humans might be less convinced about our assumptions of superiority. We could, with wilder minds educated to recognize interdependence, diversity, the sacredness of creation, promote them from their current third or fourth place status and renew the world sheltered beneath the common umbrella of awareness and the energy field—of which wildness is the clearest, handy example.

In 1980, when Mount St. Helens, the largest active volcano in the Cascade Range, erupted, scattering trees like toothpicks and decimating 22,000 square miles with lava flow, intense heat, and flames, it did not take long before plants were returning, sending shoots aloft like green gas flares. As browse returned, so did wildlife, in a picture-perfect expression of the regenerative powers of Nature. We humans might consider imitating the example of wilderness and its diversity as a better indicator of value than assigning worth to only those species that primarily serve human ends.

Yes, it is difficult to witness the enormously destructive fires of the past several years in Sonoma and Napa Counties, where I live, and to witness the suffering that accompanied them. But in terms of a threat to Nature, while *any single thing* can be destroyed, that is not the case with *all of it*. It will return. It may, however, return in a much diminished form. Neither is it preordained that our human species will return with it or that we must build our houses in the midst of forests.

Dylan Thomas's lovely line, "The force that through the green fuse drives the flower," is a circuitous way of describing Emptiness/wildness as well. The kinetic energy of formlessness is driving us, driving the clouds. It is driving the flowers to rise among the ghosts of trees. It drives us, breathes us, beats our hearts ceaselessly, and eventually, under the loam itself, continues to propel us, even there, on its own terms, transforming laughter and tears into beetles, mushrooms, worms, and mycelium networks.

When we sit zazen, because we are Nature itself, we should not be fixating on ideas of personal enlightenment as a divisible, imagined state outside of and apart from our normal awareness. The *idea* of our personal enlightenment is like the idea of a personal self that we can wash and wax, groom and clip into a perfect artifact. It's just another tricky reformulation of self-centered thinking that eventually traps us in the tiny pit of self-concern. The "I" sitting on the cushion, imagining enlightenment somewhere else, is creating a pitiless dualism from which it cannot escape. Conceiving of self and other as two different things reifies them as separate. The map is not the territory. Welcome to the land of contradiction.

More and more people, hopefully, are arriving at the conclusion that something new (or very ancient) has to occur if we are to escape the dire consequences of our species self-service. We have to drop below or step aside from our habitual, self-centered narratives and descriptions to experience the basic quality of the mind itself. This is where meditation proves itself invaluable. Sometimes this stepping aside occurs at our limits of endurance, when we have exhausted "our personality"; at other times, through consistent practice, we ripen more gradually and may be startled one moment to re-cognize (which literally means "to become aware of or know . . . again"!). An utterly familiar event, a bird's call, a slammed door, or, as Dogen once experienced, smoke swirling off the incense at his mother's funeral, can be perceived as "a letter from Emptiness." When that occurs, we have reentered the wild country where we can recover our sense of trust in wildness and understand that we possess the freedom to do something totally unexpected and new in the next instant—which is what the word *nirvana* actually indicates.

We never know when that signal is going to jingle our spinal telephone, but whenever or whatever, once we recognize the call, welcome and allow it to reconnect us with what has always been here, and we will regain our original permission to exist at times in an undivided state.

20

Misunderstanding Emptiness

·····

June 3, 2020

MY FATHER HAD A FAVORITE EXPRESSION he'd usually remember immediately after I had uttered one of my adolescent "truths" in a way that indicated my certainty of its veracity. He'd continue whatever he was doing for a moment or two and then, as if speaking to himself, would say, "A little knowledge is a dangerous thing." The older I grow, the more correct his observation appears.

There is a danger that resides in a superficial understanding of Emptiness, and it's easy to see why. If, as the Buddha proposed, all things are truly empty of a fixed self, and the implications of this are spelled out well by physicist Carlo Rovelli in his lovely book *Helgoland: Making Sense of the Quantum Revolution,* when he discusses writing of Nāgārjuna, a second-century CE philosopher.

> The central thesis of Nāgārjuna's book is simply that there is nothing that exists in itself independently from something else . . . If nothing exists in itself, everything exists only through dependence on something else, in relation to something else. The technical term used by Nāgārjuna is "emptiness . . . There is no ultimate or

mysterious essence to understand. That is the true essence of our being . . . Conventional, everyday existence is not negates; on the contrary, it is taken into account in all of its complexity, with its levels and facets. It can be studied, explored, analyzed, reduced to more elementary terms. But there is no sense, Nāgārjuna argues, in looking for an ultimate substratum."

Rovelli takes Nāgārjuna's radical departure from Western physics and its search for a "something" from which everything evolves, as a valuable gift in studying quantum theory. He is a deep thinker, but it's clear from this that the perception could also generate another train of thought. If everything is no more than a nexus of energies and awareness without permanence, then why should we not steal, murder, or oppress to achieve what we want? In such a Universe wouldn't it be like bursting soap bubbles or beating a bag of cotton? No harm done. Why, then, worry about precepts and edicts about behavior?

The Buddha was aware of this potential for error. It is the reason that his insights are strictly framed by ethics. What the superficial thinker overlooks is that if Buddha-nature, the nature of the Universe itself, expresses itself in infinite forms, the careless observer still believes in a hierarchy of values that declares some manifestations more worthy than others. They certainly are to our egos and personalities—but they are as precious as hummingbirds and infants to the Universe, because they are the Universe itself. And if that is not sacred and worthy of worship, what is? Believing that Emptiness devalues the physical world would be like walking into the Vatican, defacing a mural of the Virgin Mary, and declaring, "It's only a painting."

It is in the context of such devaluation that we need to examine events like the death of George Floyd. I'm certain that nearly every American is familiar with the events of May 25, 2020, when African American George Floyd was murdered by police, in full public view on a street in Minneapolis, Minnesota. The police had responded to a call from a store owner who'd accused Mr. Floyd of trying to pass a counterfeit $20 voucher to buy some cigarettes. Four police officers responding to "a forgery in progress" apprehended him. Videotape from the scene reveals him to have been fully compliant with police commands prior to being forced to the ground.

Mr. Floyd's death was particularly egregious, not only because of the triviality of the offense for which he was charged but also compounded by the fact that he was handcuffed and posed no possible threat to the officers. Moments before, sitting on the sidewalk, calmly chatting with an officer, fully present, tranquil, and alert. So what we witnessed on the video was a public execution by police over an unresolved issue of a possibly counterfeit $20.00 bill. The execution was a chilling display of human cruelty compounded by the policeman's taunting his victim: "Hey bro, you want to get up and get in the car now?" Aside from the irony of addressing a man you are choking to death as "brother," the officer made no motion to raise his knee from Mr. Floyd's neck, and in fact adjusted his weight to get a better purchase on it.

African Americans have been describing such murderous assaults by police since slaves were freed, but until cell phones afforded the white population video proof of their claims, the majority routinely accepted the assurances of policemen that they "feared for their lives" and the official miscreants escaped accountability and punishment. The complaints of African Americans were often dismissed as being overly sensitive.

The three policemen who aided the murder by standing around or kneeling on some other part of Mr. Floyd's body were fired immediately, and Officer Chauvin, the officer kneeling on his neck, who had eighteen complaints against him on the official record, was involved in three police shootings, and received two letters of reprimand for misconduct. He was eventually sentenced to twenty-one years in prison.

Many people wondered why Officer Chauvin had been allowed to continue his service after receiving *seventeen* previous citations for violence on his record. The Asian officer, Tou Thau, who was assisting Mr. Chauvin had eight violations and more complaints on his record, *yet none of these charges had derailed either man's careers* or prevented future offenses. How had these men escaped disciplinary proceedings? Why weren't their immediate supervisors and the mayor and board of directors not included in these charges?

The unexpurgated American history that many parents no longer want taught to their children reveals that police departments since the end of the Civil War treated African Americans as a threat to be controlled. Adjusted for population, black men are 2.5 times more likely to die at the hands of police than white men. African American women are 1.4 times more likely to die at the hands of law enforcement, according to a National Academy of Sciences study. According to a 2019 study from Rutgers University, 100 out of 100,000 black men versus 39 of 100,000 white men die at the hands of police.* As they say, we are free to have our own opinions, but not our own facts.

Leaving the nuances of racism aside for a moment, consider the social implications of this disparity of treatment. One sector of American citizens is dying at the hands of tax-funded public servants more than twice as frequently as another. *If the privileged section does nothing to insist on equal protection under the law for all citizens, would it not appear to others that they are sheltered by those privileges or do not consider the unprotected population as worthy of the rights the privileged receive?* Does this not force the question of how seriously we Americans *believe* in the values we claim to cherish—the protections of the Constitution and Bill of Rights, our laws and the standards we set for the people who must see to their enforcement?

From a big picture perspective, perhaps one in a thousand deaths of black men sounds minuscule, unless of course you happen to be related to or identify with any of them, have suffered brutal encounters with police yourself, or have difficulty accepting privileges that are

---

*Race itself is an invention of people who consider themselves superior. There's only one race—the human race—and any of its members can interbreed, which makes them the same species.

denied your fellows based on meaningless distinctions like how much melanin* is in their skin. George Floyd's death floats on the surface tension of racism and Jim Crow and centuries of deaths and protests, which began long before I was born. Such events have no sell-by date; they are as current in black communities as the Holocaust remains for Jewish people, or for Armenian relatives of those massacred by the Turks, or victims of Pol Pot's death camps in Cambodia, or the Irish murdered in the "troubles" with the British. In every case, lore passed down in family and social gatherings transmits the knowledge of the crimes from generation to generation, keeping history alive, if they have not been certified by personal experience.

And now, for just a moment, consider the implications of these executions for Caucasian people. Pastor Martin Niemöller was a German Lutheran pastor and a theologian who had a very intriguing and complex life. Born in 1892, the son of a Lutheran pastor, Niemöller's first career was as a submarine commander for the German navy during World War I. Apparently, he was a pretty good sub commander and was awarded the Iron Cross. Rather than stay in the navy after the war, he decided to become a pastor in the Lutheran Church. In the postwar period, he became alarmed at Hitler's rise to power, began speaking out forcefully against his racist views, and was imprisoned in Dachau concentration camp from 1937 until 1945. He is best known for this passage from a sermon that he gave after the war.

First they came for the socialists, and I did not speak out—Because I was not a socialist.

Then they came for the trade unionists, and I did not speak out—Because I was not a trade unionist.

---

*While I use *black* and *white* colloquially in conversation, they are shorthand. I know no humans the color of my toilet, or my father's black Cadillac. Those terms actually measure the degree to which members of the designated races can count on protections from the state. I believe it's worth remembering when we employ these words casually.

Then they came for the Jews, and I did not speak out—Because
I was not a Jew.

Then they came for me—and there was no one left to speak for me.

Less well known is the story he recounts of his visit to Dachau
concentration camp with his wife after the war.

I stood with my wife in front of the crematorium in Dachau, and on
a tree in front of this building was a white-painted board with black
lettering. . . . There one could read, "Here in the years 1933–1945,
238,756 people were cremated." While I read it, not aloud, I noticed
that my wife fainted and sank trembling into my arms. I had to support her and noticed how, at that moment, a cold shudder ran down
my spine. I think my wife fainted when she read the quarter-million
number. That hadn't moved me. Because it didn't tell me anything
new. What ran through me hot and cold at that moment was something else. That was the other two numbers: "1933–1945." I groped
for my alibi and knew that the two numbers were the wanted poster
for the living God for Pastor Niemöller. My alibi reached from 1937
to 1945. Yes, I know, from 1937 until the end you had an alibi. Here
you're being asked "where were you from 1933 until 1937" and I
couldn't avoid this question any longer.*

Pastor Niemöller is interesting because he was an imperfect man,
"unevenly developed," as we describe ourselves and other imperfect people in Buddhist practice. He was an early supporter of Hitler and made
so many anti-Semitic comments and tried so forcefully to soften Allied
punishment of the German people that after the war Rabbi Samuel
Wise, a prominent pro-democracy liberal and later founder of the
World Jewish Congress, objected to Niemöller's tour of America under

---

*Matthew D. Hockenos, *Then They Came for Me: Martin Niemöller, the Pastor Who
Defied the Nazis* (New York: Basic Books, 2018).

the auspices of the Federal Council of the Church of Christ. In a letter to them, reviewing Niemöller's tacit and active support of Nazism until his own church was attacked, Dr. Wise charged that the German pastor was attempting to sell the American people on the necessity for dealing "softly" with the Germans, who, he added, were "invincibly anti-Semitic." Stating that he was writing also as a "minister of religion," Dr. Wise said that Niemoller "has not so borne himself throughout the unspeakable Hitler years as to merit the respect or confidence of the Christian peoples of America."

The pastor gradually changed his anti-Semitic views, but the point that engages me most is that we do not have to be perfect to do what is right and good. For Christians, humans are born sinful yet can aspire to the selfless purity of their prophet, Jesus Christ. For the ancient Jews, the Talmud states, "Man should bless god for the evil which occurs in the same way that he blesses Him for the good"—stated thus to avoid the dualistic trap of a separate god for evil (Satan). To Buddhists, humans arrive in the world of form with evolutionary propensities for greed, hatred, and delusion (qualities that perhaps once offered evolutionary survival benefits). Yet, through striving to imitate Buddha's example, we aspire to clarify these kleshas (negative propensities) until we are able to express compassion for all beings, including ourselves.

We do not have to be perfect and blameless before we try to do what is right. The phrase that gained currency in the post 9/11 era, "If you see something, say something," should apply to more than suspicions concerning terrorism. Each of us embodies in our citizenship the responsibility for expressing our beliefs in our personal actions. Looking away, remaining passive, refusing to step up for whatever reason, clears the stage for malefactors and bad-faith actors who take advantage of diffidence, shyness, and lack of courage to perpetrate their own agendas.

What I would like to discuss about this subject is its relationship to enlightenment, which for purposes of discussion I'll reframe as "Perceiving the Unseen"—consciously perceiving the interconnections and the mutual dependencies between individuals and events. People interested in spirituality are often discomfited by political discussions, but politics, particularly in a democracy, is the way that people in groups express arguments and make decisions about how they want to live together. It concerns agreements and arrangements so that we can live together peacefully and fruitfully. It is a way of organizing relationships. Sometimes that organization can be corrupt, based on power rather than negotiation and consensus, but our arrangements do not have to be perfect. We do not have to hold fast to positions of purity that make it impossible for others to join with us. We are social beings and changeable. Consequently, relationships must be continually adjusted as circumstances change. This is part of the teaching of Fuketsu's speck of dust.

The police are employees. If their "bosses"—the mayors, governors, and city council members—gave firm orders that "the harassment and murder of black men and women must stop or we will indict, try, and jail you and hold you liable for egregious misconduct," such transgressions would have stopped by now. Because, even in the presence of visual evidence of abuse, it *hasn't* stopped or abated, one has to assume that the explicit orders have not been given. The only next pertinent question must be, Why?

The order to desist *not* being given, appears to this observer as a dog whistle—a frequency inaudible to most but not the intended audience. It is addressed to Caucasian constituents afraid to express their fear, complaints, or distrust about black people for fear of being labeled racists or because they are racists. Human beings of every persuasion are imperfect; therefore we can find examples in every culture on which to base anxiety and/or judgment. However, the silence from white citizens on the issue of black citizens being denied their due constitutional protections appears to be an equally unspoken reassurance to anxious constituents: *We're not going to let them get you.*

There are numerous reasons white people might fear African Americans—perhaps for seeking revenge for centuries of enslavement, Jim Crow laws, segregation, red-lining, inadequate schools and neighborhood protections, injustice, and repression at the hands of the white majority. Such a chronicle of injustice might have made the Buddha angry. My white informants, comfortable because I am a Caucasian, often assume I identify with "'whiteness'" which is an error. However, it makes them comfortable and they speak frankly, sometimes sounding like Old Testament prophets as they describe the "black rage" they imagine as a simmering tidal force restrained only by police or armed white men. They fear what might happen if the dam protecting white privilege was ever breached.

That fear is not a new phenomenon. In fact, the Second Amendment of the Constitution was demanded by white slavers fearing black rebellion, concerned that they might not be well defended by the government.

Such fears project their own imagining how they would feel and act if racial imbalances were ever reversed. Their fear of this rage grows every time an extrajudicial murder of a black man or woman occurs at the hands of the police. Once such an idea is internalized: the image of a powerful black man is immediately translated into a threat, and that sense of threat is transmitted (and may be shared) by the men they hire to ensure law and order.

An obvious response to that fear would be that the explosive potential of a pressure cooker is nullified once you turn off the heat and open the lid. Such fears also overlook the centuries of black grace, striving for citizenship, becoming first responders, joining the armed services, not seeking revenge in cities where they have come to power, and not going postal and burning the neighborhood each time a young, unarmed black man or woman is murdered by police. African Americans keep extending such grace to their white fellow citizens—despite having their successful, thriving communities repeatedly destroyed in places like Atlanta (1906), Greenwood in Tulsa (the Black Wall Street, 1921), and Rosewood (1923). Their fellow white citizens have never even voted to make lynching illegal. This is classic projection of one's unacknowledged personal rage and fear onto others. And yet, in other more egregiously war-torn places like Northern Ireland, South Africa, and Rwanda, we've witnessed examples of ordinary citizens meeting to bury ancient bitterness, express remorse and reconciliation in situations apparently more intractable than our own.

One of the ways white culture lets itself off the hook of bearing responsibility for race relations is by defining racism as one white individual being cruel, mean, or impolite to one person of a different race or color. Such a definition camouflages any responsibility for *systemic advantages* from which white people profit every day. It is like limiting the dialogue about mass murders in schools to mental health and fortifying schools, without ever mentioning the plethora of weapons of war in civilian hands and the political impotence that makes even regulating them impossible.

The white majority profits from cheaper, more available mortgages, better schools, better health care, easier access to groceries and pharmacies in their neighborhoods, less anxiety, higher pay, lower unemployment, and fewer incarcerations.* White people rarely hesitate to enter any store or neighborhood. They never have to keep their hands in their pockets as they browse to obviate a storeowner's anxiety about shoplifting; never have to pretend to be happy when they are not to alleviate white people's fears, which could be fatal for them. White people may not enjoy encounters with the police, but they almost never fear them, even when assaulting the U.S. Capitol on January 6, 2021.

Caucasians are afforded advantages and benefits they did not earn, which automatically places them in a higher social caste than black folks, in exactly the same way that dark skin places black and brown citizens into the lowest caste. Anyone who takes the trouble to look at our culture through the prism of caste can see this. The question is:

---

*On March 27, 2021, on a segment of MSNBC news interviewing the first black mayor of Boston, anchor Alexandra Witt read off a startling statistic sourced to the *Boston Globe* newspaper. It stated that the median wealth (not salary or earned income, but owned resources) for white people in Boston was $247,000 and for blacks was $8.00 (that is not a typo).

What do we do with and about that knowledge? As citizens? As spiritual practitioners? Once we have experienced the infinite interconnections between all parts of the Universe, why do we wait until people are impoverished, imprisoned, suffocated, and murdered in the streets before we intervene on their behalf?

A deceptively simple paper circulated on the internet shortly after George Floyd was murdered. It began:

I have privilege as a white person because I can do all these things without thinking twice about it.

A quick list followed:

I can go jogging.
I can relax in the comfort of my own home.
I can ask for help after being in a car crash.
I can leave a party to get to safety.

Affixed after each of these sentences was, the name a recently murdered African -American, killed in precisely the circumstances the sentence described.

No one is putting white children in cages at the border. No one is shooting white citizens to death in routine traffic stops or killing their kids for playing with toy guns. Black mothers have nearly three times the incidence of deaths during childbirth and lose 2.3 times as many children as infants than those considered white. The empirical data is clear: non-white citizens have shorter life spans, suffer higher stress, and have far less access to clean, healthy food, while white people find it less difficult to take fastidious care of themselves, eating organic food, keeping themselves healthy. When will white culture produce its Pastor Niemöller? Who but you and I will do this?

Black folks *know* and have known for years that this situation is within the power of the white majority to alter and control. By *not* controlling it, whites continue to enjoy their privileges without risk, but the irony is that they would not lose them by sharing them. They would simply live in a happier, more courteous, comfortable country. We are not behaving as allies for our fellow citizens. It's not a question of good will or having black friends. Unless we are helping to teach this issue and organize for its transformation, we are not sharing our power and privilege to help. We are not making their issue our issue. We are not demanding the full protections of the Constitution and Bill of Rights for all citizens.

The situation is complicated because there are many white people who are also treated unfairly by the system and who receive precious little help. They perceive Affirmative Action as favoritism, people getting something for nothing, and their political representatives do not explain that the primary beneficiary of Affirmative Action *is white women*. They don't explain because fueling the anger of their constituents is a powerful aid to their reelection—another example where "me" over "we" thinking harms us all.

If financial aid were class based or income based, it might go a long way toward dissipating racial resentment and envy, but it would not solve the problem of caste, the tendency of people to rank one another heirarchically. Isabel Wilkerson's book *Caste* ought to be required reading for all Americans for the light it sheds on what appear to be racial problems but may have more to do with an individual's fear of demotion to the lowest tier of any social organizing system. Isn't that fear actually a confession that we fully comprehend the benefits of our social privileges?

Enlightenment, at its root, pierces the central delusion of humans: the idea that our existence is a discrete entity, separate from all else—*we* are in here, and everything *not us* is out there. I've offered numerous examples previously in this book demonstrating that that is only half the story. What interests me as a teacher and a citizen is; What is, and how do we express, our responsibility to others? As ethical beings, as spiritual beings?

Living in a culture where the rights of some citizens are not protected as equally as our own, and complaining about their "whining" or boisterous protests against obvious injustice as one race or class is killed 2.5 times more frequently than another, obscures the fact that our silence is a form of consent. Isn't the absence of protest on the part of the *majority* both a support of the status quo and a denial of the common bonds of citizenship between us and our afflicted fellows? Is it any wonder, after centuries of looking after our own, that our country is divided, and while the divisions may appear to be camouflaged as race, they are more likely about the sharing of what some fear may be diminishing resources?

These are uncomfortable questions, I know, but for anyone considering a spiritual life based on the teachings of Buddha (or, for that matter, Jesus), such questions are unavoidable.

As a Buddhist American citizen, when I tolerate a system that privileges me at the expense of others, I am not behaving as a citizen who believes in democracy or the basic political equality guaranteed by the Constitution. I am pretending that the evil is *out there* among the racists and letting myself off the hook for not putting my voice and shoulder to the wheel for real democracy, real equality of opportunity for all citizens. I am the only part of this political system that I can control. Obviously, even if the white majority of citizens disapproves of racism, they do not feel impelled to insist *politically* that our Constitution *guarantees* each citizen rights and privileges under the law, and when they are denied one, the odds are that the jaws of that vise will one day close upon ourselves.

To see clearly may not always be pleasant, but we can't pour a quart into a pint pitcher. The quart is reality, and the pint is our limited ideas about it. We are going to have an election in November (of 2024), and no matter who wins, there are going to be *millions* of disaffected people. Angry and unhappy. That's not a prognosis for a prosperous, powerful, or peaceful nation. That scenario is being writ small in the everyday deaths and disadvantages of African American, Mexican, Latino, and Asian citizens in our nation. Murdered unarmed. Murdered in handcuffs. Shot running away, choked to death in broad daylight, their deaths captured irrevocably on video. Do we really think that going to comedy clubs and watching TikTok is going to solve such dilemmas?

I am not diminishing the many attacks on policemen who risk their lives serving the public every day. This is *not* an indictment of them, and to use it as such is falsifying my intent. However, when I observe Caucasian militiamen using the Second Amendment as a veneer to justify bearing weapons of war and body armor in our streets to intimidate voters, it's pretty clear that the only part of the Constitution they care about is the Second Amendment or they would be defending the rights of *any* citizen, male or female, African, Latin, or Asian, transgender or gay who is being abused by agents of the government or bullied by others. They would be defending the rights of Black Lives Matter activists or women demanding equal pay for equal work. They would not be hiding behind racial loyalties like it was a fan club but would be attending rallies, defending weaker or more timid Americans from provocateurs. Intentions always reveal themselves over time. What these guys apparently want to do is dress up like soldiers, act tough, intimidate others with their weapons, and be the shock troops for authoritarian initiatives where they are the only ones armed. They remind me of the weekend warriors, dentists, attorneys, and linemen who dress up like Hell's Angels to ride their Harleys on the weekend.

If we want to live in a peaceful nation, we have to engage with our own political system and struggle for change. If we do nothing, we tacitly support a system that advantages elites over the majority. We don't have to engage violently. We don't have to engage angrily. We can meditate sitting at the site of a murder or a nuclear power plant. We can call and write our elected representatives in numbers sizeable enough to command their attention. Whatever we do, it is necessary to *decide* what we represent and what values we will stand up for; to imagine the world we want to live in and then act it out to bring it into being. Without action, our best ideas are just memes on Instagram and Twitter.

I'm going to leave this alone for now, but I wanted to be sure that the subject was included in any discussion of Vernacular Buddhism. I wanted to be sure that the hidden details of our mutual bonds were expressed politically in spiritual discourses. We can deride the subject as vulgar and pretend that politics and spiritual practice are mutually exclusive, but that is a self-deception fostering cruel consequences. One of the great gifts of Buddhist thought is that it creates a frame of reference large enough so that black, white, Catholic, Muslim, Jew, or Wiccan is secondary to being a human being. Then the next question to ask is: What can I do to help? Read the next chapter.

21

Values Not Embodied in Behavior Do Not Exist

.....

July 22, 2020

MY FRIEND DAVID HARRIS, an important writer and thinker, has just published a new book titled *My Country 'Tis of Thee*. David is also a personal hero of mine—an early Freedom Rider in Mississippi helping to register African Americans to vote and who went to prison as a draft resister during the Vietnam War. He continued his resistance to the war inside, creating the first sit-ins in jail (watch the documentary *The Boys Who Said No* for more details). He formed a group of resisters in prison, fighting for prison reforms. He has lived a life of tireless political engagement in service to deeply held values of democratic principles, fairness, and inclusion. Released from prison, he ran for the U.S. Senate and continued his work as a writer for *Rolling Stone*, the *New York Times Sunday Magazine*, and a series of novels and books on important issues. David is also a serious Buddhist practitioner, a disciple of Rimpoche (Precious One) Tsoknyi, a Nepalese Tibetan Buddhist teacher, author, and tulku of the Kagyü and Nyingma traditions.

David has dedicated a great deal of time considering the moral life of his country, and when he says, "Unexpressed intentions don't count," he uses the word *intention* differently than Buddhists generally do.

For Buddhists, *intention* represents the only thing in the Universe that we can control, but we differentiate it from the normal impulse of *intending* to empty the garbage, or quit smoking, by referring to it as "fundamental intention." I would hazard a guess that everyone has a fundamental intention, whether or not they are conscious of it. It is the place our thoughts return to most effortlessly and habitually; it is as native to us as breathing. It is not necessarily positive. There are people whose anger forces them to concentrate on revenge and others whose competitiveness demands that they always win in every situation. Very few are born with a fundamental intention to serve others.

However, once we have clarified and accepted the shadow sides of our nature, and developed a sense of inter-being (Thich Nhat Hanh's lovely term) with the Universe, it is also true that feelings of kindness and gratitude well up spontaneously as we become aware of the uniqueness and preciousness of every person, animal, plant, the wheeling beauty of the night sky—the entire dazzling Universe into which we have been born. Buddhists practice organizing and focusing their intention on kindness and mindfulness, literally training our attention on remaining conscious of which face or facet of the formless is rising to mind; monitoring our own thoughts and impulses to ensure that we do not let negativity and impulses from the shadow side leak into our speech and behavior. It is something like remembering that all the billions of little wavelets in the ocean are, despite their apparent singularity, inseparable parts of the ocean. We are what we perceive.

Fixing our intention with the force of habit means that we don't have to think about every decision, every moment, but respond to all phenomena as if they are an expression of that ocean—in other words, not exactly *other* from ourselves. In that way, Buddhists do not have to memorize too many rules and can afford to be spontaneous. If we can succeed in fixing our intention on kindness and compassion with the force of habit, we can trust ourselves to monitor the shadowy sides of our human nature without worrying overmuch about leaking envy, jealousy, anger, or competitiveness. These are universal emotions and impulses, but for Buddhists, polishing and selecting among them are the raw materials of our work.

I'm sure that we've all said something at one time or another and felt, "Oh, that was a little much, I hope she doesn't take it the wrong way." Moments like that occur because our attention to what we were actually feeling may have been wobbly in that moment, or we were actually thinking about something other than the conversation we were involved in. Nevertheless, it is useful to catch ourselves in these little "holidays" of paying attention.

In David's book when he writes, "Values that are not embodied in behavior do not exist," he is saying, in effect, intention is not enough. Unless we *act* on those intentions, practice, review, and revise them, we get what we *do*, nothing more. Especially for critical issues or when lives are on the line. We do not get what we *meant* to do . . . nor do we get what we *tell* ourselves we did. Appearance counts little, and rhetoric even less in David's value system.

> Acts that fail to embody their object, fail to realize it. I call this the "do" theory. The war taught it to me.
> Values that are not embodied in behavior do not exist.

I'm sure we have all sometimes gotten "ahead of our skis" in a conversation, expressing things we believe in but may not have assiduously practiced. Bars, social media, cocktail parties, and political speeches are infused with passionate statements of belief and intention, opinionated conversations concerning politics, the environment, gender, sexual orientation, and the like. Our country has foundational, publicly stated values declaring that all people are created equal, meaning politically equal and equally deserving of the protections afforded by the Constitution. It is a grand thought, and today we are further along toward living the life it implied than the Founders were, which speaks well for the inspiration the Constitution has continued to offer us. At the time it was written, no women, Africans, or landless people were included in the democracy it outlined. Applying David's criteria to this document, we would have to say that some of those values embedded and expressed in our founding documents have been codified into law and actively protected, while others have been circumscribed and prevented from becoming law. The hundreds of new laws recently enacted to restrict voters who might vote Democratic can serve as examples of restraining behavior before it can be translated into political action.

There's an old saying that *hypocrisy is the tax vice pays to virtue.* It means that everybody recognizes what's right. Even miscreants understand where virtue resides, and lie about what they have done to remain cloaked by it. Even though a number of the Constitution's goals have not been realized, they are not to be dismissed, as they have some power to restrain the malevolent.

The United States Constitution was perhaps inspirational but essentially inconsequential to women, Native Americans, and African Americans for centuries. It was meaningless to Chinese workers imported into the United States to build the railroads and sluice gold but forbidden to bring their wives with them. When their labor seemed unnecessary, they were later excluded from even being here by democratically passed laws.

The Constitution may have been inspiring but also meaningless to American citizens of Japanese descent imprisoned preemptively as spies and forced to sell their homes and possessions at a loss during World War II. And it remains meaningless to those today arguing against the burning of books and teaching students self-comforting mythology about our country's history rather than equipping them with tools for clear thought and analysis and skills to be good citizens and competitors in a global economy.

This is an issue I'm sensitive to for a number of reasons. My father loved history, particularly the history of the Bill of Rights, which he spoke about often. He was the president of the local Jewish Community Center, who fired him during the McCarthy period because he refused to censor speakers.

I remember him coming home one evening with boxes containing a dozen or more bound copies of Thomas Jefferson's collected letters, giddy with anticipation of reading and discussing them. There is a
deeper reason for my sensitivity than his example, however.

For a number of difficult reasons, my childhood from age two to
nearly fourteen was intimately guided and instructed by an African
American young woman and her boyfriend and their close circle of
friends. They were not my biological parents, but they were my functional
parents. Shortly after my younger sister was born, nineteen months after
me, wanting a divorce and being told that if she left my father would use
his wealth and political power to take the children from her, she suffered
a crippling nervous breakdown and became completely unavailable to me.

My father was driven to succeed at his multiple labors—the
president of a railroad, an oil company, and his own stock brokerage
business—and was not to be deterred from those goals. His sister, my
Aunt Ruth, sent her seventeen-year-old housekeeper to our house to help
with the emergency, telling her that my father would pay her more than
three times the $25.00 a week she could afford. He'd give her room and
board and enable her to send money home to North Carolina.

Sue Howard was a powerful young woman, absolutely fearless and
outspoken, and within a month, when the original housekeeper was
caught stealing money, Sue took over the entire house and ran it like a
master sergeant with a sense of humor.

As very young children (I was about three and a half), both my
sister and I transferred our loyalty to her and her boyfriend, Ozzie,
as a source of safety and care. I remained intimate with them until
their deaths, and at her funeral at ninety when my black "mom's" self-
composed obituary was read aloud, along with her biological son, Bill,
she claimed me as the other of her two children.

I can't overstate the importance of the education I received from
Sue and Ozzie and their friends, Chris, John, Violet, and Jules, who
clustered in my kitchen multiple times each week eating, with music
playing, lively conversation, arguments about the Bible and politics, and

a general sense of fun. They took the time to speak to me. Appeared to see me clearly and taught me to dance, sing, and attempted to teach me to play ball. Ozzie was an a capella gospel singer in a group like the Swan Silvertones (still a favorite), and I learned about the power and spirit of gospel music before I could read. I still play it on Sundays.

Most importantly, I learned about whiteness. I don't mean being a Caucasian but rather the organized system of privileges for white people that continually plagued Sue and Ozzie and their friends. Sue was a brilliant networker, and when her son was arrested for spurious reasons, her friend who worked for the local judge got him to help her. Black people knew everything about white people because they had to. If I went downtown with my biological mom, people were deferential and polite. If I went into the same store with Sue or one of her friends, they would follow us around as if we might steal. It infuriated me, but I took my clues from Sue, who remained cool. She was one of the organizers who secured the integration of the public schools in my town, so that her son could get the education he deserved.

Consequently, it should come as no surprise that I remain an obdurate supporter of the proposition that *all* citizens receive the protections and freedoms guaranteed by our Constitution and Bill of Rights.

In that vein, many years later during the 1960s in San Francisco, I was a Digger,* and Huey Newton (founder of the Black Panthers) and

---

*The Diggers began as a core group of actors from the San Francisco Mime Troupe who believed that culture was a stronger force than politics. Most resistance to the status quo was based on Socialist or Communist ideals. We were artists and didn't want to have to do plays about heroic janitors and bus drivers; we wanted to live in a world where we could be authentic. To that end, we imagined it and made it real by acting it out. We served free food to hundreds of kids in the Haight Ashbury every day. We created the first Free Store, which offered clothes, tools, furniture, all the accoutrements of a life without requiring a job. We created a free medical clinic that met at the Free Store on Wednesday nights, staffed by medical students at UC Med Center, and we created numerous theatrical events that enlisted everyone as actors to create realities they could not imagine. We also had our own newspaper, printed on stolen Gestetner machines that cut electronic stencils for mimeographs. We became so skilled at making multicolored photos and drawings that when the company finally caught up with their machines, they said that we could keep them if we trained their staff how to use them as we did. It was this paper, *The Free City News*, that Huey Newton and Bobby Hutton came to inquire about. People interested in this period might read my first book, *Sleeping Where I Fall* (Berkeley, Calif.: Counterpoint Press, 2009).

Bobby Hutton showed up at my apartment in San Franciso to learn about the Digger newspaper that our community published to express our position directly to denizens of Haight Street and San Francisco. I supported them immediately and arranged that the Digger press adjunct, known as the Communication Company, would publish the first issue of the Black Panther Party newspaper. I continue to support Black Lives Matter not only because I'm partial to and comfortable in black culture but also because I believe that racism is a toxin weakening my nation and white folks in particular.

I support the reformation and supervision of local police forces to ensure that BIPOC (Black, Indigenous, People of Color) communities and people feel and remain safe and receive all the protections and guarantees of the law to which they are entitled. I fail to understand what is remotely controversial about such demands and consider them an overdue note signifying a debt owed to the citizens by the nation. They should not even be up for discussion. When the house is on fire, quibbling with the fireman about the type of hose they're using is stupid and dangerous.

There are those who believe that such political matters are not appropriate to spiritual practice. *Politics* is the name we apply to formal relationships between people and groups. Those relationships can be positive or negative, democratic or oppressive, and Buddhism offers tools and skills that can foreshadow positive outcomes. As with individuals, such relationships can be founded on power and will or based on cooperation and respect. It is never not spiritual to foster and defend the latter.

The "original" dialogue (and perhaps the intentions of the Founders) are currently being distorted by clever Sophists. Constitutional guarantees of freedom of speech and free expression of religion are being coopted and gaslit to support bigotry and bully LGBTQ people and to allow corporations to deny health services to female employees. Guarantees of constitutional rights for *all* American citizens, the guarantees enshrined in the Constitution every law officer and political employee swears to defend, is the real issue. I suspect arguments calling for defunding the police (as if the police were only agents of repression and not needed to serve and protect vulnerable people). We can and should *reform* every police force in America, especially when, as the *Vallejo News* reports:

> A secretive clique within the Vallejo Police Department has commemorated fatal shootings . . . by bending the points of their badges each time they kill in the line of duty. . . . The custom was so exclusive, some officers involved in fatal shootings were never told of its existence. Senior law enforcement and government officials say everything changed when a police captain tried to end the practice following the fatal shooting of 20-year-old Willie McCoy in February 2019 . . . [and] the tradition became known at the highest levels of Vallejo city government and the district attorney's office.

To be clear, such reforms will not abate one expensive, substandard mortgage sold to a qualified black or Latino customer. They will not produce capital for a small business; or create a single grocery store in a poor neighborhood food desert; or buy books and school supplies for a poor school; all of which flow from actions that reveal malign intentions, despite impassioned expressions of "how much we care." Consider the 800-billion-dollar-plus military budget to get a clear idea of what "we" care about.

Racism is a pandemic in the United States. It should be declared a national security issue, because a population at war with itself cannot agree on vital health and safety issues. This pandemic depends on white people to end it. According to the 2021 census, African Americans represent 13 percent of the population while white people, minus Latinos and Hispanics, make up 60 percent. Any political change required by African Americans or any minority population requires 38.9 percent of fellow citizens to stand up with them and insist that they will not tolerate mistreatment of *any* citizen! Passivity in the face of injustice is supporting injustice.

Consider your own awareness for a moment. It is utterly transparent, devoid of all qualities, colors, except perhaps a "brightness" and a sense of knowing. Every person on Earth shares that awareness. Beneath the superficialities of skin color, culture, and custom, what animates them is this common awareness. How can one hate that?

Wrapping it in negative narratives is to ignore the fundamental quality of our awareness which is its acceptance of everything.

Our ideas about what we do will not protect us from negative consequences. As David Harris reminds us, "Especially when lives are on the line. We do not get what we mean to do." Lives are on the line every day. Cautions are in order.

22

Karma

.....

September 30, 2020

WE WANT THE WORLD TO MAKE SENSE TO US. We would like it to be fair and just. We want those we perceive as violators of norms and laws to be punished, and those we perceive as good, rewarded. We are unbalanced by the impersonality of the Universe, which makes it nearly impossible for us to consistently remember that it is not organized for the exclusive benefit of humans, and particularly not for ourselves.

Often, we can manifest very little control over issues we perceive as problematic or immoral. We can and should stand up (or as Buddhists we often sit zazen at protests) for what we believe is right, but we should also be on guard about drawing conclusions about the entire Universe based on our personal experiences. The alternative is to settle our minds at rest, as often as possible, in a calm, elastic, receptive state.

We can practice identifying and containing our own negative impulses and darker preoccupations of thought, because they precede and announce the future we will be inadvertently creating if we believe them. If we would inhabit a brighter future, we will need to clean up this moment's thoughts, premises, beliefs, and impulses that precede and lay the foundation for it. Zazen is a karma-free practice, because in allowing everything to arise in the mind without censure within the

278 Engaged with Vernacular Zen

discipline of our immovable posture, we allow the kinetic energy of our negative, shadow sides to work on emptiness, rendering them visible to us but harmless to others. Monitoring our thoughts and feelings in the moment, interrogating the dark ones and trying to understand how they serve us, what narratives we've attached to them, and where in the body they appear to reside, builds confidence that we can manage them. Generosity and planting seeds of positive thoughts and intention is the moment-by-moment recipe for breaking the chains binding the future to the past.

I receive a lot of questions about karma and justice these days. Right now in our country and every country on Earth many cruel, unfair, and unjust events are unfolding. The Universe offers us an infinity of everything, so to some degree our perceptions of the world depend on what we examine most carefully. Everything is always available. There is an infinity of kindness, cruelty, betrayal, compassion, suffering, exaltation— all manifestations of the pregnant turmoil energy of the Universe. Everything exists in incalculable numbers, and all of it is empty of self.

Despite being old enough to know better than to expect life to be fair, nevertheless, when events like the murder of George Floyd or the calculated suppression of voters by gerrymandering or legal trickery arise, it is disturbing and raises the issue of how Zen practice might serve us in addressing such circumstances.

Quick quiz: Who in contemporary American life resorts to the phrase "not fair" more often than anyone else? Answer: Children in middle school and Donald Trump. Children use it because they are trying to understand the phrase and understand how to negotiate and defend their growing sense of self and their swelling sense of limits. Donald Trump employs it because he fully understands that there are vast numbers of American voters who feel left out of the nation's prosperity, promise, and equity and betrayed by their leaders. He understands that it is a powerful political lever and he has a genius for wielding it. It is so powerful it can make people believe that a heartless millionaire who stiffs employees, has been convicted of raping women, and may very well be on his way to jail for trying to overthrow a legitimate election for the presidency cares enough about them to be their guardian and protector.

Feeding political disappointment and anger and pretending to identify with it has been a successful strategy to draw more than 70 million citizens into his orbit. Consider that for a moment. Nearly half of the voting public is unhappy and dissatisfied with the hand that life in America has dealt them and with our government's response to help them. How successful can we determine a political system to be when half its citizens are no longer loyal to it?

Our current state might be regarded as the karmic accumulation of a nation historically and presently consumed by the acquisition of material wealth. This has organized most of its past actions and decisions, from Imperialism to the Supreme Court's assertion that political contributions are the equivalent of free speech. There are days when I feel that our fixation on material wealth has used up the near-total of our mental bandwidth. Whatever space is available for spiritual growth is the space required to question our dominant political paradigm. It is by that slender thread that the fate of democracy is suspended.

After a lifetime of political involvement, my antennae are currently tweaked by a disturbing thought, which might account for the Republican Party's descent into unprincipled lawlessness and gaslighting. What's keeping me awake nights is considering whether or not Republican defectors from democracy might be receiving quiet signals from their donors in the C-Suites and billionaire class. The corporate sector may well have concluded that the regulations safeguarding our environment and workers (clean air, clean water, worker safety, food safety standards, product liability) extract costs affecting their profit margins. They may have calculated that they and their shareholders can be richer if Donald Trump wins the 2024 election.

I hope that's not the case, and it seems more reasonable that the rightward shift of public policy since Ronald Reagan has disappointed and deprived enough uneducated voters that they have lost faith in government itself. This has for a long time been the goal of Conservative neoliberal thinkers who believe that nothing should ever impose limits on markets. Given enough time and close observation, patterns become visible that make it obvious that, in many cases, the well-being of the citizens has not been left to the honorable statistics of chance but are the results of strategic planning and collusion among people who would just as soon dismantle our country to sell as spare parts as contribute to a thriving, equitable democracy.

Fair and unfair are human inventions and concerns based on an innate respect for ourselves and others that is hard-wired into our DNA. One cannot imagine a rabbit protesting its seizure by a falcon or a gazelle berating a lion. All prey species want to live, but they have inhabited the world of living and dying for millions of years and have a less obscured understanding of both than most humans.

The implications of dependent origination inform us verifiably (and self-certifiably) that *no individual form can exist without the rest of it.* If that is true, doesn't it follow that everything we do has consequences in multiple dimensions? Remaining conscious of this is a useful counter-balance to overenthusiastic pursuits.

So, let's regard fair and unfair again. Since the Middle Ages gave way to the European Enlightenment and the industrialization that accom-panied it, people have learned how money was accumulated. Wealth was not the "divine right" of a certain class but involved buying and selling and interest and acquisition. We learned that poor people are not poor because they behaved badly in a former life or because they are inherently lazy or stupid. Neither are the rich privileged because they lived nobly and selflessly in a prior time.

When a fox eats a rabbit, is it fair or unfair? When one set of people oppresses another, it doesn't matter what our ideas about it are, the results are similar. This does not mean that we have to accept ani-mal behavior as the "natural" standard of humans as some apologists for unregulated capitalism suggested during the 1970s, arguing that capitalism should not be blamed for its flaws, because it was a natural expression of survival of the fittest, emulating the procedures of the Universe. It's twaddle, of course. What distinguishes humans from the animal world, among other things, is our ability to control instincts and behavior that do not serve us.

Survival of the fittest as an economic theory was a philosophy guaranteed to please Wall Street and hedge-fund speculators but did not do much for the 99.9 percent of souls on Earth hauling the water, setting the bricks, or working in the Post Office. We are all on this Earth together. We are all playing roles consciously or unconsciously, interacting with one another, inventing our parts as we go within ancient, inherited scenarios *that were designed by humans and can be redesigned by them.*

Every conceivable human intention is being expressed on the human bandwidth simultaneously, which includes Mother Teresa, Nelson Mandela, Jesus, Ted Bundy, Donald Trump, and Hitler—every possibility of the human mind—and it's foolish to think that because we don't see it operating in our neighborhoods or living rooms that we are somehow immune to humanity's darker intentions.

Recall Karl Marx's surplus value theory of profit, which amasses wealth very rapidly, especially when you have thousands of employees. When I was working in Hollywood and visited the homes of agents who commission their clients 10 percent of each job, I was flabbergasted at the wealth on display—grand homes, Warhols and expensive art adorned their walls, expensive furniture, multiple assistants served and ran the house—all because of this snip from hundreds of clients.

Our expectation that the Universe will correspond to our ideas of justice is another kind of human delusion. Yesterday I heard a podcast on *NY Times Daily* by a fellow who was charting human migrations due to climate change. It turns out that *currently tens of millions of people are preparing to migrate* because they can see the writing on the global warming wall. They are either going to be underwater or without water, or in a place where they can't grow crops, or where it's too hot to work outside. They're not going to be able to live as they always have.

Those of us in the developed nations, with the time to read books like this, are turning the planet into a fireball by refusing to limit our indulgences in consideration of the rest of humanity. The planet is demonstrating that we are living out of balance—taking more from the planet than it can sustainably give. Today, moderating our personal climates with air-conditioning, importing lobster and fresh fruit by jet planes in every season, or hopping on the same carbon-spewing jets for "environmental vacations" is considered "taste," "lifestyle" or "sophistication." If we do not alter our personal habits, who will?

It's the developed nations creating the markets clearing the rain forests for palm oil in our skin creams or cattle for our hamburgers; snapping up the last vestiges of fish and by-catch Hoovered from the ocean with enormous nets that destroy the coral reefs, where tomorrow's fish might have grown; the New Age, hi-tech optimists are remarkably coy about wealth and often seem to suggest subtly that wealth and taste are the rewards of spiritual development. The result is the same in every quadrant of society—there are no viable public discussions of limiting oil, driving, cattle breeding, or the production of a new plastic to draw down the carbon our culture emits into the atmosphere and which is killing tomorrow.

The poor cannot be blamed for wanting to survive, and when most of the world's population is living on a dollar a day or less, it will have to be the First World, industrialized nations who must learn to live on less.

The existential threat of global warming to civilization will not be deterred unless we modify how we live; unless government begins to set strict standards to protect the planet, and unless people develop the trust to believe that those standards are necessary. The question remains whether or not that can happen in a political system which revolves around money.

Afghanistan was once a forested environment. What we see today as a bare and harsh land inflicting poverty on its people is the result of decisions made perhaps a thousand years go. Wall Street and savvy investors are already buying up properties in cooler climates, driving the

the cost of housing up for local people who can't compete with them. This is investing in the future as a commodity. There are those who do not see "a problem" with losing a third of the world's population. The hoarders and investors in catastrophe may discover short-term escapes for a decade or so, but my seventeen-year-old granddaughter is going to live as an adult in a world with 35 percent less oxygen, because the plankton in the ocean (which outstrips even the rain forests as a generator of oxygen) are disappearing due to warming and acidity. If she continues to live in San Mateo, California, in thirty years it will be like living at 12,000 feet above sea level.

So I have to wonder: When do we begin to consider global warming as the existential emergency it actually is? When do we take disciplined, conscious action to make our governments respond? We're in it, whether we want to be or not. We're in it, whether we change all our lightbulbs to LED, install solar panels, and drive electric cars. We're in it. It's the collective karma of a "me" culture, of wanting "to be all we can be" without ever realizing we are *already* more than we can possibly imagine ourselves being. Consequently, it would be to the benefit of everyone if we paused to take a hard-eyed, deadly serious inventory distinguishing needs from wants before we shopped again.

Not to make light of small individual steps to consume less, but the problems facing us require systemic-scale alterations to our power grid, transportation models, commuting, addiction to daily meat, and a host of other items. It means that it is critical to vet the people we elect; to demand their positions on these items, which are no longer radical but may well be emergency, life-saving policies. By 2040 the global temperature will rise to 1.5°C above pre-industrial levels; we are currently at just over 1.2°C. That modest elevation of temperature has generated all the current floods, fires, droughts, and disaster reporting we are currently experiencing. Imagine increasing our environmental stressors by an additional 25 percent.

I'm not exempting myself from these observations. I live alone in a 1,700-square-foot home, which would house ten people in a less-developed country. I've done all the lightbulb changing, solar panels, no air-conditioning, and electric vehicle Band-Aids, but it's not nearly enough to make a difference. Most Americans are not aware that recycling has basically ended since China began refusing our garbage. From all the plastic-wrapped goods we're forced to buy, from the single-use plastic bags and clam-shell containers for berries, to the see-through garment bags we receive from the dry cleaners—is the culture we grew up with. It's our normal. I understand how irritating it can be to be constantly reminded of negative aspects of our daily life, but unless each of us assumes some responsibility for manifesting the changes we want, they will continue. We are being called upon by Nature herself to change our "normal," to change our expectations if we want to survive. Because we know nothing else, the change looms overlarge and frightening, but we are a clever, resourceful species, and there is nothing in changing the model that dictates that we live in squalor or without regard for beauty.

Writ large, *the issue is extraction and consumption to ensure human ease and comfort.* This is a spiritual problem. For beings who are the Universe itself, what do they not already possess? There is *need,* and then there is *greed,* and spirituality helps us to know the difference. No one fully understands the political consequences of our standards for what a normal, successful life might require. The critical issue is understanding the difference between being wealthy and being rich.

Wealth is a measure of natural systems—fresh air, clean water, stable forests, safe neighborhoods, happy families, good relationships, fulfilling work. Riches pertain to what can be bought and sold. Unfortunately, the men and women populating our political institutions are forced to contend with the demands of the rich. We have allowed money to control our political system, and any objective observer will tell you that its power is absolute. Consequently, the short-term success (reelection) of individual legislators is more vitally important to them than knuckling down to think through a long-term path out of the current mess. In order for that to work, the public must be honestly educated and offered an option where the burdens will be equally shared, if the political class is to win the trust and loyalty of voters. It's possible that most legislators (and the big capital on which they depend) have concluded that in the short term they may skate by and escape before the bill for their dereliction appears—certainly an appealing option, one far less rigorous than what will be required to change our culture.

Those perceiving the nature of the threats before us need to learn to explain them in a nonjudgmental way. We are all guilty of wanting normal lives, but our nation's "normal" is unsustainable. No one wants to be told how bad they are. You may have LED lightbulbs, but you might also have a gasoline-powered motorboat or car you love. Other people are refusing to stop importing food by jet to have fresh strawberries in February, and others are giving up beef. The big takeaway is that not one of us is pure enough to judge others as if we alone were standing outside the contradictions of our society. This is a big "WE" problem.

Obviously, no one *needs* a 66,000-square-foot home with eighteen bathrooms. While Bill Gates's foundations do laudable work around the world, we might ask ourselves about the degree to which those good deeds are counterbalanced by establishing lifestyles that inspire status competitors around the world to build their own palaces and purchase their own mega-yachts. One must also wonder if the billionaire and corporate classes paid their fair share of taxes, how much suffering here at home might be alleviated, if public expenditures were subject to the scrutiny of policy debates. The power of the Buddha's teaching created lives that perpetrated minimal harm, and established models which could easily be imitated.

Bill Gates might respond if people resisted his products to protest robbing Peter to pay Paul. However, this dharma talk is being written in Microsoft Word, on a computer he helped to develop, and so I share culpability in supporting his indulgences. That's the rub. It is the system's *premises* and ubiquitous marketing that have snared us all.

However, if enough people simply change the way they live,

protesting by developing with a smaller, less-harmful, potentially more elegant lifestyle, eventually the worldview of the "mega-class" would become out of step.

Recall the useful phrase *hypocrisy is the tax that vice pays to virtue*. When we know what's good but pursue a different path, we lie so that we're not exposed as violating an accepted standard. In that way, even negatively, moral standards like the Ten Commandments or the Buddha's precepts exert positive pressure on society. Whether we still have the time available to change course before incurring catastrophes remains an open question, but what are the alternatives?

I'll share mine. One is meditation, the daily descent into formlessness is a refreshing bath for awareness. Meditation reaffirms the transitory nature of everything we refer to as reality. It makes our prizes and successes as transitory as our culpabilities. As we grow more familiar with what our minds generate, it eventually becomes incontrovertible that much of what we perceive as facts are internally generated feelings. Interrogating those feelings and analyzing their roots, causes, and consequences protect us from acting them out and generating negative consequences. While it seems a small step, remember there's not much smaller than a grain of sand, yet multiplied billions of times, it becomes a beach. What we previously perceived as difficulty—social disruption—could become energy we can use and direct toward achieving the lives we might all feel proud of.

An extension of such thought leads me to support the practice of reparations, particularly to the descendants of enslaved Africans for the centuries of oppression and lost advantages they received at the hands of the white majority—Jim Crow laws, "separate but equal" facilities (that were never equal), and economic practices like red-lining, punitive mortgages, denying agricultural loans to black farmers, or stretching out the time of processing those loans until they were too late to be of help in planting an annual crop.

White people have been living on the fruits of privilege, capital and opportunity, denied black people for centuries. This has nothing to do with having owned slaves or not. White people have received privileges denied to black folks for centuries, and it's a debt that must be paid if the nation's racial problems are to ever be healed. We owe amends and reparations to Native Americans for ethnic cleansing and genocide. There is not a white foot walking today that does not cross Indigenous land and step over their graves. Their religious treasures have been stolen and locked in museums, and they continue to live in unbelievable poverty—cars on cinder blocks, shabby housing, bad water and medicine—in the richest nation on Earth. Justice postponed is justice denied, and the karma generated by that is one of the great divisive forces preventing our country from unifying around common goals— which is to say, a national security issue. This sense of debt can be overwhelming, particularly the longer it is postponed. There may be other consequences that we need to repair. We killed three million people in Vietnam, Laos, and Cambodia and left their countries littered with toxins and landmines that are still dismembering children today. Is there not some honorable debt to be paid there? Even apology? Does national pride insist that we, alone among humans, have never made a mistake? Preemptive war against Iraq? Deregulating the banking system? Please, the people know better.

In Twelve Step programs, which have remarkable results in treating addictions, step four is to make a searching and fearless moral inventory of ourselves. Step eight is to make a list of all persons we have harmed and becoming willing to make amends to them all. And step nine is to make direct amends to such people whenever possible, except when to do so would injure them or others.

My argument is simple, that as a nation we have become addicted to riches and maintaining the highest status. Every addict understands that behind their addiction is a lot of "stinkin' thinkin'" and the insistence of guilt and shame, which they will go to any lengths to suppress. My country cannot have compassion for itself, apparently, and will not until it has faced steps four, eight, and nine of the Twelve Steps. Until that day, we are postponing the joy and self-respect we used to feel. It starts with ourselves, with the simple act of sitting down. Democracy is concerned with gathering more grains of sand in your bucket than your competitor's. The accretion of tiny integers is not something to be overlooked. If you doubt it, consider the power and efficacy of pollen. When we don't interrogate our lives with fine-tuned attentiveness and a calm mind, whether we are performing our "good works" and spiritual practices or not, we are vulnerable to the intrusions of negative impulses and thoughts getting away from us. We are not just nice people. We have the full potential of human beings inside of us, positive and negative, and when our attention lapses, we can be quite dangerous. I try to remind myself often that I am often the problem I am trying to solve.

We all tend to forget that each and every human represents the full spectrum of thoughts, feelings, impulses, sensations, and consciousness to which the species is heir. There are no good guys. Evil is the opposite pole of good, and neither exists as an absolutely identifiable, stand-alone quality. For *good* we could substitute *generous, empathic,* and *nurturing,* and for *evil* we might substitute *ruthless, amoral,* or *sadistic*—all words that describe identifiable behaviors. Good and evil, however, suggest fixed, permanent states that we *assume* are always identifiable, but if that were the case, people might not be repeatedly sending delegates who vote against their interests back to Congress.

It is uncomfortable to press this point, but important. With the recent invasion of Ukraine, the subject of war crimes is once again in the news. We say this as if we understand it as a universal standard, and certainly the intentional killing of civilians in battle is universally condemned. But when it comes to our own troops killing civilian men, women, and children in My Lai (1968), Haditha (2005), and Jalalabad (2007), we define those incidents as tragic events, not war crimes, and as such they fade rapidly from public scrutiny.

"No one is above the law" means just that. Unless we can apply and consent to a common standard for a concept like war crimes and hold ourselves to the same standard we hold others, it is as meaningless as a parent who's smoking while they lecture their child about the dangers of tobacco. Consequently, when other countries criticize the United States for refusing to join the International Criminal Court (because we cannot face allowing American soldiers to be judged by others), it imperils our moral standing in the world. Such hypocritical behavior is really an extension of our belief in American exceptionalism. Are we really arguing before the world that we can take exception to world rules and norms and still rule?

Once again, this is where meditation proves precisely useful. If it arises in meditation that I see myself riding in a gold Cadillac, surrounded by winsome acolytes strewing flowers in my lap, I don't have to believe it. I know it's not an omen from Buddha or a sign of my moral superiority. I can hold fast against the impulse to judge it at all and allow it to dissolve into Emptiness. If I observe myself vanquishing enemies, or shooting people I don't like from a sniper's position, it is no more potent than the former train of thought, but in meditation it alerts me to negative qualities of my nature so that I can be on guard if they arise.

If we repeat such a process often enough, we arrive at a deep familiarity with the boundaryless mind itself. We see for ourselves how ephemeral our mental prompts and impulses are and can actually contain them within the form of our meditation and render them harmless there. We need expend no futile energy pretending they do not exist.

Danger for ourselves and others arises only when we allow those impulses physical expression—first energizing our desires and then our actions. Considering the question in its broadest parameters, we *can* extend our investigations to include examining the premises of an acquisitive, industrially extractive society and determine ways of increasing beauty and opportunity in sustainable ways. This may be a prerequisite for our short-term survival.

If we intend to survive as a species, we are going to be required to make big changes in the number of calories of energy we use per person, regardless of the short-term economic consequences. This will probably require reallocating the spending of tax dollars to pay for the programs and retooling required. It will no longer work simply as a mechanism for rewarding the wealthy and leaving what's left to run the nation. Under the pressure to adjust to global realities, we may wonder what, if anything, a military/intelligence budget more than eight times larger than all of our allies combined can actually do for our defense against a heated planet, mass extinctions, and the cost of requisite changes to our way of life. We might do better instituting a Marshall Plan for Latin America to make their economies more just and their societies more stable so that millions no longer need to flee their homes for our shores.

These are national problems, and the costs will have to be borne by the nation. That will involve everyone (and every industry paying their fair share). This may appear to be "redistribution of wealth" to Conservatives, but it is unfair to expect workers in the coal and petroleum fields to accept poverty because the nation has been forced to change its practices. It is unfair to expect beef and pork growers to do the same. There are still 1,800 illegal, coal-fired power plants operating that will have to be shut down because of carbon emissions. Shareholders will pay some of that cost, so will consumers, but it is a more acceptable price than making the entire planet unlivable. It's better to have half a loaf than no loaf, and instead of "preemptive wars" and paying billions to test and store catastrophic nuclear weapons on layaway until the first accident occurs, we need to be saving funds to carry our populations through the economic dislocation that will arise from changing from an extractive into a sustainable economy.

This will be true for every developed country on Earth, and it will also be true that those countries will have to bear some of the costs to help undeveloped countries reach some sustainable plateaus without going through our centuries of extractive and polluting procedures. *We* have a responsibility *to* others and *for* the social inequities our system has created and fostered and by which many of us have been privileged.

Poor people in America already feel left behind in comparison to those who are wealthier, and that envy often complicates the noblest schemes to solve social problems. They see affirmative action as "colored" people getting something for nothing and overlook the fact that the primary beneficiaries of affirmative action are white women.

The turmoil and fear of the adjustments required to ensure the full protections of law to all citizens is producing violent reactions within our population, but I believe the target is misplaced and will discuss later how the replacement by other races that working people feel is actually their replacement due to unregulated capitalism, particularly noticeable in the United States because of the dominant power of money operating in our political system.

Even as President Biden is working today (September 20, 2021) to pay for infrastructure repair and social justice reforms by raising taxes on the wealthy, several of the *Democratic* votes he needs to pass his plan have to date stifled it. A senator from a coal-producing state (with family in the coal business) flexes his muscles to ensure that provisions of the Clean Air Act do not pass. The other, a senator from Arizona deeply indebted to the pharmaceutical industry, is blocking the bill because of its provisions to regulate the costs of drugs. Their wealthy donors have been protected against finding a larger tax bill in their mailboxes (of no consequence to the scale of their wealth), and, consequently, most of the fiscal burden of requisite changes will be expanded to include the upper middle class and working people, while simultaneously ensuring that the incomparably wealthy billionaire class pays no extra taxes. This is a recipe for global catastrophe, future dissatisfaction, and unrest in every political sphere, but it is small potatoes measured against the enormous tax cuts Presidents Reagan, George W. Bush (extended by Barack Obama), and Donald Trump afforded their wealthy donors and financial institutions. According to Bobby Kogan, senior director for federal budget policy at the Center for American Progress, 75 percent of the increase in our national debt and deficit (related to income) is due to tax cuts favoring the wealthy. I'm sorry, the folks we're sending to Congress and what we demand from them is bankrupting the store.

All the above strategies and curtailed programs are ensured success because of the way we pay for our elections. In most European countries, the nation itself pays. Candidates go on every TV station to be inter-viewed for about three weeks, the people vote, and life returns to normal. In our money-dependent system, electioneering is endless, with multiple stations dedicated to covering politics 24/7, and the larger the controver-sies surrounding candidates and elections, the more viewers they win, the more they can charge for advertising, and the greater the bonuses of the commentators. If this feels like a recipe for cultural suicide, you're correct.

People are imperfect, and the problem with our elections is the same as the problems in Buddhism—there are people in them. There are obvious alterations to our system that would return power to the electorate, but I doubt we'll see them in my lifetime, unless there is a Great Awakening among voters and they demand it.

Our political system would be radically more fair and responsive to the democratic will of the people if three changes were enforced:

- Full federal funding of elections: Elections paid in full by taxpay-ers, each candidate receiving the same amount of money with no additional funds allowed. (In lieu of this, strict federal limits on candidate *spending* might accomplish the same goal.)
- Corporations should not be allowed to spend tax-exempt dollars on influencing public policy for *the benefit of their shareholders*. Their employees are free to vote and contribute as they like.
- It must be illegal for lobbyists to make any tangible contribution to legislators (money, junkets, speaking fees, future employment, etc.), which would be unnecessary since their campaign costs would be underwritten by taxpayers. This would even the playing field among lobbyists, allowing information rather than influence to seep into congressional offices.

Any political veteran reading this knows instantly that it is a lost cause. It is. Money is so woven into the system that corruption (inten-tional or unintentional) is endemic. However, the impossibility to consider such a change should make it obvious to readers how taboo the subject is to open, candid discussion. It appears logical that if legislators are ever to be once again responsive to the will of the voters, they should be in their employ. As things stand now, other than organizing focus groups to determine the buzzwords and issues that will win them votes, congressional and senate *loyalty* is reserved for the owners of private fortunes and the finance/insurance/real estate/energy sectors of the economy.

I mention it here, in the same spirit that Buddhists take impossible vows—beings are numberless, I vow to save them, etc. Vows are not logical or based on the possible. They are aspirational and aimed at charting behavior over vast periods of time, trusting that it if it is worthy, it will be picked up, modeled, and passed forward. If they are articulated there may be some dim hope that positive changes will occur. Without them, the chaos will continue while more and more people will lose faith in democracy as our system continues to deteriorate, rotting from within.

Wealthy industrial cultures exist in multiple countries, where industrialists and elites understand that strong unions keep workers feeling safe and reduce turnover, making adequate training of employees worthwhile and reducing urban turmoil. It should be clear that unless we negotiate ways of living with one another that are sustainable (meaning, among other things just, democratic, and fair) instead of short-term "gotcha" moments, we are running the game of America as if it were a sports event, transforming it from an infinite game to a finite game without ever asking ourselves: If the game "ends," what do we have? Buddhism, particularly in a vernacular expression, may be the most radical tool we have available to address the root of the problem.

Meditating on self and other will demonstrate to nearly anyone in short order that either/or victories will not work for the country in the long term. This is why parliaments are more successful at actual representation of the people than a two-party system can be. While it's true that we are "individual" existences, it is as demonstrably true that we are all parts of a whole, and so the appropriate question is: Who would want a diseased right arm? Either the body-politic is made healthy and whole, or its illness will spread until it is irrevocably weakened.

23

On Loss: Issa's "And Yet . . ."

·····

October 7, 2020

IT'S DIFFICULT NOT TO SPECULATE too often about loss these days. Everywhere I've been in the past months, people have appeared stressed, unhappy, restless, bored, hyperirritable, craving sociability and human contact, and struggling with loss of jobs and income. Many have mentioned that they could handle the pandemic's inconveniences when they believed that the Covid-19 shutdowns might be for only three or four months. Now, it's clear to all that the pandemic will extend into the next year and probably beyond.

I woke this morning (September 9) before sunrise, and the sky was black. When I emerged from zazen at 7:00 a.m. it was still black, and two hours later someone called me, alarmed, exclaiming, "The sky is black!" It was so dark I suspected it might have been an eclipse, but it was smoke from massive forest fires incinerating vast areas just north of where I live, blotting out the light. Later, the day turned more ominous.

People are on overload.

Kobayashi Issa was born Kobayashi Nobuyuki on June 15, 1763, in the village of Kashiwabara (present-day Nagano prefecture), Japan. He had a life filled with sorrow and difficulty after his mother died when he was three, and his father's new wife was a cruel and unloving step-mother. Teased relentlessly at school for being motherless, he spent his days alone, and fifty years later he wrote a haiku commemorating that loneliness.

> 我と来て遊べや親のない雀
> ware to kite asobe ya oya no nai suzume

> *come and play*
> *with me . . .*
> *orphan sparrow*

His stepmother banished him at fourteen, and he became a lay follower of the Pure Land school of Buddhism, writing poems under the pen name Issa—Priest's One Cup of Tea—referring to himself as a priest of the Haiku Temple. A deeply spiritual man who was obviously influenced by Buddhism, he appears to have been a lay practitioner. Issa wandered for more than forty years, begging for his sustenance and writing haiku. He left more than twenty-two thousand haiku poems as a legacy and is ranked by the Japanese among the top four haiku masters of their culture, along with Basho, Buson, and Shiki. He married at fifty, and on the death of his second child, Sato, a daughter who died at two, he wrote the following:

> 露の世は露の世ながらさりながら
> Tsuyu no yo wa tsuyu no yo nagara sari nagara

> *This dewdrop world*
> *Is but a dewdrop world*
> *And yet, and yet . . .*

This translation is by Gary Snyder from his book *Danger on Peaks*. Gary observes in his essay that Issa's "And Yet . . ." is our perennial practice and may be the root of dharma. We've all seen dew in the morning, sparkling for only a short time before it evaporates beneath the sun's heat. For Issa dew emblemizes the transiency of things and events. As a Buddhist and poet whose heart is fully open, his *and yet* speaks to our all-too-human sense of loss and grief. He understands how reality is conditioned. He understands transience, that all things are impermanent, but his *and yet* signifies indelibly how difficult mourning and grief are to bear and that they are never separate from all of life, no matter how deep our understanding may be.

Suffering does not occur because people are not sufficiently enlightened or spiritual. Buddha called suffering and affliction Noble Truths. It is the bedrock reality of human existence, and there is no one who escapes it. Grief is the price we pay for loving and loss. We do not choose between experiencing and not experiencing grief, but rather between bearing the loss with dignity or running to the distractions of the bar, mall, casino, compulsive sex, or drugs. There is nothing in Buddhist practice that makes us immune to the loss indicated by those words—*and yet*.

Psychologist John Wellwood coined the phrase *spiritual bypassing* to describe those who try to hide their emotional difficulties behind a bulletproof facade of imperturbability, passing stoic woodenness off as being too developed to display emotion.

Such behavior is a direct by-product of the search for a *personal* salvation instead of practicing to save all beings. Spiritual bypassing is a difficult double-bind to dodge. It's a variety of magical thinking: "If I can remain untroubled, maybe I won't age and be moving toward death. People will respect me if I am in control of my emotions." The focus remains on the self—well-rounded and half an inch in diameter.

When my granddaughter was an infant, she had severe asthma attacks and had to be taken to the hospital emergency room multiple times. The doctors would have to draw blood from veins in her arms that appeared smaller than hairs. I or her parents would have to hold her still, inches away from her face, which was distorted by fear, pain, and betrayal, and were helpless to explain to her why we were holding her still to be stabbed with needles. The "Why" in her eyes was as tangible as a slap.

Her parents and I understood that this had to be done, but we had no way to detach from her pain and fear, no way to explain it to her, and consequently no way to comfort ourselves, either. Sometimes all that we can do is be completely present as witnesses in the moment, no matter how horrid it might be. Within such moments, in its actual textures, qualities, and parts, sometimes the undiluted taste of existence is indisputably driven home.

What is the loss I am referring to? It is the consequence of attachment and affection. It's the real price of a ticket to the Kingdom of Love. Occasionally, when I come across a dead creature in the woods, or a dead bird in front of my window, I experience it as a shock. I have a sudden pang for that creature—a titmouse who snapped his neck against my window, a gopher mauled by the jaws of my dog or cat, an entire red fox I stumbled across in a pasture recently whose life was abruptly cut short. When I noticed too many bees drowning in the water dish I leave out for the birds, I floated a snippet of twigs in the dish so they could escape. I can't help but put my finger under them and lift them free of the surface tension. It's beyond thought, simply a creature-to-creature impulse. I watch them shake their wings and eventually dry off in the sun and fly away. That bee wants to live, and so do I. We both come from nowhere and are working our way back. How can I not have tender feelings for these little propagators of flowers and fruit, these chemists of honey?

There's an ancient story of a woman named Kisa Gotami, who lived in the time of the Buddha. She was wandering absently, carrying her dead baby, blinded by grief. She visited the Buddha and begged him, "Help me. I'm suffering so much I can't stand it."

The Buddha told her: "Put down your baby, and I'll look after it. I want you to visit every household in the village, and I want you to collect a mustard seed from every house where death has not claimed someone," and he sent her off.

Buddha didn't touch her forehead and inject some magic wisdom into her that lit her up like a bulb. He didn't tell her that all things were empty of self (true enough). He told her the absolute truth, that in this world of form everything is impermanent. It's the fundamental rule of the infinite game we call Life. He instructed her in this way because the absolute truth would do more to save her by reintegrating her into the actual world where her heart might be opened to the suffering of others and where she could claim her grief, stop seeking to flee it, and burn it to ash. In her actual life, she might understand that the pain of her loss was the consequence of her love for her child and the cost of having a body.

We know that life is not a Hallmark card, but somehow when grief touches us, when we are reminded that each thing (except all of it) is impermanent, it's unnerving. The body doesn't want to die, even though I suspect the body knows how to die quite well. It's been doing that for eons. Animals know how to die. I used to hunt and fish for nearly the first third of my life, and I witnessed many animal deaths. When there was no escape, the animal resigned itself to its fate. Our mammal bodies have been dying for millions of years, and I suspect, beneath our narratives and anxieties, they understand the process, even if our egos don't.

There's no way to avoid the loss inherent in impermanence, and while there may be people who would prefer to live without love in the hopes of avoiding that pain, I don't know any. There's no way to run away from the pain in your knees when you sit long periods zazen. The only thing you can do with it is to become intimate with it, and, curiously, the decision not to flee but to stand fast alters the quality of the pain itself. Investigate it. Separate the warp and the weft of it; let the light in. Discover its specific textures and qualities and learn the true taste of your suffering, which is also the true taste of being human.

When you do that, something changes. The flight from pain, the pushing it away, repressing it from consciousness, exhausts us and somehow increases the difficulty of it. But if we examine it with a tranquil mind, we may come to understand that in this world pain and discomfort are inevitable; clouds will sometimes cover the sun. It will get cold and uncomfortable or extremely hot. They are the characteristics of being alive, and they are also the price of loving life.

And yet reminds us that the impermanence is all we have. Impermanence is what renders entities precious. No one has powerful emotions about artificial flowers, because they are not dying. It is the transitory, fragile nature of flowers that decrees them precious. It is that way with everything. If we deny it, we bypass our own humanity for the sake of some imagined tranquillity and will discover in that logic only cold comfort.

Emotions are as real as anything else. No more, no less. It's not that every feeling requires expression, but neither should they be denied. Spiritual bypassing is the social neurosis of practitioners and communities who believe that enlightenment exists in some imagined realm beyond the passions and *samsara* (ancient Sanskrit word referring to an endless cycle of death and rebirth and suffering) of our daily existence. Such practitioners appear to have been captured by the belief that any display of emotion is a red flag that will alert others to their spiritual immaturity.

There is also a way to twist the assumption that Emptiness could lead people to believe that impermanence can justify nihilism and conclude too facilely that if everything is impermanent and the "self" illusory, why should moral behavior matter? If a human being is, for instance, no more substantial than a soap bubble, why does killing or taking advantage of them matter?

To preclude such detours, the Buddha established guardrails in an ethical framework before beginning to teach. He understood that if those insights were understood solely through the personality (the small mind) and the intellect they could easily be misconstrued and misapplied. Impermanence in no way connotes valueless.

My father used to warn me that a little knowledge is a dangerous thing, and extrapolating Buddha's teaching to suggest that impermanence obviates moral behavior is a perfect example of that dictum. The deeper truth is that Buddhist thought does not privilege one side of a duality, like *self* and *other*. We don't discuss good and evil or dualisms often, because Buddha-nature always contains both. Though we navigate the torrents of life in our borrowed kayak of a body, simultaneously we should not be so fooled by appearances to accept that we and the river we run have separate existences. In a world characterized by interdependence, if anything is sacred, it's *all of it*. Everything comes and goes, and while any single thing can be destroyed—all of it—Buddha-nature cannot be.

And yet (these two evocative words express so much). *And yet*. In the world of form, of individuated bodies and the apparent separation of self and other, attachment and aversion are inevitable. Because we overstress the importance of self we can undervalue the worth of other. In truth, every single entity of creation is a nonrepeatable expression of Buddha-nature—like a snowflake. A housefly may not mean much to us, but it meant enough to the Universe to create it. Each thing has an inherent and absolute value and is, in its own way, a Buddha modeling Buddha-nature in one of its infinite forms.

In stressful situations, many people seek comfort and relief in spiritual practice, thinking it will somehow save them from sorrows, woes, the rigors and disappointments of life. We may believe that enlightenment is a state existing on the other side of a fence that we can hurdle by practice and meditation. We may believe there is a separate enlightenment that will, once attained, free us from all suffering, difficulty, and unpleasantness, forever. Snyder once referred to such confections as *sexless nirvana*.

And yet . . . for 2,500 years men and women have experienced kensho and enlightenment and preserved and transmitted the Buddha's teaching. If they hadn't, I would not be writing today. It is our greed that seduces us into believing that we can live permanently in such peak states. I believe I've mentioned the Default Mode Network before, an area of the brain that keeps us stabilized and focused on our orthodox perceptions. It conserves a great deal of energy by maintaining our focus as a way to ensure our survival. Issa's haiku "And Yet . . ." reminds us that we don't exist perennially in an enlightened state. For our life to move and change it must be *afflicted* by what I sometimes imagine as "peppered winds" of the Universe; the affliction generating samu-daya—arising—(the Second Noble Truth) within us, instilling us with the desire to move or change our state, impelling us toward what we want. It is enlightenment itself moving us, supplying the motive energy, that transforms chaotic impulses and random encounters into a life that models the Buddha's. *Enlightenment* is not a static noun but a verb.

It is compassion that protects us against a nihilistic interpretation of Emptiness (inter-being/impermanence) as meaningless. It is our empathy and wonder at our Universe, including the little housefly on my fingertip, washing its face and grooming its wings and following its own unimaginable purposes. It is easy to swat but impossible to do so if we ever grant it full consideration as Buddha-nature.

During sesshins, the scraps of each meal are collected from our bowls and offered to the "hungry ghosts" (ants and insects) outdoors. I don't cite this consideration to signal virtue or advertise Buddhism's compassion. It arises spontaneously on seeing suffering and wondering if there is anything one can do. If Zen has done anything to help me, it has obliterated the distinctions between little and big, important and unimportant. Flies have their work to do, and our intersections with one another needn't be lethal. It saddens me to find their bod-ies between my windows and the screen, where they died trying to escape. It is difficult not to wonder if they experienced anxiety.

Everything is like that.

O

Impermanence is never an excuse to allow compassion to evaporate or to fail to remember the transitory nature of everything, includ-ing our own lives. These expressions are precious *because* they are impermanent—and because they are precious to us, we grieve when we lose them . . . *despite* our understanding of Emptiness. This is the bone-dry country of Issa's poem.

It's important to our practice to remember that impermanence does not hinder us from being kind or being studious and committed to wisdom. Impermanence does not render things valueless or prevent us from treasuring the expressions of human mind and culture of ages past. Nor does perception of impermanence prevent us from sweeping the sidewalk in front of our store or home, washing our windows, helping the homeless, or extending courtesy and respect to everyone we encounter.

The necessary question is: How do we live as transients in an impermanent world? What practices are useful and which can we jettison?

For arguments sake, I'll offer that there is only one thing in the Universe that we can control, and that is our intention. Zen Buddhists try to train their intention with the force of habit to kindness and compassion. The emphasis rests on "try"—trying continuously to marshal our attention to remain in and be open to the present moment. We are all fallible and should not pretend that we are not. However, that fallibility should not be an excuse for failing to make the effort. And we do fail. It is something that only happens to the living; consequently, Buddhists refer to what we do as a practice. When we inevitably fail, miss the mark, or disappoint ourselves by failing to achieve our standards, the practice of righting ourselves like a sailboat, returning to our upright intention is our moment-to-moment work. Our ballast, righting us, is our Buddhist vows. Carried out wholeheartedly, the intention of kindness is our compass, directing us on our way along the Buddha's Eightfold Path. This path has a purpose. Speaking about it with my teacher one day, he responded emphatically, as if I were missing the point, *"If you are not kind and helpful to people, who cares what kind of spiritual experience you had!"*

We behave as enlightened beings when we attend our Buddha-nature—Buddha's wisdom—and vows. When our acts are thus directed, we are behaving in an enlightened manner. Following the Eightfold Path *is* enlightened action as we continually cross-check our decisions and impulses against our Buddha-nature. A Zen master who utilizes dharma as a merit badge, camouflage for seduction, or quest for personal power and social status is just another hustler in this dewdrop world. We may have the same problems as before, but as Katagiri-roshi once observed, "They are in the bamboo tube of practice, even the snake of our craziness," so they are contained and do not generate negative consequences.

We may assume that a life we desire is the life we should expect, or even the life we deserve because we're kind and good people. We may feel that we will be exempted from the final bill for our rented bodies. Zazen helps us see things as they really are and to accept them as the workings of Universe, operating with impersonal laws and logic even if we do not understand them. It is not teaching us to master superhuman detachment, allowing us to regard whatever we might observe inside or out (and we may not always be clear on the distinction) without emotional response. That is not what the Buddha taught.

Even if it were possible, such a teaching would leave most of humanity behind. Of course, we want to monitor and control our attention, but we also inhabit these "flesh sacks," bearing their own experiences and generating responses according to the fluctuations of hormones and events. Our bodies and sense organs are full of feelings, perceptions, thoughts, sensations, hunches, and intimations. That is our actual life. They are our actual mind.

And yet, remembering the universal sorrows of the dewdrop world, it becomes reflex to add as little harm and suffering to it as we can, to care for each moment as if it were a precious, newly minted constellation placed in our care to be groomed for future maturity.

Such compassion toward the world feels natural and is certainly not exclusively Buddhist. Compassion is our natural human state of readiness, and evidence of it exists in every culture and tradition and is also part of our genetic heritage.

Archaeologists have discovered Neanderthal graves where the interred bodies could not have survived their grievous wounds had they not been cared for by others. The graves are filled with flowers and pollens, obviously placed there as offerings. As far back as human history extends, and no matter how much murderous evidence we amass to buttress arguments about the rapaciousness of human nature (a mental pet of those who favor unregulated capitalism as an economic system), it is equally true that we, like many of our evolutionary antecedents, specifically bonobos,* are as genetically directed toward compassion and caring for one another as we are toward violence.

From a Buddhist context, human nature is really no nature— boundaryless, indefinable, the same pregnant energy roiling the Universe. To extend kindness, to act on the understanding that everything wants to live is our practice. An insect struggling to escape a water dish is using every ounce of its energy to live. When you put your finger under it and lift one out, it shakes the water from her wings and wiggles her butt until she's dry and can fly away. I don't know if they feel gratitude, lucky, or if they feel anything, but *I* feel tenderness toward it, toward the flowers that nourish her, and to the foods she pollinates that makes my world comprehensible. My indisputable relationship with these little beings dictates my care for them.

The county where my tiny farm is located has, over the past two decades, replaced the dry-farm, unirrigated orchards of apples and plums with water-intensive vineyards and marijuana plantations. Wine in particular has become a signifier of taste and social status and so rests in a cocoon of social silk. Wine fosters social cohesion, stimulates the palate, and is generally considered an unalloyed positive. However, most vineyards use fungicides on the crop to protect the grapes, which negatively affects bee populations by killing the enzymes in their saliva that turn pollen into beebread, the food they make for their larva. When I try to discuss this issue with vintners and wine connoisseurs they may cluck good naturedly or inform me politely that they have "bigger fish to fry." But do they really?

---

*Adherents of the tooth-and-claw school of nature make much of the violence and murderous behavior of chimps toward rival bands. But bonobos, whose sex organs face front and who can have face-to-face sex, may be even closer relatives, and their social life is distinctly based on sharing and partnership, even of sexual partners, where the highest calling appears to be keeping the peace.

Indigenous populations used to consider the consequences of decisions for seven generations to ensure that today's decisions would not impinge on tomorrow's life. What are we to make of corporate and manufacturing decisions that make sense for profits but destroy the natural world, using rivers, the atmosphere, and oceans as sumps for manufacturing effluents, and bearing none of the costs or consequences?

Buddhists take vows to save *all* beings, so we cannot really exempt ourselves from our part in causal chains harming them. Can we afford to kill honeybees? Can we afford to poison human populations with oil production, gasoline engines, and coal-fired power plants simply to enrich a small percentage of our species? What do you think?

The problems of global warming are enormous and frightening, and we can't blame people for fearing the social disruption that could shatter social norms and agreements if not done carefully. However, doing nothing has cost us many deaths and trillions of dollars and, more alarming, is spawning vast migrations of populations across the globe, populations impelled by the mandate of staying alive. Such masses will arrive with tidal force, overwhelming all borders in their search for food, grazing, water, and livelihoods. We could well be facing not the end of humanity but of civilization. What would life be like if the entire Earth began to resemble war-torn Afghanistan and Iraq?

The logic of interdependence demands that we broaden the parameters of our inclusion and understand that it is not only people who are suffering but millions of species as well. If any among us might believe that science can free us of these mutual relationships, or believe that billionaire's' rocket ship jaunts will deliver us to some other inhabitable planet, please speak up now. If we colonized Mars, it would only be a matter of time before the undisciplined behavior of the chosen few colonizing it would result in war and exploitation rendering it unlivable. There is no escape from the demons of humanity except learning to detach from them. We are all like kayakers shooting the Grand Canyon rapids. We can't control the river, but we can develop our skills and play with its energy and develop our resilience and patience. These are the tools we need to live successfully. We do what we can, radiating compassion and kindness because the world is literally us. If I'm made of sunshine, if I'm made of microbes in the soil, if I'm made of water, if I'm made of your efforts as well, my life is certainly inseparable from all of it.

This dewdrop world
Is but a dewdrop world
And yet . . . and yet.

24

Contradictions

.....

April 14, 2021

Contradictions in Human Nature Based on
the Genjo Koan—the Koan of
Actual Living

ANOTHER OF MY FAVORITE Suzuki-roshi dharma talks is titled "Good and Bad. Half and Half." It is a perfect complement to Fuketsu's speck of dust.

In this talk, Suzuki-roshi discusses the inherent contradictions in human nature and how the way-seeking mind arises, usually when we have some problem that feels insoluble. Normally, when we want to study something or solve a problem, we concentrate on it, isolating it from the rest of our life. Think of going to church on Sundays, temple on Saturdays, or attending a Zen center's public lectures and discussions on Sundays. Concentrating on your spiritual life one day a week. Quite often that suffices for most people, but while quite normal, and certainly okay, that's neither *practice* in a Buddhist sense nor a way-seeking mind.

Eventually, we will all, at some point, encounter contradictions in life we can neither straddle nor resolve. It may be aging or some sense that ordinary life has become meaningless or is no longer working for us. It may express itself as a feeling of having nothing to rely on. That's the soil in which the way-seeking mind sprouts. That's where the quest for help or some need advances to the foreground and claims the forefront of our awareness.

When I was young, I dedicated whatever energy was left over from self-criticism and wondering if every house in Englewood was as unhappy as mine. I was searching for something I could commit to with total belief and vigor. I began to campaign for Adlai Stevenson for president (at fourteen), march and speak up for integration and civil rights, travel to Washington to oppose nuclear testing. I honestly believed that my efforts and sincerity would make a difference in ensuring a better, more inclusive future for everyone. I became adroit at ignoring the shadow aspects of what I was doing—being closed-minded about the opinions of others, arguing angrily with them, dismissing those who disagreed with me. I chose sides as if they were unrelated to one another, arguing only for the virtue of mine, appending all evil to my opponents. This carried me quite a long way.

I pursued my goals in the same way for decades, but by the time I passed my midtwenties, my own sense of truth began to push back. I was unable *not* to notice how, in my "perfect world" of the Left, the counterculture and communes, where my peers and I were living and claiming to be the next evolution of America, a sizeable number of problems were metastasizing, inside and outside our communities. Despite our rigorous efforts, in the midst of the organic brown rice and veggies, collective work, minimal material footprint, and the sexual and chemical free-fire zones, some of our children were not thriving, some of the women grew tired of listening to men pontificating all the time. One of our kids had eaten a slice of pumpkin pie filled with LSD that was stashed carelessly in the refrigerator and spent a terrified afternoon among adults who were not prepared for such an upset.

Years later, I was shocked to discover that one of our communes had a child molester among the population. Sexual tensions and betrayals could suddenly flare and disrupt community harmony. Relationships between men and women were not always as wholesome, equal, generous, and supportive as the men believed they were. We had not evolved beyond fixed attachment to opinions, and some barking-mad ideas, and neither had the nation. At a certain point I could no longer not notice these contradictions. I realized that the new world my comrades and I had been assiduously constructing had some serious flaws in its foundations and design. No matter how beautiful the finished building might have appeared in the architect's renderings, out where the rubber met the road, problems were multiplying faster than the zucchini. Children were getting older, and many parents felt our homeschooling did not suffice. They moved away, closer to town and easy access to schools. As families became established, commune life became more orderly and demanding of quiet and certain basic considerations from others. The imposition of any order conflicted with the laissez-faire attitudes of two or three years earlier. A group house couldn't allow Wino Eddy to be playing his congas at four in the morning, when mothers were waking to breastfeed at five. In the final analysis, despite ideals and goals I continue to believe in and practice, the new world we were constructing was not serving the American people as a model they clamored to replicate. The death knell to any remaining New Age optimism was when the American people elected Richard Nixon and Ronald Reagan as president and governor, respectively. If I was honest, the way things were going were also no longer serving me.

We can work hard. We can concentrate. We can persist, but if we are not tracking our internal life and exerting the discipline on our shadow sides, nothing will work out as we hope. I suppose that was the conclusion that led me to Buddhist practice.

Previously I had been fascinated by indigenous cultures because, of all people, they were the repository of encyclopedic knowledge of the continent we were inhabiting. They knew how to live here without ruining it, using nature as their hardware store, grocery store, and pharmacy. I searched them out and kept my mouth shut and my ears open and spent a lot of time with Karuk people in Northern California, running around with Rolling Thunder, a Paiute-Shoshone medicine man, who'd come to the Haight searching for Diggers, and saying he'd had a dream that we were the ghosts of Indians who died at the Battle of Little Big Horn. It sounded like B.S. to me, but "good" B.S., and despite sometimes resembling a carnival barker, I had witnessed Rolling Thunder doing some extremely impressive things. I had taken lots of peyote and sat up all night in the highly ritualized tipi gatherings of "road" people, but none of them were of my culture. What's more, I knew that I would never be cut into the deepest levels of Native wisdom without a sponsor. On the other hand, Buddhism was a world religion—I figured that they had to take me, and that at the deepest level all religions shared the same transcendental truth. That is the train of thought that led me to Buddhist practice.

By nature, human beings are half positive and half negative because that is exactly how the Universe is composed. All of us, each of us has negative energy, a shadow side, engrained in us as a birthright. It is the evolutionary baggage all humans have carried forward from our earliest days, and we can understand how, in a lawless and uncertain world, greed, aversion, and delusion might serve positive purposes. The problem is that in a nuclear world of nine billion souls with nuclear weapons, that ancient heritage has us teetering on the edge of world suicide.

Does the following scenario appear remotely familiar to you? When we want to accomplish something, we might make pledges like, "I want to develop more. I'm going to stop watching TV late at night (or porn, Twitter, Instagram, or Facebook), throw out all of my coffee, buy green tea, get up early every morning, and sit zazen."

And then, after a late and festive night and a dark and chilly early morning, we say, "Oh, I was so busy yesterday, I'm exhausted. I'll just sleep a bit longer and do better tomorrow." We may oscillate—"Maybe I'll just take twenty minutes more sleep, but I *am* gonna sit zazen. Okay, maybe I'll take five minutes. Actually, I won't sit today, but I'll get up with a fresh start tomorrow."

The more disciplined we become, the more alert we become to our little self-deceptions. The more conscientious we become, the more clearly we begin to observe ourselves and the more rigorous we become with our expectations of ourselves. Instead of feeling badly 50 percent of the time, we begin feeling badly 95 percent of the time, because we have finally begun to examine ourselves more scrupulously and allowing ourselves less slack to roam off course. The consequence is that we wind up with less certainty about how spiritually developed we are, and at that point we can either bluff or get serious and make some sort of commitment. When we make a commitment, it's important to keep it. It's better to say, "'Okay, for one month I'll try to sit zazen twice a week'" and then keep that commitment, than it is to say you'll sit every day and fail. If after a month twice weekly is too little, or you feel you could do more, make a new commitment for a month and stick to it. When we finally understand that our human nature *itself* is half positive and half negative, we discover the true rationale for mindfulness and monitoring our own behavior. We discover that we are often the problem we are trying to solve.

The fact is that as our culture advances in one direction, so do its composite parts—positive and negative—and the sum total of our difficulties appears to remain intact.

Racism has been an ugly and public stain on our national honor for 250 years and today white supremacists march in our streets and gun-crazy teenagers murder people in black churches and Jewish temples, new laws are being passed where white people now determine the manner in which black history must be taught. Young people are not free to explore their gender (depending on where they live), even as women are losing the right to control when, how, and if they give birth. At least one judge on the Supreme Court has expressed an opinion that the Constitution does not protect same-sex relationships, sex, and marriage.

When we realize the ineradicable presence of positive and negative aspects of our personality, quite often we don't know how to respond. As long as we have this human nature, it appears impossible (to the small mind, anyway) to ever achieve a spiritual culture in the human world. *And yet,* what can we do but try?

My father was a highly successful businessman for a good while. He appeared to mint money and prosper at everything he did. In 1962 one misstep bankrupted him and sluiced his entire fortune: a stockbroker's business, multiple farms and cattle, hounds and silken rugs, down the drain. I was embarrassed about this wealth when I was young—perhaps it had something to do with being delivered to school and dropped off in front of my friends in a chauffeured car. In my teens, I argued with him about inequity and the need to care for others, or how life was unfair for Sue and Ozzie* and their friends. My father would always respond with a parable about a lifeboat at sea, with three people and only enough food for two. He never really fleshed out the story to my satisfaction, but the implication I was supposed to take away had something to do with survival of the fittest. Personally, I could never envision murder and cannibalism as an admirable option to strive for. (My father ran a brokerage house on Wall Street, though, so perhaps should be forgiven.) Neither could I envision many scenarios where cooperation and chance might not offer them all the possibility of survival if they cooperated.

What bothered me most about this metaphor as a boy was the lack of effort and the lack of *aspiring* to be helpful. It's important to remember that Buddhist vows do not embrace merely the possible. They are vows that we intend to fulfill in spite of prevailing facts and attitudes, no matter the odds. They are vows we will model in our lives in the hope of inspiring others, to keep them alive and pass them forward to successive generations. However, we do that *knowing* that it's the nature of reality that things will be difficult, will fail, and also go south. So

---

*Sue Howard was a young African American girl who came to work for my family at 18 after my mother had a crippling breakdown. She soon took over the house and in short order became the emotional anchor and safehouse for my sister and I. She and her boyfriend (and later husband) Ozzie Nelson were two of the most important people in my life. They remained in my home town and we stayed close until she died in 2019. My kitchen was filled every day with her friends, discussing the world, the bible, politics and relations with "white-folk." It was from them that I learned to see and understand what "whiteness" meant as a privilege.

what? It means we have to behave in a manner we can sustain forever. If we're too rigid, too insistent on purity, too judgmental, exhaust ourselves through refusing to rest or taking too many stimulants, we will never last the course, because there are never going to be *just* people who think and believe as you do, in this world.

Not understanding the perennial existence of shadows, we are not always alert for their unintended appearance and consequences. Considering ourselves "the good people," as our leaders reassure us that we are, is too facile a solution for this complex and demanding world. When we don't acknowledge the full spectrum of our human potential, we will always excuse, overlook, or ignore the wreckage we leave behind us as we pass.

If the standards we apply to President Putin do not also apply equally to ourselves, we are not supporting the rule of law but rather asserting our own privileges. When we remain fixed on being perfect (exceptional) and demand perfect justice, perfect spirituality, perfect economy, we make the perfect the enemy of the good, defeating our best intentions.

We can discuss spiritual life as much as we want. We can read as many spiritual books as we want, microdose at the tech office, or drink ourselves blind on the weekends. We are not going to help anyone, least of all ourselves if all our investigations are one-sided. Remember the opening lines of Gary Snyder's poem "This Tokyo"? *"War. Peace. Religion. Revolution. Will not help."* If we can't develop the courage to see Buddha-nature fully and clearly, we can never claim to understand our own nature, either.

Buddha's teaching is not based on an *idea* of who we are, or a theory about the world, but on seeing "things as it is." You can, too. We can all understand that affliction exists. Negativity exists. Our problems exist, and yet Buddha insists they are Noble Truths. In his book *The Feeling Buddha,* David Brazier points directly toward negativity as energy turning the world, "thickening the plot," as Gary Snyder once described it. The energy is like gasoline, which, if contained, can be put to good use like driving an engine, but allowed to burn freely it can become uncontrollable. Our passions and energies are also energy that can be put to careless use or to good use, but only if we can face them squarely and develop the discipline to contain them.

Some people jump to an easy conclusion and insist, "Well, if human nature is always the same, it's useless to practice. It's useless to try to change things." But *Buddhists are not trying to improve reality.* That's an important point. Big Mind already contains *everything.* It is the source of every problem and every conclusion and certainly the source of our own undisciplined and dark impulses as well as our nobler ones. If we are in conflict with Big Mind, and cannot accept the world as it is, we will never subject ourselves to discipline—which is to say, never transform our anarchic nature into noble, dignified, and helpful lives.

Buddha accepted the reality that human nature is both positive and negative. He based his study on that fact, and he taught us how to live with it. If you try to change that bedrock reality you are not modeling the Buddha's wisdom.

The Eightfold Path, the Sixteen Precepts, the Four Noble Truths are all teachings on how to deal with, manage, and neutralize the discordant, 50 percent of our nature. That's what the deal is.

So, what *can* we do? We can move toward our intentions, testing them step by tentative step, testing our environment, to ensure that circumstances have not changed since we accepted our mission, and developed some strategy for it. We press forward, always testing our faith against our doubts. *Because* we have both positive and negative energies, it means we have the ability to see even the tiniest improvement in our work. We are never going to eradicate all shadows unless we eradicate the sun. Suzuki-roshi once described "a paper's thickness of difference between good and bad." That's enough. If we can see the paper's thickness of difference, we're moving things in the right direction and are not confused. That is not inconsequential. We also need to learn patience and persistence, because sometimes even the smallest improvements require a great deal of time and energy.

It makes no difference what kind of situation or problem we have. *What's important is to work on something.* That's what takes our focus. That's what shifts our focus from our addiction to our small minds. There's a problem—Oh! Let's get to work! Let's work on it. It's not just thinking about me, and what I can achieve as a Buddhist. Will I get a blue rakusu or a black one or a brown robe? Our intention should be leading us to doing something for everyone or nothing if there's nothing. apparent to do. How can we be helpful? is a question we can always ask. And how do we allow other people to help us? How do we know when to leave things alone. We are never going to be a sheet of paper that has only one side.

Realistically, if we want the future to be different from the present, we have to change the present. We have to work on ourselves. We have to sit zazen. We have to have trusted friends whose efforts we respect to advise us and jerk our chain when we are off base. We live in this vast realm where we have inconceivable freedom. Nirvana is actually the revelation that in the next instant we are absolutely free to behave differently from the moment before. But to take advantage of that freedom, we need discipline. If we misuse that absolute freedom, just to do something for ourselves, we are only redecorating.

We have absolute freedom to follow the path of negativity, to kill, to harm, to cheat, to steal, to misbehave sexually. Jehovah will not strike us dead. We can do whatever we want. But that doesn't stop the flow of consequences we set in motion, the law of cause and effect that Buddhists refer to as karma. It's indisputable. Even the street addicts I used to know honored karma when they said, "Payback is a motherfucker."

The mind is like a horse. It can be well or badly trained, can follow the command of our intention and intuition or take us where *it* wants us to go. The more conscientious and attentive we are, the more strict we will be with ourselves and the more we can trust ourselves. But if you have ever been on a horse and had it bolt, jump, or throw you, you know that a ride can go badly wrong in an instant.

When we can get in touch with Big Mind, when we understand that it is far more trustworthy than our small personality, to the degree that we become interested in this practice, we have started on a noble and dignified path outside of the tiny domain of the self. This trust in absolute Emptiness, preceding all form, color, impulse, sensation, and consciousness is the only article of faith that Buddhist practice requires us to have. Again, however, it's not the kind of faith one has in miracles, because eventually you will certify it for yourself. It is synonymous with having faith in our inner nature as identical with Buddha's. Your "I" is Buddha's "I." The old-timers used to say of the students to whom they transmitted their authority: "His eyebrows have tangled with Buddha's."

We don't know what is going to come next. We don't know what to do. But we can aim our intention toward being helpful. Even if we are only a paper's width away from negativity, it is enough.

We appeared in this world, just like the little wavelets dimpling the ocean's surface I referred to in an earlier metaphor. We will arise into form for a while and eventually settle back into the formless ocean. Our birth foreshadows our death. We were born with that sentence hanging over us, which means we should not waste our time in trivial pursuits. But what we refer to as dying is the ocean, which generated us, reclaiming us. In some sense we're going nowhere. Perhaps the ego can't handle that, but the body can.

To see things otherwise is to regard the world from the viewpoint of the transient self. The Heart Sutra reminds us that "dharmas don't appear, or disappear, are not tainted nor pure." Our "guest," this sack of meat, is one of the billions of little wavelets peaking in the ocean and then collapsing back into the ocean. Nothing about that affects the ocean itself. Awareness itself will not disappear from Earth, but it was never a personal possession to begin with. And finally, the entity we so confidently identify as "us" is also the ocean from which we have never for one instant been separate. So, we don't have to worry about that too much, so why not concentrate on what we can control?

Even if we attain enlightenment, we should dedicate it to something. We have this practice. We should do something with it. Ask yourself: *What do I want to do*? Don't be overeager, because you are going to be doing as much bad as you do good, but, tentatively, what's something you'd enjoy doing? My first wife is an accomplished Japanese tea-ceremony practitioner. It's a very strict and demanding form that she's practiced for forty years. She once told me of a fellow student who confessed that she came to tea ceremony because it was the only thing she could think of that did not make her feel anxious. What a wonderful reason to begin something. What are you going to do with your twenty-four hours?

Finally, the point is not that our practice is right or wrong, or good or bad, the question is: Are we making a constant effort? Are we focusing our intention consistently, moment after moment after moment? Practicing kindness? Practicing how to be helpful? Despite the knowledge that it's completely impossible for us to avoid our bad karma, the Buddha did teach us a way that will minimize harm. That seems like enough to begin, doesn't it?

25

Buddhist Anarchism

.....

January 26, 2021

GARY SNYDER WROTE AN ESSAY TITLED "Buddhist Anarchism," which I first read more than fifty years ago. It has been foundational in my understanding of what I imagined Buddhist practice might be, and reviewing it as the final chapter of this book seems appropriate to me.

Rereading this essay was like bumping into a cherished old friend, someone you're reenergized to introduce and share with all your pals. So I'd like to review this article, share some quotations from it and discuss them, because it's not only formative to my understanding, but it also addresses some current misunderstandings about the differences between spiritual and secular life that I think are important. It speaks to a view of Buddhist practice perhaps in the minority today, but a minority among which I consider myself an active member.

I've been criticized before for raising political issues in my dharma talks by people who remind me (often quite aggressively) that they tuned in to my talks for balm and comfort not an examination of the world's discord. If you are interested in Buddhism as a morphine suppository to temporarily smother your pain or discomfort, you need to ask your doctor for a triplicate prescription. You are wasting your time listening to me, because that's not my understanding of what the Buddha intended to accomplish.

Buddhism asserts that the Universe and everything in it is intrinsically interdependent, in complete harmony and mutually responsive. It may not feel that way when we regard the world and its follies, cravings, and cruelties through the lens of our prejudices and personality. What Buddha perceived was the transpersonal common source of the Universe as pure energy. Though he did not name it after himself, Buddhists now refer to this formless energy as Buddha-nature or Buddha mind. This roiling, formless energetic common denominator incessantly expresses itself as the tangible forms of our reality, including our thoughts, feelings, impulses, sensation and consciousness. *This* is our actual self, not the learned and constructed personality we have come to treasure as a "self." The personal realization of this from-the-beginning-state cannot be had by and for oneself alone as a personal goal, because it's not fully realized until the self, and its concerns, are temporarily allowed to fall away.

I imagine that many of you may have begun your Zen practice as I did, searching for some balm or release from difficult feelings, afflictions, and suffering. The contradictory nature of my thinking when I was young led me to imagine enlightenment as an anodyne to all wounds, a fence I could hurdle or pierce and once on the other side, my life would generate peace, harmony, and goodwill with the reliability of an automobile engine. That idea lured me into sitting zazen, sweeping and cleaning and washing dishes at Zen Center, learning to housebreak some of my more intemperate impulses (and believe me, there's nothing like ten years of undisciplined, narcotized indulgence to polish intemperate impulses to a high sheen).

Desire to pierce that imagined enlightenment barrier forced me to restrain my opinions when they weren't asked for, to accept the strictures and the formal dress and personal restraints of behavior at Zen Center in hopes that such surrender would pay the tab for my one-way ticket to enlightenment. Those lessons were extremely helpful. I *needed* domesticating. My mind needed training, and I don't want anyone to believe that I am discrediting any of the valuable lessons I learned from monastic practice.

Today, however, my practice is secular in and of this dewdrop world. As long as we're considering ourselves an isolated integer separated from the rest of the Universe, we're out of luck. We sit on our cushion and we imagine ourselves over *here* and enlightenment over *there,* and they don't and won't meet. We're not going to bring them together because we're operating within a world Balkanized by language. Buddha's description of the Universe and all creatures in an intrinsically harmonious state of complete wisdom, love, and compassion is a unified whole. Snyder once elegantly translated that description as "*the hawk, the swoop, and the rabbit are all one.*"

However, it bears mentioning that the wisdom, love, and compassion are not designed for anthropocentric comforts. The hawk can be eaten by the eagle and the rabbit by everything. It all makes sense from the biggest perspective.

Living that perception is the trick. We may only perceive it for a few hours or minutes, but that's sufficient to recalibrate our perspective. Buddhists have always felt that the precepts and Eightfold Path are the visions of Buddha's enlightenment, and following them faithfully is in itself enlightenment. They both exist as a description of reality and as the product of his enlightened vision and will sustain you whether or not you achieve some radical awakening. Suzuki-roshi expressed this explicitly.

> To obtain enlightenment is not so difficult. Basically, he [Buddha] says that if you practice, if you practice well, it will come. You don't have to worry about it. What is difficult is to renew that enlightenment, moment after moment.

Hakuin, the great Rinzai Zen master, certainly would have agreed with that. He had many kenshos in his life, but the one he related to as his fundamental "opening" was the revelation that the Eightfold Path *itself* is enlightenment. It's not a map to get there. It is the recognition and the modeling of an enlightened life.

Buddhist philosophy identifies that which interrupts our manifestation of love, harmony, and compassion as ignorance, but historically, Buddhist philosophers have not often analyzed the degree to which suffering is amplified by social factors. For many centuries, Buddhists in every country were under the protection of and lived at the will of an Emperor. Politics was off-limits. In the West however, Buddhism has been liberated from that ancient obeisance and now often includes social and political factors as realms of suffering where meditation, compassion, and self-lessness have a positive role to play. Vietnamese Zen master Thich Nhat Hanh, who lived and taught much of his life in Plum Village in France, paid primary attention to social factors and social behavior in his teaching. Alan Senauke, the new abbot of my home temple, Berkeley Zen Center, has been working in Myanmar, where restrictions of human rights and *Buddhist* depredation against the Muslim Rohinga community have been labeled "crimes against humanity." American Buddhists have been meditating in front of nuclear power stations and taking stands on social problems afflicting the well-being of ordinary people, including structural and political problems. My former teacher, Robert Aitken, and his dharma heir, Nelson Foster, founded the Buddhist Peace Fellowship in 1978 for nonviolent social and environmental engagement.

Buddhists don't yell and scream when they demonstrate. They usually sit zazen or register their positions with dignity and with respect for themselves and those who oppose them. The message they transmit is more than a slogan. It includes dignity, self-possession, and discipline, which is designed to build trust and confidence among those who witness the demonstrations. In this essay, Snyder makes a clear and cold assessment of the contributions of Mahayana Buddhism—currently the most popular form in the United States and Europe—which encourages enlightenment for all beings. It offers a grand vision of universal salvation, but when we assess its *actual* achievements, it has remained largely confined to practical systems of meditation and monastic practice situations, toward the end of liberating a few dedicated individuals from psychological hang-ups and cultural conditioning.

In other words, of the millions of people studying Buddhism, not so many enlightened souls are dedicated to saving *all* beings. Enormous energy and effort go in to teaching this wisdom tradition and introducing people to it. But when we compare the number of people practicing Buddhism to the population of the Earth and our effect on the problems of the Earth, I think that we Buddhists have to admit that if we intend to contribute to our species remaining on this planet, we need to become much more effective.

This narrow focus can be attributed largely to the fact that from the fifth century BCE up until the fifteenth century CE, Buddhism survived and flourished under the umbrella of state power. Those states were monarchies, usually autocratic and definitely not democracies. As a consequence, the teachers and masters made whatever accommodations were required to maintain their institutions and continue the teaching. Even the grandest temples did not always save them from vindictive pogroms. When their royal patron was defeated or out of power, many Buddhists were executed and their temples ransacked or destroyed, with events toggling back and forth like this for centuries.

During that period, Buddhism was quite willing to ignore or accept the inequalities and tyrannies of whatever political system sheltered their practice. It kept its lips buttoned and attention focused on the business of transmitting Buddha's wisdom. Perhaps Jesus made similar accommodations when he counseled turning the other cheek. He was certainly prescient enough to know how the pharaoh or Pontius Pilate would have responded had he preached violent retribution. Expediency is a severe master.

Snyder observes that this "acceptance" of political repression and tyranny imposes a kind of death sentence on Buddhism, smothering many meaningful and appropriate expressions of compassion. Wisdom without compassion never feels pain and offers the intellect clear sailing. However, it's only our activated compassion that awakens and grounds us to the suffering of others and other forms of life. Compassion is what tempers our intellect, warms it up. Intellect is cold steel, razor-edged, and can be pitiless. Compassion instructs it what to cut, what not to cut, and what to bind and nurture.

So, nearly fifty years after reading it, the following paragraphs still remain extraordinary to me.

No one today can afford to be innocent or indulge themselves in ignorance of the nature of contemporary governments, politics, and social orders. No one can afford to be innocent or indulge themselves in ignorance. The national politics of the modern world maintain their existence by deliberately fostering craving and fear. It's a monstrous protection racket. The free world has become economically dependent on a fantastic system of stimulation of greed which cannot be fulfilled, sexual desire which cannot be satiated, hatred which has no outlet except against oneself, the persons one is supposed to love, or the revolutionary aspirations of pitiful, poverty-stricken, marginal societies like Cuba or Vietnam.

The conditions of the Cold War have turned all modern societies—Communist included—into vicious distorters of man's true potential. They create populations of "preta"—hungry ghosts, with giant appetites and throats no bigger than needles. The soil, the forests, and all animal life are being consumed by these cancerous collectivities; the air and water of the planet is being fouled by them.

This is as appropriate today as it was forty-eight years ago, but Gary presses his argument.

There is nothing in human nature or the requirements of human social organization, which intrinsically requires that a culture be contradictory, repressive, and productive of violent and frustrated personalities.

We can see today how radical Buddha's renunciations were. He lived in a world like ours, with vast inequities of wealth and power, and yet, every day before teaching, the Buddha went into town and begged for his daily meal. He returned, washed his bowl, feet, and hands, plumped up his pillow, and *then* sat to teach. Buddha lived precisely by the standard to which he held his disciples, and that standard was a renunciation of security, of wealth, of status, of power.

It's true he had had advantages. He was a prince and probably possessed a prince's confidence. He knew how to move in the royal realms. He knew how to talk to the elites, but he did not trade his access for personal wealth. He received from them places where his disciples could sit in safety and study. Buddha had no castle, no gold or jewels in his robes.

From the very beginning, a radical edge inherent in the Buddha's insight sliced through the presuppositions of everyday society. On some levels, perhaps monks come closer to actualizing that edge since they reduce the footprint of their personal lives so extremely, but monks alone don't make up a society. So those of us who are secular practitioners, who follow the example of Vimalakirti—a contemporary of the Buddha, reputed to be second in wisdom only to the Buddha—have not strayed far from the ancient understanding. There is no Buddhist temple in Japan that doesn't have a picture of Vimalakirti with a full head of hair in layman's clothing. Whether he was an actual person or a collage invented by Mahayana Buddhists as an example of how one could live according to the precepts and dharma doesn't matter. That's the lineage that I number myself among—my teacher's students were known as Vimala Sangha and still exist in Mill Valley.

As secular practitioners, we have a little more complex path to follow than monks. We have children to raise and educate, we have houses we must rent or pay mortgages on. We can condemn such attachments as indulgence or regard them as the opportunity to become intimate with the afflictions and difficulties of our fellow citizens. For those of us who have benefited from white privileges and educations that taught us to analyze and study history and social and political forms, why wouldn't it be an adjunct of our work to disseminate that information and to critique those forms that increase suffering?

The implication of nirvana is the truth that *in the very next instant,* we can do something fresh and new. That's a root definition of *freedom.* In the very next instant, in a world of formless energy, where nothing is permanently fixed, we can surprise ourselves by doing a handstand in this emptiness. The ruins of past empires dot the globe, reminding us that no institution or political system is permanent. Civilization is an inherited habit. In any instant we can analyze its rules and operating orders and, where it pinches or is cruel, resist it and support those doing the same thing.

We can only do this if we're willing to sacrifice some degree of our own comfort and complacency; to admit that the idea of who I am is simultaneously a tool for organizing the senses *and* a never-was fiction of a self humans have been developing and grooming over lifetimes.

So, before we proceed, I'm going to leave the last word to my mentor and first exemplar of Buddhism, Gary Snyder, now ninety-three and in good health, still razor-sharp and indomitable. I offer it to readers with a deep bow of gratitude for all he's taught and shared with me through the five-plus decades of our friendship.

The mercy of the West has been social revolution; the mercy of the East has been individual insight into the basic self/void. We need both. They are both contained in the traditional three aspects of the dharma path: wisdom (prajna), meditation (dhyana), and morality (sila). Wisdom is intuitive knowledge of the mind of love and clarity that lies beneath one's ego-driven anxieties and aggressions. Meditation is going into the mind to see this for yourself—over and over again, until it becomes the mind you live in. Morality is bringing it back out in the way you live, through personal example and responsible action, ultimately toward the true community (sangha) of "all beings."

This last aspect means, for me, supporting any cultural and economic revolution that moves clearly toward a free, international, classless world. It means using such means as civil disobedience, outspoken criticism, protest, pacifism, voluntary poverty and even gentle violence if it comes to a matter of restraining some impetuous redneck. It means affirming the widest possible spectrum of non-harmful individual behavior—defending the right of individuals to smoke hemp, eat peyote, be polygynous, polyandrous or homosexual. Worlds of behavior and custom long banned by the Judeo-Capitalist-Christian-Marxist West. It means respecting intelligence and learning, but not as greed or means to personal power. Working on one's own responsibility, but willing to work with a group. "Forming the new society within the shell of the old"—the IWW slogan of fifty years ago.

Acknowledgments

THIS BOOK WOULD NOT EXIST WERE IT NOT for the pandemic. So many people were stressed by being sequestered and afraid of this invisible illness that, at the request of a number, I began doing dharma talks on Facebook, at first once a week and then every other week. The response was heartening. There were occasions when nearly two thousand people showed up, which was a flattering inducement to continue.

Even a deadly virus can and has made valuable contributions to our culture, in the acts of courage it fostered, the extraordinary science that generated life-saving vaccines in record time, the heroic deeds of doctors and nurses and first responders who exemplified high sacrifice and boundless love as well as the unsung courage of so many designated essential workers, forced to serve those of us like myself who could afford to remain sequestered. And finally to the anxiety and fear it produced that impelled many, myself included, to seek deeper refuge in spiritual practice.

My friend Ruby Lee edited each and every videotaped lecture, excising chitchat and fumbling. I'm very grateful for her care and diligence. Without her precise visions and labor, the finished tapes would be much less agreeable and accessible. The originals are all posted on my YouTube channel, Hosho Peter Coyote.

Kensho Judith Gilbert, an old friend from San Francisco Zen Center, dedicated many hours and days transcribing the original talks and passing them on to me for editing. When it was assembled as a book, she cast an eagle eye on the entirety, alerting me to errors of fact, grammatical blunders, and areas requiring clarification. I am deeply indebted for the time and energy she spent serving as a whetstone to what otherwise might have a much duller blade.

Special gratitude to literary agent Joe Kulin, who found a home for my previous book, *The Lone Ranger and Tonto Meet Buddha* (which may epitomize the nearly unsellable book). Somehow Joe found a good fit at Inner Traditions, and his easiness, his patience, and his doggedness in pursuing this one have won him the right to exhaust himself by trying to see it published.

I have great affection for the folks at Inner Traditions, who were precise, helpful, organized, and downright cheerful in all the numerous labors required to get a book to press. A deep bow in particular to Elizabeth Wilson for her eagle-eyed copy editing, and my apologies for torturing my project editor, Renée Heitman, with corrections and editorial changes made well past her "final, final" deadlines to me. To Kelly Bowen, who made all the contractual details a breeze. To publicists Manzanita Carpenter Sanz and Gail Torr, thank you. I'm deeply grateful to all and apologetic to any whom I've overlooked in expressing gratitude.

To friends too numerous to list here who read the manuscript and gave me good advice, I remain indebted. And, as always, to my teachers, formal or not, but which must always include Gary Snyder, Lew Richmond, Dan Welch, Edward Brown, Ed Satizahn, Jane Hirshfeld, Linda Ruth Cutts, Steve Weintraub, Tenshin Reb Anderson, Fu Schroeder, Taigen Dan Leighton, Blanche Hartman, Vicki Austin, Dokai Ronald Georgeson, Gaelyn Godwin, and all the sanghas I've practiced with or lectured to. My sincerest apologies to those whose names eluded me when composing this list, and, of course, any errors, bloopers, and misstatements are my own responsibility and not theirs.

Annotated Bibliography
of Further Reading

THE BOOKS BELOW are books I refer to often and recommend for further study. Some stress technique and form, some are analyses of the Buddha's teaching, and others will acquaint you with the mind of Zen. They are all valuable.

Aitken, Robert. *Taking the Path of Zen*. San Francisco: North Point Press, 1982.

> This work provides a very basic how-and-why book by a very fine teacher I studied with for several years.

Anderson, Tenshin Reb. *Being Upright*. Boston: Shambhala Publications, 2001.

> Reb is a lineage holder in Suzuki-roshi's lineage, one of my earliest dharma friends, and a very senior teacher. He introduces readers to fundamental Zen Buddhist practice. Who was Shakyamuni Buddha and what was his core teaching? What is a bodhisattva and the bodhisattva vow? Why should we acknowledge our ancient, twisted karma? What do the vows of taking refuge in Buddha, dharma, and sangha really mean? The author explores the Ten Basic Precepts well and deeply.

Brazier, David. *The Feeling Buddha*. London: Constable Publishers, 1997.

> This is a very practical and clearly articulated and concise re-look at the Four Noble Truths and their implications. The same goes for the Eightfold Path.

Chodron, Pema. *When Things Fall Apart.* Boston: Shambhala, 2016.

Pema Chodron is a teacher in the Tibetan lineage of Chogyam Trungpa. I have never met her, but I have read and appreciated her books and don't hesitate to recommend her to readers who would like to deepen their practice.

Cohen, Darlene. *Turning Suffering Inside Out: A Zen Approach to Living with Physical and Emotional Pain.* Boston: Shambhala, 2002.

Darlene Cohen was an early friend at San Francisco Zen Center and was one of the three teachers training me during my priest's training. She suffered early from crippling arthritis, and her writing about living (and enjoying) life with chronic pain is instructive for any difficult situation.

Dalai Lama. *A Flash of Lightning in the Dark of Night: A Guide to the Bodhisattva's Way of Life.* Boston: Shambhala, 1994.

A bodhisattva is one who puts himself last, vows to help all beings cross the barrier to enlightenment, and will go last. It is a tall order, and the Dalai Lama himself is regarded as a living embodiment of such a being. This is a very inside look.

Fischer, Norman. *The World Could Be Otherwise: Imagination and the Bodhisattva Path.* Boston: Shambhala, 2019.

When I was preparing for my transmission, my teacher urged me that if anything were to happen to him, I should seek to continue with Norman. A very well-known and respected teacher, and a poet—perhaps it's because of that and my own addiction to writing poetry, that I so like this book about involving the imagination in our practice.

Nhat Hanh, Thich. *The Heart of the Buddha's Teaching: Transforming Suffering into Peace, Joy, and Liberation.* New York: Harmony Books, 1999.

Thich Nhat Hanh was in many places regarded as a living saint, and anything he has written is worth your time spent learning to know his mind.

Okumura, Shohaku. *Realizing Genjokoan: The Key to Dogen's Shobogenzo.* Boston: Wisdom Publications, 2010.

Dogen was one of the giants of Zen, a founder really, who brought the practice to Japan from China. This brilliant book by Shohaku Okumura concentrates on the first chapter of Dogen's Shobogenzo and teases out themes and teachings that apply to all of Buddhism. Okumura-roshi brings a very pure form of Japanese understanding with him, abetted by a perfect grasp of English. You can't do better.

Richmond, Lewis. *Work as a Spiritual Practice: A Practical Buddhist Approach to Inner Growth and Satisfaction on the Job.* New York: Broadway Books, 1999.

———. *Aging as a Spiritual Practice: A Contemplative Guide to Growing Older and Wiser.* New York: Gotham Books/Penguin, 2012.
Chikudo Lewis Richmond was an early disciple of Suzuki-roshi and my teacher for a dozen years. A self-effacing and quiet man, his insight is profound and brilliant, and several of his books, including this one, have become best sellers. He has studied with every Japanese teacher that came to California and is very clear-eyed about which aspects of practice are Japanese and which are parts of Universal Buddhism. He has remained a trustworthy guide even after I received transmission from him.

Suzuki-roshi, Shunryu. *Zen Mind, Beginner's Mind: Informal Talks on Zen Meditation and Practice.* Boston: Shambhala, 2006.

———. *Not Always So: Practicing the True Spirit of Zen.* New York: HarperCollins, 2002.
Suzuki-roshi was the founding teacher of San Francisco Zen Center and the founder of my lineage, an endless well from which to drink. Further information can be found in Suzuki's disciple David Chadwick's invaluable record of Suzuki's work at the website Cuke.com. You can see Suzuki-roshi on video at San Francisco Zen Center's website (SFZC.org) and buy supplies at their store. I remain very honored that San Francisco Zen Center asked me to record the audio version of his wonderful book.

Thurman, Robert. *The Holy Teaching of Vimalakirti: A Mahayana Scripture.* University Park: Pennsylvania State University Press, 1976.
Vimalakirti is the root teacher of my secular practice. Vimalakirti was reputed to be the most profound man next to the Buddha. Whether a real man or a composite representing the newly emerged Mahayana ideal, he was a layman of wealth and means who visited the bars and racetracks and brothels to teach dharma. My teacher's sangha was named Vimala Sangha, and I and nearly every Zen center in Japan feature his picture on an altar.

Index

Abhidharma, 120
abortion, 70–72
Abrahamic religions, 52–53, 57, 97,
     161, 165, 248
  and dominion perspective, 245–46
accepting, 66, 148–49
  and condoning, 142–43
achievements, human, 99
acquisition, 279
addiction, 287–88
affirmative action, 264, 290–91
affliction, 118. *See also* dukkha
  dukkha as, 7
  and neurosis, 15
  as part of reality, 13
African Americans
  median wealth of, 262*
  and police, 200–201
  racism against, 254–57
Aitken, Robert, 71, 83–84, 321, 327
Akusala, 61
"A little knowledge is a dangerous
     thing," 253, 299
America, taking advantage of
     powerless, 213
American Buddhists, number of,
     249–50
Ananda, 50

Anderson, Reb, 149, 162–63, 327
"And yet . . . ," 295–96, 300, 303
anxiety, 204–21
  becoming intimate with it, 215–16
  and helping others, 219
arising, samudaya as, 17
aspiration, 312
atman, 9
Avalokitesvara, 56, 121–25
awareness, self as, 94

Baizhang, fox story, 134
Baker, Richard, 79–80, 86, 208
balance, 226
bamboo tube metaphor, 105, 175
Beginner's Mind, 122, 148, 199–200,
     202
"being the boss of everything," 234
belief, 118
  believing in nothing, 141–45
Big Mind, 94, 100, 176, 314
  allowing ourself to be instructed by,
     181–82
  and body-mind dichotomy, 93
  and cherishing what we use, 188
  practice supported by, 227–28
  trustworthiness of, 316
Bill of Rights, 271

birth and death, Dogen on, 12
black / white issues, 200–201, 260–67, 272–76
Blue Cloud, Peter, 37–38
Bly, Robert, 242–43
Bodhidharma, 176–77
bodhisattva
    defined, 62
    vow of, 73, 123, 174*
bonobos, 304
boundaries, necessity of, 109
Boyle, Gregory Joseph, 99
Boyle, Paul, 172
Bozos on the bus, 219
Brady, Tom, 155, 232
Brahmajala Sutta, and wrong views, 21
Brazier, David, vi, 6–7, 12, 19, 22, 24, 210, 313, 327
Brown, Jerry, 80, 241–42
Brush Dance, 46
Buddha, 142
    accepted reality, 314
    advice to mother of a dead child, 297–98
    as Buddha-nature, 58
    enlightenment of, 11
    everyone is a, 32
    gratitude for, 103
    intention of, 27
    is not a god, 103
    life of the, 10–12, 115–17
    renunciations of, 324
    on the self, 89
    taking refuge in the, 57
    why he taught, 119
Buddha-nature, 141–42
    as common denominator, 21

and Emptiness, 54
and science, 196
Buddhism
    and agnosticism, 165
    as an intuitive practice, 73
    as mirror of human diversity, 4–5
    myths in, 53–54
    not trying to improve reality, 314
    the problem is it's got people in it, 103, 154
    secular practitioners, 324–25
    what the Buddha taught, 1–75
Buddhist Action, 33
Buddhist anarchism, 318–26
Buddhist Conduct, 33–35
Buddhist Effort, 45–49
Buddhist faith-based practices, 100
Buddhist Livelihood, 35–37, 42
Buddhist Peace Fellowship, 321
"Buddhist persona," 20
Buddhist practice, 106. See also
    individual topics
    not an end to suffering, 163–64
    role of faith in, 161–70
    as using energy, 24
Buddhist Speech, 33
buffalo, extermination of, 243
busyness, 222–35

calm, and meditation, 62, 228
capitalism, 41, 223
Carse, James, 231–32
ceremony, and form, 102–14
Chan, 169–70
Chodron, Pema, 328
Chogyam Trungpa, 150

Christianity. *See also* Abrahamic
    religions
  the God of, 52–53
climate change, 225, 242, 281–83
Cohen, Darlene, 328
Communism, 222–24
compassion, 301, 322–23
  as fundamental instruction, 55
constancy, 226, 230–31
Constitution of the United States,
    270–72
consumption, 284
containment, 234
contradictions in human nature, 307–17
corporations, 38, 229, 292
Council of Nicea, 52–53
Covid, 205–7, 217
Coyote, Peter (author)
  as actor, 43–44
  on becoming a priest, 212–13
  biography, ix–x
  and busyness, 222–24
  early disillusionment of, 308–10
  early years of Zen study, 130–32
  granddaughter story, 296–97
  and his father, 136–38, 271–72, 312
  and Indigenous cultures, 309–10
  and jerks in the SF Zen Center,
    104–5
  kensho of, 119–20, 135
  overview of his Zen practice, 78–87
  and priest training, 109–10
  upbringing by African American
    housekeeper, 272–73
  wanting a Ferrari, 47
  working with the ranch foreman,
    230–31

craving, 8. *See also* samudaya
creation myths, 52, 245*

Dalai Lama, 32, 328
  on non-necessity to change one's
    religion, 75, 170
  and vegetarianism, 69
dangerousness, of each of us, 96
death, 34–35, 173–74, 179
Default Mode Network, 132, 300
delusion, defined, 118
dependent origination, 9, 43, 117,
    138–39
desire, 8–9, 17
dew, 295–96, 306
dharma, 58–59, 316
  taking refuge in the, 57–59
  as truth, 142
Diggers, 18, 273*, 273–74
disputes, stress of, 100
divorce, 113–14
Dogen, 136, 175, 178, 183, 185, 252
  on birth and death, 12
  "Form is form, and emptiness is
    emptiness," 125, 197
dokusan, 157
dominion, as Western perspective,
    245–46
"Don't invite your thoughts for tea,"
    69, 143
dukkha, 6–16, 163–64, 204–5, 220
  Buddha's definition, 8
  defined, 6
  as energy, 16

East and West, 325–26
effort, constant, 317

ego, 138–40. *See also* self
  as not the enemy, 59
Eightfold Path, the, 26–50
  as a circle, 26, 41
  as enlightenment, 321
  summarized, 29
emotions, reality of, 299
Emptiness, 115–29
  defined, 52
  and dependent origination, 194–97
  Heart Sutra and, 115–29
  understanding and
    misunderstanding, 253–67
energy, per person use of, 39–40
enlightenment, 130–40, 259–60
  aftermath of, 101
  changes everything, 14–15
  and dukkha, 9
  as human experience, 4
  the idea of, 132
  necessity of human realm for, 108–9
  not a salvation from all suffering,
    14, 130, 319–20
  renewing, 320
  and Soto practice, 131
  as a verb, 301
environmentalism, 250
ethics, Buddhist, 25, 254
European enlightenment, 244–45, 248
evil, good and, 60–61
extraction, 284

faculties, five, 162
fair and unfair, 280
fairness, 292
faith, 161–63
  in Abrahamic religions, 161–62
Buddhist faith-based practices, 162
  in Buddhist practice, 161–70
  as confidence, 165
  and insight, 168
  and true self, 168–69
Fayan, on Bodhidharma, 176–77
Fischer, Norman, 5, 328
Floyd, George, 254–57, 278
form, and ceremony, 102–14
"Formal practice / Informal mind," 62
"Form is form, and emptiness is
    emptiness," 125, 178, 197
Foster, Norman, 321
Four Noble Truths, the, 6–50
  brief summary, 6–7. *see also*
    dukkha; samudaya; nirodha;
    marga
fox story, 134
freedom, 325
  concept of, 236–38
  defined, 108
Fuketsu, his speck of dust, 180–90, 226
Fundamental Vehicle, 120

Gach, Gary, 51
games, 231–32
Gaté, gaté, paragaté, parasamgaté,
    Bodhi, Svaha!, 126
Genjo koan, 184, 188, 227, 307–17
"gift wrapping" (of Buddhism), 4
global warming, 242, 281–83
good and evil, 60–61
goodness, personal, 96–97
Gotami, Kisa, 297–98
Grace, Dick, 219
greed, 284
  restraining, 224–25

Greens, 80
grief, 296–98
Grizzy Man, 240–41
guru tradition, 152

Hakuin, 28, 131, 320–21
han, 172
happiness, 15, 199
harmlessness, 68–70
Harris, David, 268–69, 276
    "Values that are not embodied in
    behavior do not exist," 109, 211
Hawken, Paul, 250
Heart Sutra, 121–29, 316
    text of, 123–26
helping others, 34, 94, 187, 225
Herzog, Werner, 241
Hillel, Rabbi, "What is hateful to
    yourself . . . ," 55
Hinayana school, 53, 120
Ho, Kyong, 15–16
holistic view, 139–40
Hongzhi, 177–78
hooking up, 111
host and guest, 171–79, 316
house-cleaning (internal), 98–99
Howard, Sue, 272–73, 312*
Hsueh-tou, 181, 184–85, 187
human beings
    as animals, 238
    capacity to express everything,
    61
    half positive and half negative,
    310–11
"hungry ghosts," 301
Hutton, Bobby, 273–74
hypocrisy, 271, 286

"I," 118. *See also* self
    and attachment, 95
    nature of, 23, 88–100
    non-existence of, 92
"If I speak, I am a liar," 128
"If you are not kind and helpful . . . ," 302
impermanence, 18–19, 89, 298–99
    and compassion, 301–3
"Indian problem," 243
Indigenous peoples, 309–10
    considering consequences for seven
    generations, 305
    invading the spaces of, 229
indriyani, 162
inequities, social, 290
infusing the ordinary, 78–87
intention, 48, 269–70, 302
    defined, 114
    fundamental, 27
inter-being, 170, 269
interdependence, 305, 319
interrogating states, 210
intuition, 73, 202–3
Investigating, 66–67
Invisible University, 79
Iraq military campaign, 96–97
Issa, Kobayashi, 294–96

James, Henry, on Native Americans,
    247
Japanese aesthetic, Zen and the,
    78–81, 85, 149–50
jobs, 42
Judaism, 52, 97, 161, 245–46

karma, 277–93
Karuk people, 46, 309–10

Katagiri-roshi, and putting life into a bamboo tube, 105, 303
Katie, Byron, 216
Keizan, 119, 177
kensho, 14–15, 101, 131–32
    and disappearance of "I," 134–35
    as human experience, 4
killing, dictates against, 97
kleshas, 259
koans, 131, 180

language, arising of, 238
liberal, defined, 214*
Lieff, Judy, 165
loss, 294–306

Mahayana school, 53, 121
Mara, 116
marga, 26–50. See also Eightfold Path, the
    defined, 7, 26
marriages, 110–14
Marx, Karl, 281
materialism, 279
materialistic practice, 131
McCarthy, Joseph, 223–24
meditation. See also zazen meditation
    allows mind to be mind, 143
    as antidote to "ill-being," 99
    benefits of, 166, 228, 252, 286
    defined, 325
    and free zones, 209
    as means for calming, 62
    as search for heightened state, 144
    and softening of fixed boundaries, 93
Merton, Thomas, 222, 225, 233
Middle Path, 28–29

migration, 281
Miller, Arthur, 223
mind, is like a horse, 315
mind-body, 59, 67, 90, 145, 228, 240
mindfulness, 218
    defined, 48–49
money, 290–93
monks, 324
morality, defined, 325
Mount St. Helens, 251
Mumon, Yamada, 83

Nāgārjuna, and Emptiness, 253–54
naming objects, 90–91
Nam Myoho Renge Kyo, 162
Native American culture, 247–49, 287
    considering consequences for seven generations, 74
Neanderthal graves, 303–4
Newton, Huey, 273–74
Nhat Hanh, Thich, 94, 125*, 321, 328
    biography, 166–67
    on faith, 167
    on half-smiles, 144
Niemöller, Martin, 257–59
nirodha, 7, 22, 22–25, 49, 234
Nirvana, 44–45
    implication of, 325
    as not a metaphor for escape, 25
noble, meaning of, 12
normal existence, as the miracle, 144
"not fair" phrase, 278–79
"Nothing-Special-Zen," 86
Not identifying, 67
Not Knowing, 148, 192, 199–200, 216
not one, not two, 90, 94
"not-self," 89

okesa, defined, 109–10
Okumura, Shohaku, 221, 328
ordinary, infusing the, 78–87
organization, necessity of, 102–3

pace, 230–31
passivity, 259
path with a heart, 114, 163, 230
patience, 234–35
payback, 315
Plum Village, bells in, 30
poise, 226
police, 260, 274–75
policeman, being stopped by a, 200–201
political system, creating fairness in
    our, 292
politics, defined, 274
Pollan, Michael, 132
posture, of zazen, 220
poverty, how it is generated, 41
practice, defined, 106
prajna, 165
    defined, 122
precepts. See also Ten Clear Mind
    Precepts; Three Pure Precepts
    defined, 51–52
    history of, 62–63
    an introduction to the, 51–75
    usefulness of, 73–75
present moment, and Zen practice,
    10, 93, 171–73, 209, 302
priests, Buddhist, varieties of, 5
profit, 281
projection, defined, 33
promises, and vows, 111
proprioception, defined, 88
Pure Land Buddhism, 169–70

purity, 43, 104
"Put no head above your own," 69, 147

Quick Fixes, 108

racism, 260–67, 272–76, 311
RAIN, 66–67
rakusu, defined, 109–10
Ram Dass, 152
readiness, 198
Recognizing, 66
recycling, 284
reincarnation, 21, 24–25, 56, 173–74
    and suffering, 9–10
religion, organized, 104
reparations, 286–87
respect, of self and other, 241
responsibility, accepting, 74
riches, vs. wealth, 284
Richmond, Lew, ix–x, 26–27, 85–86,
    172, 329
"Right," as in Right Understanding,
    etc., 26
Rinzai school, 131
Roberts, Harry, 45–47
Rogers, Martha, 196
Rolling Thunder, 309–10
Rovelli, Carlo, 253–54

Samadhi, defined, 49–50
samudaya, 17–21
    as arising, 17
    defined, 7
San Francisco Zen Center, 79–85, 104–5
sangha, 31, 142
    and doing things, 106–7
    taking refuge in the, 58–59

as teacher, 158

Sarvāstivādins, 120

satori, 14–15

saving all beings, 27, 38, 49, 62, 65, 108, 170, 174*, 225, 305

Schroeder, Fu, 31

scorn, vi

secular practitioners, 324–25

self, 59, 88–100
    assumption of a, 9–10
    as awareness, 20, 94
    as delusion, 88–89, 190
    and dependent origination, 138–40
    forgetting the, 118
    as king, 240
    as not discoverable, 54–55, 195, 319
    and other, 251–52

self-involvement, 220

Senauke, Alan, 321

sesshin, defined, 83

sexuality, and teachers, 153–55

shadow side of human nature, 310, 312

Shakespeare, 198

shamans, 250

shamata, defined, 30

shame, abandoning, 18

Shantideva, on mind, 233–34

Shariputra, 120

shikantaza, 83
    defined, 93–94

Shippee, Paul, 6

sitting, 157–58

skandhas, 8*, 91, 123

skillful means, 150

Snyder, Gary, x, 150
    "And yet . . . ," 295–96
    author's relationship to, 81–84

on Buddhist anarchism, 318

on contributions of Mahayana Buddhism, 321–22

on East and West, 325–26

on frontier, 243–44

on sexless nirvana, 300

"This Tokyo," 189, 313

on the unified whole, 320

on wilderness and wildness, 59, 107, 199, 236–52

social imbalances, and Zen, 80–81

Socialism, 222–24

speck of dust, 180–90
    meaning of the phrase, 182–83

spiritual bypassing, 13, 19, 296

Stalin, Joseph, 223

standards, 230–31

stillness, 233–34

stopping the mind, 197

Strozer, Teah, 51, 66–67

suffering. See also dukkha
    and Buddhist practice, 163–64
    cause of, 296–98
    and craving, 8
    and dukkha, 7–8
    and helping others, 34

surplus value theory, 281

survival of the fittest, 281

Suzuki-roshi, 329
    "being the boss of everything," 234
    on belief, 118, 141–42
    on cultivating your own spirit, 192
    "Don't invite your thoughts for tea," 143, 215
    on eating eggs, 188
    "Everything is perfect . . .," 211
    good and bad, 226–27, 307–8, 314

on headaches, 144
on the "I," 94–95
on instructions from Big Mind, 185–86
on knowing, 193–94
on letters from emptiness, 136
on letting thoughts in, 69
presence of, 145
on pride, 227
on renewing enlightenment, 320
on saying "Yes," 142, 210–11
simple ceremonies of, 4
on training, 189
"You're perfect the way you are . . . ," 152
on Zen and Hinayana, 121

Tassajara Bread Bakery, 80
tax cuts, 291
teachers, 146–51, 150–60
    expectations of, 150–53
    and intimacy, 158–59
    qualities of, 133
    as sources, 73–74
    undeveloped, 133
    and uneven development, 156–57
    in the Zen tradition, 153–54
Ten Clear Mind Precepts, 63–65
"The ground you fall on . . .," 220
Theory of Unitary Human Beings, 196
Theravadins, 120
things as it is, 24, 59, 77–190, 198
    defined, 3, 313
thirst, 23
"This Tokyo" (Snyder), 189, 313
Thomas, Dylan, 251
Three Poisons, 66–67
Three Pure Precepts, 60–75
    summarized, 60

Three Refuges, 55–58
    defined, 55
    taking refuge in the Buddha, 57
    taking refuge in the dharma, 57–59
    taking refuge in the sangha, 58–59
Three Treasures, 146–60
    defined, 106–7
Thurman, Robert, 329
Tibetan Buddhists, on anger, 20
time, 171–72, 171–79
time-being, 175
transmission, 79*
Treadwell, Tim, 240–41
triggers, 57
Trump, Donald, 32–33, 278–79
trying our best, 183
tulkus, 173–74
turning word, 31
Twelve Step programs, 287–88

Unity, 52
upaya, 150

Vachagotta, 89
Vallejo Police Department, 275
"Values that are not embodied in
    behavior do not exist," 109, 268–76
vegetarianism, 68–69
Vietnam War, 217–18
Vimalakirti, 324
vows, 69, 293
    to avoid evil, 60
    to do good, 60–62
    living by, 40
    not to be possessive, 64
    not to disparage the Three
        Treasures, 65

not to harbor ill will, 65
not to kill, 63, 68–70
not to lie, 63
not to misuse sexuality, 63, 70–73
not to praise self at expense of
    others, 64
not to slander, 64
not to take what is not given, 63, 70
not to use intoxicants, 64
and promises, 111
to save all beings, 27, 38, 49, 62, 65,
    108, 170, 174*, 305
usefulness of, 106

wealth, 290–93
    vs. riches, 284
"we are always the problem . . . ," 33
weddings, 110–14
Weitsman, Mel, 131
Weitzman, Sojun, 193
Wellwood, John, on spiritual
    bypassing, 13, 19, 296
West and East, 325–26
What can we do? 227–28, 314–17
"What is hateful to yourself . . . ," 55
What vs. How, 228–29
white people
    black / white issues, 200–201,
        260–67, 272–76
    systemic advantages of, 262–64,
        273, 286–87
wilderness, 107, 236–52, 244
wildfires, 241–42, 251
wildness. See also wilderness
    denotations of "wild," 238–40
Wilkerson, Isabel, 264
wine, 304

wisdom, 163, 325
    metaphysical, 127–28
    mundane, 127
    three ways to consider, 127–28
    transcendent, 128
Wise, Samuel, 258–59
Witt, Alexandra, 262*
Wobblies, 82, 82*
woke, defined, 212
working on something, importance
    of, 315
Wright, Gabriella, 34–35

Yongming, 119
    on faith, 169–70
    "You're perfect the way you are . . . ,"
        152
Yurok Indians, 45–46

zazen meditation, 190, 226. See also
    meditation
    as ceremony, 106
    as doorway to Buddha's mind, 57
    helps us see things, 303
    as karma-free, 277–78
    and mind training, 159
    and personal enlightenment, 251–52
    and posture, 220
Zen. See also individual topics
    engaged with vernacular Zen,
        191–326
    and Hinayana, 121
    as not a religion, 119
    translated into American vernacular,
        2–5, 86
    and we're all in this together, 250
Zitner, Sheldon, 211

BOOKS OF RELATED INTEREST

The Lone Ranger and Tonto Meet Buddha
Masks, Meditation, and Improvised Play to Induce Liberated States
by Peter Coyote

Flight of the Bön Monks
War, Persecution, and the Salvation of Tibet's Oldest Religion
by Harvey Rice and Jackie Cole
Foreword by the Dalai Lama

Riding the Spirit Bus
My Journey from Satsang with Ram Dass to Lama Foundation
and Dances of Universal Peace
by Ahad Cobb

Instructions for Spiritual Living
by Paul Brunton
Introduction by the Paul Brunton Philosophic Foundation

Effortless Living
Wu-Wei and the Spontaneous State of Natural Harmony
by Jason Gregory
Foreword by Damo Mitchell

The Hundred Remedies of the Tao
Spiritual Wisdom for Interesting Times
by Gregory Ripley

Being Nature
A Down-to-Earth Guide to the Four Foundations of Mindfulness
by Wes Nisker
Foreword by Jack Kornfield

Hara
The Vital Center of Man
by Karlfried Graf Dürckheim

INNER TRADITIONS • BEAR & COMPANY
P.O. Box 388 • Rochester, VT 05767
1-800-246-8648 • www.InnerTraditions.com

Or contact your local bookseller